*The Man Who Gave Away His Island*

# The Man Who Gave Away His Island

*A Life of John Lorne Campbell of Canna*

## Ray Perman

BIRLINN

First published in 2010 by
Birlinn Limited
West Newington House
10 Newington Road
Edinburgh
EH9 1QS

*www.birlinn.co.uk*

ISBN 978 1 84158 894 0 (hardback)
ISBN 978 1 84158 929 9 (paperback)

British Library Cataloguing-in-Publication Data
A catalogue record for this book is available from the British Library

Designed and typeset by Iolaire Typesetting, Newtonmore
Printed and bound by MPG Books Limited, Bodmin

For Fay Young

# Contents

# List of Illustrations

# Foreword: The House of Contradictions

The owl-lamp on the Steinway grand, quartos
Of Schubert, Mozart, Moore's Irish Melodies,
The carved funny animals, the barque under glass,
The curious mirrors of carved bones
Made by the French prisoners in Edinburgh Castle,
Books on birds and minerals, cases of butterflies,
The family miniatures on ivory, piles
Of the New Yorker, Paris Match, The Scotsman,
The friendly bottles, ash-trays, cigarettes,
The cat-clawed Chippendale and the dog-haired cushions,
    photographs
Of Uist and Barra and of distant friends, all this
Learned and happy accumulation, held together
By the presence of John and Margaret Campbell.[1]

The poet Kathleen Raine, waiting to play her card, recorded a small part of the vast clutter that greets visitors to Canna House and found clues to the character and past of the building's owners. Many items were probably in the same positions they had occupied 28 years earlier when she had first visited the island. They are still in place today – an eclectic collection made over long lives of curiosity, inquiry, action and compassion.

I first saw that room in 1977, the year before Raine wrote those words. Arriving in Canna by boat from Mallaig on a clear spring day, it made an impression like no other place I had been – an island of contrasts. On the north side, cold blue shadows cast on the sea by 600 foot cliffs. On the south, warm sunlit meadows of vivid green. Organ-pipe columns of hard basalt granite, soft beaches washed by a clear sea – one of white sand, another of black.

The man who had fallen under the island's spell 40 years before and against formidable odds had bought it and nurtured it, was waiting for me on the pier. John Lorne Campbell, leaning on a shepherd's stick, was dressed in a shabby tweed jacket and a black beret that appeared too big for him. While other passengers started to walk along the unmade road, John ushered me into an incongruous blue Volkswagen Beetle for a journey of just a few hundred yards to the front of the imposing stone mansion visible from the water. He answered my questions tersely, but otherwise made no conversation.

You cannot see Canna House from its gate. A dark tunnel of *Escalonia* bushes, which have been allowed to grow so they meet overhead, hides the view until, emerging into the sunlight, the house is square before you. Leading the way up short steps and through an oak door with a dolphin knocker, John Campbell hung his beret in the porch alongside several other hats which included a conical straw sun-shield of the type worn by Chinese workers in paddy fields and a solar topee, the pith helmet beloved of the British Raj. I found later that John wore different hats for different tasks. On the floor was a croquet set, in a corner fishing rods, nets and a pendant flag from the top of a buoy.

I had only seconds to take in the enormous two-handed broadsword leaning in the corner of the hall, the glass cases standing on a cupboard – one containing an aneroid barometer continuously recording atmospheric pressure on a roll of paper, the other a stuffed Spoonbill. A red and white ship's lifebelt leant against a far wall. A printed sign on a door ordered: 'Quiet. Hangover Zone.' We passed quickly through the dining room, which would have been elegant with silverware on a mahogany sideboard, white marble fireplace and portrait of a red-coated general presiding over the table, were it not for the carved and broken slabs lying on the floor of the window bay, like toppled tombstones.

I was greeted by Margaret, the antithesis of her husband: he tall, upright, reserved; she small, warm, welcoming. But John had not paused and I followed him down two steps to a large room with windows facing the garden. There were then, as there are now, filing cabinets, boxes and piles of papers on a large rectangular surface, which on closer inspection proved to be a billiard table with a wooden cover over the baize. The far wall was covered with charts of the seas around the island – still there, but now yellowing. There was another stuffed bird, a capercaillie, a stack of the satirical magazine *Private Eye*, a fax machine, a telephone and a photocopier. John, I learned later, loved technology. He was what would be called today an 'early adopter'. This was before the internet age, but with a typewriter, fax and copier he was connected to the world.

I was a journalist come to get a story on ferry policy. Dr Campbell, as I always called him, was campaigning vigorously against the 'Small Boat Scheme', a proposal to replace the ferry which provides the island with its lifeline to the mainland with a service of light craft run from a nearby island. It had set him against not only his neighbouring proprietor on Eigg, but an array of bureaucrats and politicians.

He was clearly energised by the fight, eager to explain his argument. As a *Financial Times* reporter, I was trained to demand precise numbers and verifiable facts. I had expected anecdote and prejudice from the eccentric laird of a remote island. Instead I got a folder of official documents, transcripts of evidence, and details of the class of passenger certificate required for a vessel crossing the Sound of Canna (which, John explained, has more exposed seas than those on the more sheltered side of Rum facing the mainland). He had tabulated the exact number of days during each of the past few years on which the ferry had been unable to sail because of bad weather.

Listening to him and reading the evidence I became convinced that not only would the Small Boat Scheme be a disaster for Canna, but that by backing it, the Highlands and Islands Development Board was going against its own policy. How could they not see this themselves? I asked. The answer was damning: 'Because they are not practical men.'

The John Lorne Campbell I first got to know was nothing if not a 'practical man'. At the age of 70 he was still a working farmer and fisherman, running a business in a location which presented daily challenges that town and city-dwellers never have to face. I learned only later that he was also a scholar who had devoted a second lifetime to the Gaelic language and a third to the study of butterflies and moths.

In the years that followed, I got to see more of the house. To sit where Kathleen Raine had sat, not playing cards but listening to Margaret playing the piano, John the flute and visiting musicians the violin and cello. To see the books, not just the library (the 'Hangover Zone') of books, papers and recordings, but in every room and on shelves lining every corridor and landing. The more I learned, the more I became intrigued by the puzzles.

John believed his library of Celtic languages was the most extensive anywhere in private hands and contained many rare books. But he thought his most valuable works might be his bound volumes of the *Mickey Mouse Weekly*, faithfully collected over decades. Shortly before he died he parcelled them up ready to go to an auctioneer to be valued. They are still in their wrappings.

Other curiosities emerged as I got to know him better. John the scientist meticulously pinned and labelled drawers of butterflies and moths, showing the subtle variations in the patterns on their wings, like Darwin's Galapagos finches. But he dismissed the theory of evolution for the most obtuse reason. The radical land reformer wanted to destroy the old order, but revered his 'honoured ancestor' who had assembled a vast Highland estate. The ardent Scottish nationalist loved that most English of games, cricket, and bought a copy of *Wisden* every year. The shrewd investigator saw through charlatans in print, but was so trusting in face-to-face meetings that he could be deceived and cheated. The generous man who would spend a fortune, without thinking, on his island or his Gaelic work, wrote to me approvingly of the bargain second-hand furniture he had bought at the Corpach cattle sale.

Perhaps most surprisingly, the warm, welcoming and confident man I care to know could appear rude and unfeeling to others – the result of paralysing shyness.

Canna House has been owned by the National Trust for Scotland for nearly 30 years, but is not open to the public. It is not a museum. Apart from a few damp patches and the peeling wallpaper, it is much as its former owners left it. Cats come and go at will as they always did, Patchin the dog still sits in the doorway looking out over Canna harbour to Rum. The piles of magazines and newspapers have long since been cleared, as have the friendly bottles and cigarettes. The ashtrays have been cleaned.

Unopened bottles of long-forgotten brands of whisky, salvaged from the SS *Politician* after it foundered on the rocks of Eriskay in 1941, are still in John's desk. The musical instruments: brass, wood-wind, pipes, are still there, with a drawer full of flutes, all of which John could play. Only very recently did I dare to try to get a sound from the bugle which sits on the hall table, which John blew to summon guests to dinner. Compton Mackenzie's kilt still hangs in a cupboard. Cheap clockwork toys and novelties sit on antique tables and cabinets, a reminder of how a serious man could find amusement in simple things.

It is still possible to imagine John Lorne Campbell and Margaret Fay Shaw moving from room to room. They do not haunt the house, but it continues to be inhabited by them and provides many more clues to the unfolding story. The portrait of Archibald Camp-bell, the red-coated general in the dining room. The recording equipment and Margaret's heavy camera – now museum pieces, but the most modern available in their day. The billiard table where games of 'penny pool' were played. John modified the rules from those invented by Compton Mackenzie on Barra – but the islanders still beat him. And the visitors' book with its extraordinary list of names from Europe, the Americas, New Zealand – a kaleidoscope of friends and acquaintances, most invited, some who invited them-selves – all providing a different way of seeing a man at the centre of his world.

Many people have helped me to try to understand this complex man but none more than John. It is unusual to start a list of acknowledgements with the subject himself, yet without the narra-tives and insights he gave in books, notebooks, articles and letters it would not have been possible. Did he intend his biography to be written? His hand-written notebooks were never published, nor shown to many people, but John, the diligent scholar, begins one with a list of sources and references to which the reader can turn for more information on aspects of his life. I am sure that he wanted his story to be told one day.

Whether he meant me to write it is much less certain. Looking again through a long exchange of letters, I rediscover enclosed articles and off-prints which seemed irrelevant at the time, but which now complete another part of the picture. Several times I have spent hours in the British Library or the National Library of Scotland trying to trace an article from the 1930s or 1940s only to find that I already had a copy, sent to me by John 20 years ago. I know I am not the only person to have received such unsolicited gifts. Perhaps he hedged his bets.

John was a meticulous keeper of files. It would have been impossible to find my way through them without Magda Sagarzazu, but she has been much more than just a guide to the Canna House archive. In writing, John could be a harsh critic and applied his uncompromising judgements to himself as much as to others. Some of his autobiographical notes were obviously written as therapy at a time when he was weakened and depressed. Some letters were written when he was angry or irritated. The richly layered personality which emerges from those pages is not always admirable or agreeable. It was Magda who helped me put those documents in perspective and prompted me to rediscover why I liked and respected the man.

Many of John's friends have been generous in their help and encouragement. Ann and Warner Berthoff, both distinguished professors of English and visitors to Canna for 60 years, have not only given me much personal information, but helped me with the structure of this book. Few first-time authors of my age can have had the privilege of a one-to-one tutorial from an authority on form and meaning, as I had from Ann in a caravan in Canna on a cold and stormy June day.

Hugh Cheape has been my guide to Gaelic, as well as an important participant in this story. Donald MacInnes also helped me with translations. Since I do not speak the language, this cannot be the definitive account of John's work in Gaelic, and I am sure that I have underplayed its significance as a result. Another book remains to be written by someone more qualified. Neill Campbell allowed me to quote from the Inverneill family papers and has been always supportive and encouraging. Gilmour Thom lent me the diaries of his father and great-grandfather as well as a unique collection of original letters relating to Canna in the nineteenth century. Sheila Lockett, another important person in John's story, graphically evoked the atmosphere of Barra and Canna in the 1950s. Charles Fraser, much more than just John's lawyer, has been a source of inspiration.

The National Trust for Scotland readily granted me unfettered access to the Canna papers and its own files, where Ian Riches, the archivist, was patient and helpful. Many other friends of John and Margaret have contributed memories or let me read letters.

The people of Canna, new and old, have always been hospitable and taken a great interest in the progress of the book. I am especially grateful for the friendship of Winnie MacKinnon, even though it was occasionally expressed by prodding me to get on more quickly.

Fay Young, my wife, is not only a writer and editor, but lived a lot of this story with me; she knew both John and Margaret and loves Canna as much as I do. She has read the manuscript more than once and her professional expertise has been invaluable.

Inevitably there will be omissions and mistakes and I would welcome corrections or constructive criticism.

After lunch on the day of our first meeting in 1977, John took me to bail out his boat – a sturdy work vessel, not a laird's yacht – and then to walk up Compass Hill. He strode easily, while I, less than half his age, panted beside him. Around the horizon we could see Barra, the Uists, Benbecula, the Cuillins of Skye, Rum and the mainland. Below us was the land which John had bought and struggled for 40 years to protect and sustain.

He knew every inch of it. What the soil structure was and what would grow where. In the house there are many identical maps of Canna, each one neatly annotated to identify a different hoard of treasure: the best places for lobster fishing, the plan of native tree plantings, the haunts of migrating birds and butterflies. But here, laid out below us, was the ground itself. From the highest point on the island, the beginning and end of his property was clearly defined by the sea. As I was to discover later, the boundaries of responsibility which he both inherited and bequeathed, were never so easily defined.

Ray Perman
*Edinburgh, January 2010*

# CHAPTER ONE

# The Honoured Ancestor

> There are few more impressive sights in the world than a Scotsman on
> the make.
>
> J.M. Barrie, *What Every Woman Knows*, Act II

John Lorne Campbell was born into a land-owning tradition, but in
contrast to Canna, there was no vantage point from which the entire
estate could be seen. As a tall, curly-haired boy who loved wander-
ing the woods, meadows and shores, wherever he went, whichever
direction he faced, he saw land belonging to his family. It had been
this way for over 100 years. There was no reason to believe it would
change.

The estate defined their identity. The family were not just 'the
Campbells', they were 'the Campbells of Inverneill'. It was more
than just nominative convenience – although that was useful in a
county like Argyll where Campbell was a common surname. The
land they owned provided their income and, much more impor-
tantly, their social status, and it was essential that everyone knew it.
John's grandfather, Duncan, was known throughout the county as
'Old Inverneill' and his eldest son and heir – John's father – also
Duncan, as 'Young Inverneill', or, as he preferred to style himself,
'Duncan Campbell of Ross', after the part of the family estate which
he occupied and managed.

In the seventeenth and eighteenth centuries, the Campbells had
been 'tacksmen' – senior tenant farmers, one step down in the
hierarchy of the county of Argyll from freehold-owning lairds, but
men of substance nevertheless who had a position in society and
commanded respect. Their fortunes took a decided turn for the
better with the rise of Archibald Campbell, John's 'honoured
ancestor', whose portrait was, two centuries later, to look down
on the dining room of Canna House. Born in 1739, from modest

beginnings he rose quickly through ability, determination and hard work and came early to the attention of the Duke of Argyll, head of Clan Campbell and one of the most influential men in Scotland.[1] He could not have been born into a better clan. According to the historian Ian Grimble, the Campbells had made themselves one of the most powerful tribes in Scotland by displaying a hereditary flair for joining the winning side in all the major conflicts.[2] Encouraged by his aristocratic patron, Archibald Campbell studied hard and joined the army, a common Campbell career move.

By the middle of the eighteenth century Scotland was benefiting from its union with England in 1707 and its access to the fast-expanding British Empire, in which Scots were playing a disproportionately prominent part. As Chief Engineer of Bengal, Archibald Campbell had started trading on his own account, an activity the East India Company encouraged, probably to offset the low salaries it offered. The family story was that he had chartered two ships and filled them with silk to be sold in Britain at a profit. If only one made it safely, his fortune would be made, but Archibald had luck as well as daring. Both ships made it home and he became fabulously wealthy.

In 1773 he took advantage of a harsh economic downturn which forced many Highland lairds to sell and used some of the riches he had accumulated to buy Inverneill, a large estate on Loch Fyne, the first of several purchases. After his return from India he added fame to his fortune, as commander of the 71st Regiment of Highlanders in the American War of Independence. His military exploits in the New World did not begin well. Sailing into Boston harbour, he was unaware that the British had been forced out and the port was now in the hands of the revolutionaries. After a short sea battle he was captured with his men before he even landed and spent the next two years in prison. At first he reported 'the utmost civility and good treatment from the people of power at Boston',[3] but after reports of the harsh treatment given by the British to captured American officers, including the notorious Ethan Allen, leader of the Green Mountain Boys, Archibald was thrown into the town gaol at Concord.

His time in prison was not exactly comfortable, and he described it in a letter home:

I am lodged in a dungeon of twelve or thirteen feet square, whose sides are black with the grease and litter of successive criminals. Two doors, with double locks and bolts, shut me up from the yard, with an express prohibition to enter it, either for my health or the necessary calls of nature. Two small windows, strongly grated with iron, introduce a gloomy light to the apartment, and these are at this hour without a single pane of glass, although the season, for frost and snow, is actually in the extreme. In the corner of the cell, boxed up with the partition, stands a . . . which does not seem to have been cleared since its first appropriation to this convenience of malefactors. A loathsome black-hole, decorated with a pair of fixed chains, is granted me for my inner apartment, from whence a felon was but the moment before removed, to make way for your humble servant, and in which his litter to this hour remains. The attendance of a single servant on my person is also denied me, and every visit from a friend positively refused.[4]

Grim conditions, but not nearly enough to deter a Scotsman on the make. Being a prisoner did not stop Archibald adding to his Argyll landholding. In 1776, from his cell, he instructed his brothers to buy the Knapp estate, bordering Inverneill. The addition of the Ross estate, including Taynish and its neighbouring peninsula three years later, gave him 13,000 acres of land stretching from Loch Fyne to the Sound of Jura and bringing in annual rents which in today's money would be worth hundreds of thousands of pounds.

Later freed in an exchange of prisoners, which included Ethan Allen and several of his men, he went on to distinguish himself in the southern American colonies and as governor and defender of Jamaica. A second spell in India saw him become Governor of Madras and knighted as Sir Archibald. He returned to Britain in 1789, but his luck had run out and he died before he could enjoy his possessions. A grateful nation allowed him a burial in Westminster Abbey, where his memorial slab lies beneath a statue of his contemporary, George Frideric Handel. Never again did the family rise to such heights, but Archibald was never forgotten and always remained a symbol of what it had been and what it might have been. He had no children, so his land passed to his brothers, John and Duncan. It was Duncan who became the ancestor of the Campbells of Inverneill.

By the beginning of the twentieth century, the size of the landholding and the fact that it had been in the family's ownership for over a century (although some members liked to give the impression that it had been much longer) gave John Campbell's grandparents status in the inward-looking society of the Argyllshire gentry. They were not aristocracy, like the Duke of Argyll, whose castle at Inveraray was only 30 miles north of Inverneill, but they ranked above lesser landowners, tacksmen, mere tenant farmers and, of course, those whose money had arrived recently. How you had come by your money mattered. 'Old Money' inherited its fortunes, 'New Money' made it through 'trade' – a word uttered with such disdain that it might have meant stealing, but was much more likely to mean commerce. Families in this last category were to be looked down on and avoided.

Argyll is not an island, but before the First World War it might as well have been. It was a land apart from the rest of the country, marked by its remoteness from towns and cities. Even today, with metalled roads and fast transport, the journey from the Argyll coast to Glasgow, the nearest city less than 90 miles away as the crow flies, can take three or four hours, the road winding around the shores of lochs Lomond, Long and Fyne and climbing along high valleys through steep rocky hills. In the early years of the twentieth century, with dirt roads and horse and foot travel the journey could be tortuous.

The economy of the county was based on agriculture but cattle and sheep had to be walked by drovers to the markets of the south. In the winter, snows or landslips could close the passes for weeks. Not for nothing is the most famous road through the mountains known as 'Rest and be Thankful'. Donald Sutherland, who grew up in the county, wrote a memoir describing the time:

In 1900 Argyllshire knew not telephones, motorcars or aeroplanes. There were no radios, cinemas or television sets. Some of these things may have existed elsewhere, but not in the county of Argyll. Person to person communication, when not oral, was by letter or telegram. Postcards were looked upon as vulgar. One travelled by steam loco-motive, paddle-steamer and by sail. For short distances behind, or on, a horse. When you dined away from home you also spent the night, if not the weekend, with your host. Where you now spend a weekend, your visit would then have lasted a week.[5]

This closed community had its own social rules. 'Social strata were more clearly defined and more carefully preserved than they are today,' commented Sutherland. 'Horizontally speaking, the top layer consisted of the County. One became County by owning an estate in Argyllshire or by having oneself born into a landowning family. Status within that class depended less on wealth than upon length of establishment.' Then came professions – lawyers, clergy and doctors. 'Tradesfolk were kept very firmly in their places, possibly because some of them could have bought up half the county without serious inconvenience.'[6]

The fact that Sir Archibald had accumulated the family wealth of the Campbells of Inverneill by importing goods from India and by lending money to his regimental and diplomatic associates, and that a later ancestor was an opium dealer, was conveniently forgotten. The passing generations had laundered the fortune into County respectability.

The family had all the outward signs of success: land, money and esteem. But there was always a feeling that it could – indeed should – have had more. If only Sir Archibald had lived a few more years he would surely have received a peerage, the family reasoned, elevating them to the aristocracy and above the social status of most of their neighbours. Sir John Campbell, son of Sir Archibald's older brother, had been made a baronet in 1818, but the honour had died with him a year later. Old Inverneill made two attempts to revive the title so that he could style himself 'Sir Duncan Campbell of Inverneill', but he was rebuffed by the authorities on both occasions.

The family liked to claim descent from the Campbells of Craignish, one of the oldest and noblest branches of the clan, but the link was tenuous, through one of the sons of 'Tearlach Mor' (Big Charlie), a man with a fierce and unpredictable temper who had twice been obliged to move home to escape the consequences of murders he had committed. Nevertheless, the Inverneills wanted this man as an ancestor – the problem was that they could not prove it. There was no documentary evidence that the supposed son of Tearlach from whom they claimed descent actually existed.[7]

The Inverneill, Knapp and Ross estates had originally been farmed, the family living off the rents from their tenants and the income from the 'home farms' they managed themselves, or from incidental activities like kelp burning (producing potash from sea-weed), charcoal burning or obliging their tenants to have their corn ground at the estate mill and their horses shod at the estate smithies. There were also lead mines on the Inverneill estate. But with the agricultural productivity of large estates declining, Old Inverneill had turned much of his land over to shooting and fishing to take advantage of the higher sporting rents available in the boom years of the late nineteenth century.[8] He was himself a superb shot and fisherman, skills he passed on to his oldest son. Born in 1880, the younger Duncan – John's father – had been educated for the privileged life of the Scots landed class. He was sent first to Cargilfield, an Edinburgh preparatory school, then to Rugby. Out-side the ancient foundations, Eton, Winchester and Harrow, Rugby was judged to be one of the best of English public schools. Duncan lived in School Field House, a few years ahead of the poet Rupert Brooke. His tall good looks, sporting prowess and academic abilities made him popular and successful. He became Head of the School and a member of the shooting team. He topped his schooldays with a scholarship to Pembroke College, Oxford, to read Classics.

The fact that, despite his academic achievements, Duncan left Oxford two terms before taking his degree and went to work in a Yorkshire engineering company in which his father was a share-holder and director, may have caused comment in the drawing rooms of the Argyll big houses. After all, Old Inverneill sold the Knapp estate in 1887, the obvious inference being that money was short. Keeping up large country houses – not to mention town houses in London or Edinburgh – and educating sons at the most exclusive schools and universities cost a great deal. There were also dowries to be provided for daughters to ensure good marriages, and family settlements to provide for younger sons. These were essential expenses; standards and traditions had to be maintained. However, Duncan's first job in an industrial firm must have seemed rather odd. The family had no links to the north of England and engineering must have seemed perilously close to 'trade'.

Debts were not unusual among the gentry, they were the price of having to maintain traditional country middle–class values and standards against the odds. The landowning class of Argyll considered itself the custodian of the 'British Way of Life', a self-appointed role for which it believed it received no thanks and constant knocks. Lloyd George's 'People's Budget' of 1910, in which the Liberal Chancellor had sought to increase the burdens on the 'idle rich', was, they believed, a gross injustice, raising income taxes and death duties. Then there was the high cost of repairs to large houses, the government's 'betrayal of agriculture' in 1920 when guaranteed high produce prices were abandoned, the 'unreasonable' increases in agricultural workers' wages, and high rates that had to be paid to local councils at a time when their income from rents was falling.

'Everything,' John Campbell wrote later, 'seemed to conspire to keep the "Fine Old Landed Gentry" down. What money there was, was in the "wrong" hands, of "hard-faced men who had done well out of the war" or "Americans". The Landed Gentry, who had officered the infantry during the war and suffered many sacrifices, had been treated politically and economically with gross ingratitude. Yet whisky was still only 12s 6d and labour could be hired for 30s a week.'[9]

The Argyll gentry did occasionally travel outside the county, but for the most part their lives revolved around the big houses of their friends and neighbours with whom they shared a common heritage, interests and prejudices. Social life was vitally important and the better families vied with each other to provide weekend house and shooting parties. Again, Sutherland sets the scene: 'Spring, summer and autumn brought a constant round of visiting and visitors. My mother, a very social person by nature, spent at least three months of the year in other people's houses and our own spare bedrooms were seldom empty from one year's end to the next.'[10]

Duncan Campbell's older sister Olive kept an album conscientiously recording each social event.[11] Two facing pages would feature a picture of the host's home – often a sprawling mansion with turrets and battlements surrounded by a deer park or formal gardens. The printed house name would be cut from a letterhead or visiting card and house guests would sign their autographs, a memento of a happy weekend. In a five-year period from 1901 she recorded parties at Inverneill itself, Minard Castle, Shirvan, Skipness, Ballimore, Kilberry, Gallanach, Craignish Castle, Ormidale, Kilmory, Castle Toward, Glenakil, Inveraray Castle and Ardchattan Priory – and those were just in Argyll. Further afield the family visited Eastham House, Cheshire, home of the Tobins, Duncan and Olive's mother's family; Hooton Grange and Crowthornes, also in Cheshire; Dunstan Hall, Burton-on-Trent; Aramstone and Bryngwyn, Herefordshire. The Argyll gentry felt an affinity with their cousins, the landowning Protestant Ascendancy of Ireland, so there were trips to the Royal Dublin Society Horse Show in 1903 and a house party at Ashmere, Rathgar. Olive also travelled to Wales to house parties in Bridgend, Cardiff and Llangollen.

'The climax of all this visiting was reached in September when the Argyllshire Gathering took place [in Oban]. The Highland Games were attended by everyone who was anyone in the county and every laird and shooting tenant brought his own party. The Games were followed by two regattas, there were the Royal West Highland Yacht Club and the Corinthian Yacht Club, every room in every hotel was booked weeks in advance, there were the Gathering Ball and the Yacht Club Ball and for these a perfect frenzy of entertainment. Thirty or forty yachts anchored in the bay,' wrote Sutherland. 'Today such a show might be found at Monte Carlo, but nowhere else in Europe.'[12]

The only fitting jobs for the sons of lairds were the army, navy, diplomatic corps, the law or, for younger sons, the Church, which invariably meant the Anglican Episcopal Church of Scotland. Tenants and farmworkers might be Roman Catholics, or Presbyterian members of the Established Church of Scotland, lairds, at least in Argyll, seldom were. One of the winning sides Clan Campbell had chosen was that of the Protestant Hanoverian succession of the German King Georges over the Catholic Stuart dynasty of James, the 'Old Pretender' and his son Bonnie Prince Charlie, changing their religion and political allegiance at the same time. John's family had sided with the Jacobites in the rising of 1715, but by 1745 they, along with the rest of Clan Campbell, were firmly in the Government camp.

Military service was also a feature of gentrified life. Oldest sons were expected to go into the army during their fathers' active lifetimes, resigning their commissions when they succeeded to the estate or took over its management. The Campbells of Inverneill had a long and illustrious military history. The walls of Inverneill House were covered in guns, swords, drawings of battles and portraits of ancestors in uniform going back to the Napoleonic and Crimean wars, the Indian Mutiny and, more recently, the Boer War. The 1914–18 war added greatly to the military hardware: bayonets, gas masks, binoculars, steel helmets, Verey pistols, hand grenades; there was even a captured field gun on the lawn, until it was melted down for scrap in the 1940s.

'The atmosphere in the house,' John wrote later in his notebook, 'was of the glorification of the military spirit.' The American War of Independence, which Britain lost, was hardly acknowledged, despite the part played by Sir Archibald. With this background, it was natural that John's father, Duncan Campbell, should in due course join the 'family regiment', the 8th Battalion of the Argyll & Sutherland Highlanders, of which Old Inverneill, his own father, had been colonel. He was commissioned as first lieutenant and saw active service in West Africa, before returning to civilian life. By 1904 he was working in a shipbuilding company in Dumbarton, a busy shipping and engineering town on the north bank of the River Clyde, one of the main arteries of the industrial revolution in Europe. It was there he met Ethel Waterbury and asked her to marry him.

What she was doing in Dumbarton we do not know, but possibly she was in transit to or from the United States. Ethel was American, the daughter of John Waterbury, a rich and shrewd New York banker and businessman, whose business affairs often brought him to Europe. He doted on Ethel, the oldest of five daughters, and Duncan Campbell, young, handsome and the heir to Scottish estates, must have seemed a good catch for her. The couple were engaged at Inverneill and introduced to Argyll society, which would have approved of the scion of one of its best families marrying into money, even though it was American money. No one was saying that wealth was the sole motive for the marriage, but it was not unusual for the sons of the aristocracy or the gentry to seek out fortunes from the across the Atlantic to bolster their families flagging finances. Duncan and Ethel married in Morristown, New Jersey, the

Waterburys' family home. Olive recorded the event in her album, pasting in photographs which showed Fairfield, the Waterbury residence, as much larger and grander than any of the halls she had pictured in Argyll. The following year, on 1 October 1906, their first son was born. They named him John (possibly for his American grandfather) Lorne, a Campbell family name. He was born in an Edinburgh nursing home, then taken to Duncan's estate at Taynish.

CHAPTER TWO

# *A Divided Family*

*Taigh an aghaidh a chéile*
*Cha n-fhendar dha seasanih*
[A house divided against itself cannot stand.]
Abraham Lincoln.
Written by John in Gaelic at the start of one of his notebooks.

Taynish House stands at the end of a narrow finger of woodland extending three miles south from the village of Tayvallich, at the head of Loch Sween. It is ancient country. More than 10,000 years ago the retreating glaciers of the second ice age serrated the Argyll coast of Scotland into high peninsulas separated by deep sea lochs. Vegetation came with the warming climate and by 6,000 years ago much of the land was covered in trees, which provided shelter, fuel and food for men when they began farming the productive meadows and fishing the seas and lochs. Early settlers moved north as the climate improved, and inhabited the land for millennia, leaving behind them only the stone remains of houses and small forts and a handful of artefacts. They were displaced eventually by Picts, Scots from Ireland, who brought with them the Christian religion and the Gaelic language, and Vikings from Scandinavia. For centuries Argyll was fought over by Scots and the Viking Norsemen, but it is the Scots who have left most mark on the land. Some places still retain their Gaelic names and many more are anglicisations of the originals, although Taynish may owe its name to both invaders: Tay, from *Tigh*, Gaelic for house, nish from the Norse *nise* for nose or point.

The Atlantic oak woods of the Taynish estate and the salt marshes going down to Linne Mhuirich, the water that divides the estate from the rest of the peninsula, are a pristine natural habitat. The trees are hung with lichens – old man's beard and lungwort – a sign of clean air. In the humid atmosphere under their dense canopy thrive ferns and mosses with magical names: Mouse-tail, Tamarisk, Feather Fork and Forest Star. Today the estate is a nature reserve and looks very much as it must have done in the first decades of the twentieth century when the growing John Lorne Campbell, a rosy-cheeked, long-limbed boy, liked nothing better than to wander alone through the woods. He found them a source of wonder and fascination.

John did not see much of his father, who was away working elsewhere in Scotland, or later in London, where Duncan's father-in-law secured him well-paid jobs with American companies. John's mother detested the close Argyll society and did not get on with Olive Campbell, her husband's strong-minded older sister, who had been crippled from a childhood illness, never married and took an increasingly active interest in the management of her father's estates. She held very firm views on how things should be done to be accepted in the county and she expressed her views forcefully. Ethel spent as little time at Taynish as she could, preferring London or, later, Paris.

John, and his brothers Charles (known as Tearlach after his supposed ancestor), Colin and George, born at three- or four-year intervals, were often left in the charge of their nurse, Miss Martin, a dour Scots Presbyterian. 'Martin was supposed to be an excellent infant nurse,' John wrote later. 'That, as far as I can see, was the limit of her qualities. She was a hell-fire Calvinist, jealous, possessive and domineering, who got on badly with the other domestic household servants. I am convinced that my parents were afraid of her. Always, it seemed, she was on the point of exhausting their patience and always when my parents were on the point of dismissing her, a new child would be expected and she would become again indispensable.'[1] Martin, John felt, formed a 'third pole' of jealousy in the family with his mother and Aunt Olive. In the middle of this triangle, the boy was pulled in each direction in turn.

Deprived of the influence of his absent father and mother, John often visited the sprawling mansion at Inverneill, to which his grandfather had added an ostentatious three-storey square block in the Scottish baronial style, out of proportion to and sympathy with the original farmhouse. To the young boy this newest part of

Old Inverneill's house had a brooding presence. He imagined it to be much older than it actually was. It felt cold and damp, with a hostile and haunted atmosphere. John was superstitious and never slept in it without keeping beside his bed the traditional Highland talisman, against ghosts – Bible, rowan wood and a cold steel knife or dirk.

His grandfather, always in Highland dress, ruled the house in the manner of a Victorian patriarch, conducting family prayers every morning with the domestic staff required to attend. He was the last of the family to have had an association with India, having begun his working life there until called back to manage the family estates. It seemed to John that his friends and acquaintances consisted entirely of lairds and colonels – remote and stuffy figures – and he represented a way of life which was swiftly passing. He embodied the Highland tradition, he expected loyalty, obedience and hard work from his employees and tenants, but accepted a lifelong obligation in return. He would provide their homes and livelihoods and, if necessary, defend them. John loved to go into the woods or onto the water with his grandfather. It would be decades before he realised how much of the values of the Highland gentry he had absorbed from these times.

In contrast to the austere grey stone of Inverneill, Taynish House was white-harled under a slate roof and sat comfortably in the landscape. Its distinctive semi-circular bays had been added to the ends of the house 100 years after it was built in 1630. Each spacious bay room had three windows, making dining room, drawing room and the two largest bedrooms light and airy and giving them views over the gardens or the estate. Instead of the big formal walled garden at Inverneill, with its mock turrets at each corner, the Taynish gardens were small and gave way quickly to woods and meadows edged with mature beech, lime and sycamore trees. The farm buildings, including the vast two-storey stone barn and the unusual octagonal dairy, were close at hand so young John often encountered his father's farm workers and tenants. On the shore of Loch Sween, a five-minute walk from the house, a circular bath house had been built so that the laird could take hot salt-water baths. It was said that Lillie Langtry, the music hall star and alleged mistress of the Prince of Wales, had once bathed there.[2]

The estate teemed with wildlife. In the woods were red squirrels, badgers, stoats and roe deer; in the air buzzards, tawny owls, woodpeckers, jays, wrens, curlews, larks, snipe, woodcock and songbirds. There were annual visitors like swallows, redstarts, wood and willow warblers, waxwings, eider ducks, barnacle geese and swans. At the water's edge otters made their holts and fed on the abundant fish in the lochs. 'Between Taynish and its island [in Loch Sween] the sea bottom is a miracle of beauty, black starfish, sea urchins, crabs and sea anemones,' wrote a later occupant of the house.[3] Here young John learned his love of animals and plants, which was to stay with him all his life. Here too he began to acquire knowledge and skills, from the age of nine identifying and cataloguing in his notebook the moths and butterflies which abounded in the marshes, meadows and bogs; Purple Hairstreaks, one of the northernmost colonies in Britain, red and black Cinnabar moths and orange and brown Marsh Fritillaries. The notebook is still in Canna House, a blend of child-like wonder and surprising sophistication.

In the absence of his parents he retreated to a solitary world of nature, becoming irritated when forced to go on walks with his younger brothers. With his father away working, John was not taught to shoot, as Duncan had been taught by his father, and never learned to regard birds and animals as targets to be killed for sport – a severe social disadvantage with the County, which despised those who could not or would not shoot. Left to himself he developed views which were increasingly to distance him from the life of the gentry, not only in his attitude towards wildlife. In 1911, when without his consent his parents enrolled him in the Junior Primrose League, the nursery wing of the Conservative Party, John immediately rebelled, the first of many political rebellions. He later claimed to have become a Liberal at that point, despite being only five. This would have been another rift between him and the staunchly Tory County.

★

If life among the nature of Taynish seemed idyllic, the calm came to an abrupt end in the summer of 1914. 'After that,' John wrote later, 'nothing was ever the same again.'[4] The family had been taken to

London. Although only eight, John sensed the gathering gloom among the adults over the political situation in Europe, particularly between Britain and France on one side and Germany and its allies on the other. As the summer went on, the mood darkened as 'the impossible became the improbable, the improbable became the possible and suddenly the inevitable'. The whole of Europe seemed to slide into war.

There were immediate changes for the family. Duncan and his brothers, John's uncles, Lorne and Neill, all of whom had been territorial officers, were recalled to their regiment. Duncan, promoted to captain, injured his leg while on an exercise and so was confined to administrative and training duties in Britain – an accident which may have saved his life. The Argyll & Sutherland Highlanders were involved in some of the heaviest trench warfare in France and Belgium. Attrition among the front-line troops and the junior officers who led them was severe and, compared to previous conflicts, the war was exceptionally violent and bloody. For the first time the civilian population at home got first-hand reports of what was happening at the Front. Newspapers carried pictures of ruined buildings amid the mud of Flanders and the daily casualty lists grew longer as the war went on. By 1916, when John was sent to Cargilfield, the Edinburgh prep school his father had attended, 'there was hardly a boy out of over 100 who was not in mourning'.[5] John joined them as Lorne was killed in 1917 and Neill in 1918.

But the war had other effects which were unseen by John at the time. It brought about the final collapse of the economies of the Inverneill and Taynish estates. During the war years the income from rents and sporting lets plunged and the wisdom of turning the land over to shooting looked very short term. At the same time the shortage of men for agricultural work meant that wages on the home farms rose and the need to fund the war meant that taxation increased. The estates were now not paying their way, let alone providing an income for John's family. Duncan had sold Scotnish, part of the Taynish estate, just before the war, but it was not enough to stem the outward flow of money. The family was dependent on Duncan's earnings and Ethel's allowance to stay solvent, although Ethel's father, John Waterbury, was keen to advance money to finance improvements to the estate.

John hated school at Cargilfield. It was an abrupt change from life at Taynish and he was unprepared for it. Denied his solitary escape to nature, he was now caught in 'a barbaric society, with its cliques and bullying and terrifying authority'.[6] Although in Edinburgh, the school was geared to the English public school system to which the Scots upper middle classes aspired to send their children. Boys were allowed to wear kilts, but anyone with a perceptible Scottish accent was looked down on. John spoke with an English accent and the only Scottish history he knew was from the reading of the novels of Sir Walter Scott, which were set as holiday tasks and put him off Scott for the rest of his life. The only saving grace, as far as John was concerned, was that school freed him from female control by Miss Martin, Aunt Olive and his mother.

He found Rugby School, when he arrived in 1920, to be much more civilised, with the boys' natural tendency to form cliques channelled into support for the houses to which they were assigned. John followed his father into School Field House. He felt less excluded than he had at Cargilfield but still suffered in comparison with Duncan, whose sporting and academic achievements and facility for leadership he could not match and was not allowed to forget. He made a slow start academically, until it was realised that he needed glasses.

The feeling of inferiority intensified when his brother Charles arrived at the school three years later. In contrast to John, Charles was confident and sporty. Their constant irritation with each other led them to be nicknamed 'Huffy Major' and 'Huffy Minor'. John could not steer clear of all sport – in fact he developed his lifelong devotion to cricket at Rugby – but tried his best to escape the supposedly voluntary (but in practice compulsory) military training in the Officer Cadet Corps. To avoid as many of the activities as possible he joined the school band as a trombonist and graduated to other brass and woodwind and finally to the school orchestra. The excellent musical and instrumental teaching stood him in good stead; he learned a love of music and the ability to play a wide range of instruments. He later looked back on Rugby as a reasonably happy time and – apart from holidays in Scotland – preferred it to visits to his parents' homes in London or Paris, where his father had been sent as representative of International Business Machines (IBM), another job secured by his father-in-law. There was an unspoken rift between John's parents and home visits were characterised by sullen silences, which their sons found hard to understand or to bear.

John left Rugby in the summer of 1925. He felt he had stayed too long and should have left after his eighteenth birthday the previous Christmas. The last two terms added little to his education, but instead of allowing him to go straight to Oxford, his parents insisted he spend time in France learning the language. He regarded it as another wasted year and another instance of his maturity being postponed. He was sent to 'crammers' run by English schoolmasters, which offered little contact at all with French people. Three months with a French family would have done him more good, he felt, although he had the feeling that his parents wanted to guard against any contact with the Catholic religion or the opposite sex.

His upbringing had been sheltered and his lack of contact with girls rankled most. He had spend his schooldays in single-sex institutions – fine for those boys with sisters and therefore the possibility of meeting sisters' friends in the holidays, not so good for the eldest of four brothers. When he arrived at Oxford he was not equipped to compete with young men with the experience and self-assurance to win the favours of the few female undergraduates there at that time – and in the 1920s, Town and Gown did not mix. Contemporary photographs show John to be tall and handsome, but he felt himself to be immature, painfully shy and fatally lacking in confidence.

Ironically, in his third year he found lodgings at 22 Beaumont Street, a house that he quickly discovered had a reputation as a place where the stars of college rugby teams could bring their girlfriends for 'amorous purposes'. During one holiday he told this to a friend in Argyllshire, but the story got back to his Aunt Olive, who was horrified and called her uncle, the judge Sir Alfred Tobin. He in turn called the Proctors, who were responsible for university discipline, demanding they raid the building. They declined, on the grounds that to do so would risk having to send down (expel) half the university rugby team. John, however, found it impossible to concentrate in such a busy house and moved to less notorious lodgings.

Oxford in the 1920s was rebounding from the years of austerity following the 1914–18 war. It was the period of 'Bright Young Things', the gifted and gilded youth later chronicled by Eveyln Waugh – himself an undergraduate at the time – in his novels *Brideshead Revisited* and *Vile Bodies*. In the latter he describes the 'Masked parties, Savage parties, Victorian parties, Greek parties, Wild West parties, Russian parties, Circus parties – all the succession and repetition of massed humanity . . . Those vile bodies.' John Campbell may have glimpsed this side of Oxford life, but he was certainly not part of it – excluded by his paralysing introversion and lack of money.

He might be heir to Scottish estates and have been educated at one of the country's more expensive public schools, but he lacked the funds of many of his contemporaries. John received no financial support from his father and his fees at school and university were paid by his American grandfather, who also arranged for an allowance of £375[7] a year – enough to live on but not to support a lavish party lifestyle, even had he wanted one. His notebooks make no mention of parties, punting on the Cherwell or the Isis or May balls. Nor do they give any female names, or lasting friendships made with contemporaries. The only people he kept in touch with after Oxford were his professors and tutors. While many found their period at university a time to try new experiences, meet people from different backgrounds, gain confidence and to grow up, John summed up his time at the university as: 'an obscure year as a freshman, an ill-adjusted and depressed one as a second year and an overworked and secluded third year in lodgings'.[8]

The year between school and university had meant that John had been away from study and he only just scraped his place at St John's College, although this may partly have been the result of his decision to read Natural Science, rather than follow his father in reading Classics. He had done well in sciences at Rugby and complained that having to wear glasses to read made it difficult to decipher the Greek alphabet, but there was an element in his decision of wanting to escape more unfavourable comparisons with his father's Classical scholarship. In the event he found science a struggle. He was not good enough at maths and found the routine laboratory work tedious.

In October 1927 John became 21. His great-uncle, Sir Alfred

Tobin, had rented Taynish for the shooting season and his Aunt Olive was in residence as hostess. She organised a grand party for John's coming-of-age in the massive stone barn at Taynish, inviting friends, neighbours and the estate tenants, some of whom John had never met before. There was food and dancing which resonated on the thick wooden boards of the first-floor loft. Neither of John's parents attended. His father, working for IBM in Paris, had taken his holidays to attend the annual shooting competitions at Bisley. His mother claimed that she had been kept out of the way by Olive who had held the party early, before the start of the Oxford term, without telling Ethel. This may have been the case; there was no love lost between the two women. Whatever the truth, John received neither the 'key of the door', nor his father's confidence in learning the financial health of the estate. He came of age in years only; he still felt himself to be denied access to the adult world. But the party was a happy occasion, nevertheless. The tenants, believing John would one day be their landlord, presented him with a gold watch and cufflinks, which he cherished. In return he had learned a few words of Gaelic: *'tha mi gle thoilichte a bhith comhla ribh an nochd'*. ('I am very pleased to be with you tonight.') He was touched by the warm response this simple sentiment elicited.

Back in Oxford John carried on with science for one more term, and then he began to think of changing course, but to what? With no guidance from his parents about what his eventual career should be, he settled on Rural Economy (agriculture). He could not face having to repeat his first year, so looked for a course where his science passes would be accepted. But an eye to his future after university also persuaded him that he was training himself to take over management of Taynish.

The Oxford course, although thorough and modern – including modules on soil structure and contemporary theories of animal husbandry – was mostly theoretical. There were demonstrations, but practical farming was not included and the students were not expected to do any physical work or get their hands dirty. John seems not to have minded this at the time. It is unlikely that as laird of an estate the size of Taynish he would have imagined himself actually working the land – certainly neither his father nor grand-father had done so. He did reasonably well during the course, but agriculture did not consume his interests either. His university notebooks betray an increasing fascination with another subject entirely. John's notes on Agricultural Law, for example, begin with the title at the top of each page written in English, but in the letters of old Irish script. By the end of the book the title is written in Gaelic. Notes on soil structure are titled in Gaelic from the start and his doodles increasingly contain Celtic words – and not only in Scots or Irish Gaelic. There is *Cwmrag* (Welsh) and *Kernûak* (Cornish). The notebook abandons agriculture altogether after a while and ends in a discussion of Gaelic grammar. Livestock notes eventually give way to an essay on the existence of written literature in Scots Gaelic.

In the early decades of the twentieth century Gaelic was still commonly spoken among the working population of Argyll and John often heard it spoken by his father's estate staff and their families, who lived close by Taynish House. Tenant farmers on the estate spoke Gaelic – although they were careful not to do so in the hearing of the 'folk from the Big House' – and there was a Gaelic service every Sunday in the Church of Scotland kirk in Tayvallich, the nearest village.

The language had once been spoken by all social classes in the Highlands and Islands, but after the failed Jacobite rebellions of 1715 and 1745 it became associated with political dissent and the Catholic religion. The landowning and professional classes increasingly spoke English and disdained the native tongue. There was an official campaign to discourage and even suppress the language, backed by repressive legislation which not only discriminated against Gaelic, but for a while outlawed other symbols of Highland culture, such as tartan. There was also a campaign to supplant Gaelic in education, led by bodies such as the Scottish Society for the Propagation of Christian Knowledge (SSPCK), although its attempts to provide English-only schools had to be abandoned when it was discovered that children who had learned English by rote made no effort to understand what they were saying. Among themselves and at home they continued to speak Gaelic. Catholic priests still preached in the old language and, despite the prevailing orthodoxy, many ministers in the Presbyterian Church of Scotland continued to preach in both languages.

By the end of the nineteenth century official hostility to Gaelic had lessened, but it was still associated with poverty, under-achievement and reduced social and economic chances, and was steadily eroded by the 'quieter and more gradual changes' of anglicisation and economic improvement.[9] In 1908 an editorial in the *Glasgow Herald* maintained: 'The first requisite for a High-lander is such a knowledge of English as will open up to him the lucrative employment from which ignorance of English must shut him out.'[10] The decline of Gaelic had been apparent for 150 years, but became far more rapid with the dawn of the twentieth century. In 1765, just less than a quarter of the Scottish population was estimated to speak Gaelic and in some counties – including Argyll – 100 per cent of inhabitants spoke the language.[11] By 1879 the proportion of the Scottish population which could speak Gaelic had fallen to less than one in ten, while in Argyll, although the proportion speaking the language was over 80 per cent, five sixths of these also spoke English and only 10,000 of a total 75,000 people in the county spoke Gaelic alone.[12] The census of 1921 showed only 25,000 Gaelic speakers in Argyll – still the third highest total of any county, but less than a third of the total 40 years before – and all but 500 were bilingual in English and Gaelic.[13]

After Queen Victoria's rediscovery of the Highlands and her remodelling of Balmoral Castle in mock baronial style, the Argyll gentry began to play up their Highland ancestry – wearing kilts, learning to play the bagpipes and attending Highland Games, such as the annual Argyllshire Gathering in Oban. They were even prepared to use the occasional Gaelic name or word. John's brother Charles signed himself 'Tearlach' in the Inverneill visitors' book and John's Aunt Ysobel topped and tailed her letters to John with Gaelic endearments, but it was not the done thing to show too much interest or knowledge. John was told that his grandfather, Old Inverneill, understood Gaelic well, but he would never admit to it or speak it.

A shudder ran up the spines of the gentry when they considered what was happening to their counterparts in the Big Houses of Ireland, with whom they felt an affinity. The association of Highland Gaelic with Irish as a way of denigrating the language was nothing new: some Scots writers had been doing it since the Middle Ages.[14] But in the first decades of the twentieth century it took on a new and sinister connotation in the minds of the Scots landowning classes. In Ireland a 'Fenian conspiracy' – Gaelic-speaking and Catholic – with its land redistribution policies and occasional acts of murder and terrorism, was threatening not just the old order, but the very existence of the British Empire itself. The County was not slow to see the similarities.

John's interest in the language had been sparked in 1926, the year he went up to Oxford, when, attending a Highland Games in Oban as a junior steward, he overheard four young men from the islands speaking Gaelic. He was struck by the purity of the men's accents and beauty of the language: 'I had never heard Gaelic spoken like that and I said to myself "that's something I should have".'[15] His father had offered to pay the Taynish gamekeeper to teach John the bagpipes, but John persuaded him instead that he should begin to learn Gaelic from Hector MacLean, a Tiree man who was the estate factor. The lessons consisted of reading the New Testament together in Gaelic.

When he arrived at Oxford John sought out John Fraser, a Highlander and academic who had become Jesus Professor of Celtic in 1921. Oxford was unique among English universities in having a chair in Celtic, which had been founded in 1877 and was first held by the distinguished Welsh scholar, Sir John Rhys. Fraser, a native Gaelic speaker from Inverness-shire, who had previously been a professor at Aberdeen, was the second incumbent. John Campbell started attending Fraser's lectures and classes and became secretary of an embryo Oxford Gaelic Society. It was a small and rather eccentric group. Fellow members included John Bannerman, then a post-graduate student at Balliol and a rugby blue, and his friend, the Marquis of Graham, later 7th Duke of Montrose, who was, like John Campbell, reading Agriculture. Both men went on to have political careers, Bannerman as one of the founders of the Scottish Nationalist movement, although he left it in the 1930s to become a Liberal. Montrose emigrated to Rhodesia and became a minister in the government of Ian Smith until his white supremacist views became too much even for the Rhodesian Front Party. The Oxford Gaelic Society read Irish from Keating's seventeenth-century *History of Ireland* and Scots Gaelic from *Caraid nan Gaidheal*, an anthology of Gaelic prose from the pen of the Rev. Dr Norman MacLeod.

Professor Fraser was an unusual academic and became a friend and mentor to John until his death in 1945. As well as studying the classical texts, Fraser was interested in the living language. He urged John: 'The language has not been properly recorded. You have to go among the people. Whenever you hear a word or expression you've not heard before, write it down in your notebook, because the dictionaries don't reflect the whole language.'[16] It was an open and inquiring attitude not common in universities at the time, where oral evidence was regarded as unacademic, but it struck a chord with John. For the time being, however, his interests and energies had to go into more conventional academic pursuits.

# CHAPTER THREE

# Homeless and Jobless

The year 1928 was to have several far-reaching consequences for John, although it would be years before he was aware of them all. His switch from science to agriculture was made that year, but he also began an ambitious project which was to distract him from his formal degree course. He started to research his first book.

It would be five years before he completed *Highland Songs of the Forty-Five*[1] but when it was published in 1933 it marked him out as a serious scholar and a fearless – if not reckless – commentator. For a first book from a man still only 27, it was soaring in its ambition. The Highland army raised by Bonnie Prince Charlie in his doomed attempt to reinstate the Stuart dynasty had often been portrayed as a mindless rabble out only for the plunder they could steal along the way and, in the absence of evidence to the contrary, this was widely accepted by leading historians. Ordinary Highland soldiers mostly spoke Gaelic and many were illiterate. There were no surviving written accounts of what they thought and did, but they composed and sang songs and some of these had been transcribed and preserved.

By studying some of these songs John sought to prove that the Jacobite army understood the cause it was fighting for, had a sophisticated knowledge of the political issues of the day (such as the Act of Settlement, which prohibited a Catholic from succeeding to the throne) and were less ignorant than was commonly supposed. Many knew the Bible, some Latin and Greek words and had a considerable knowledge of Gaelic lore. Furthermore, while the troops of the Duke of Cumberland, commander of the army which defeated Charles Edward Stuart at the Battle of Culloden in 1746, had been burning and looting, the Highland army had shown restraint.

To prove his theory John set himself a huge task, considering that he was supposed to be studying agriculture and was working on the book only in his spare time. He used as his source material 70 songs from the period he discovered in collections of Gaelic poetry and manuscripts in the Bodleian Library in Oxford and the British Museum in London. These he analysed for political content, reducing them to 32 for publication. In the book's preface he acknowledged the help of Professor Fraser in the translation as well as encouragement and proof reading – but the bulk of the work he did himself, a considerable feat for someone who had been learning the Gaelic language seriously for only two years. He included a scholarly discussion of the difficulties in translation, of Gaelic rhyming schemes and metres and a list of 'loan words' imported into Gaelic from Scots, English, Norse, Norman French and Anglo-Saxon. The songs themselves were published in facing pairs – the original Gaelic on one side, his own English blank verse translation on the other. He included footnotes, numbered lines and, for 14 of the songs, the music to which they would have been sung. He also included biographies of the 12 authors. The final book was a mature and accomplished academic work.

But its most remarkable feature – and the best clue to the John Lorne Campbell who was to emerge later – was the strength and audacity with which he pressed home his argument. In his introduction, he roundly condemned 'many Scottish and practically all English writers' on the period for their ignorance of 'the language spoken in half the area of Scotland'. This man who described himself privately as shy, immature and lacking in self-confidence, found no difficulty in expressing himself forcefully in print. Without formal training in historical research, or any academic qualification other than in agriculture, he nevertheless attacked the reputations of some leading Scots historians of the period, including Peter Hume Brown, a former Professor of History at Edinburgh University who had also been Historiographer-Royal for Scotland, and D.N. Mackay, who had recently published an acclaimed book: *Clan Warfare in the Scottish Highlands*.[2]

John's enthusiasm for the Jacobite cause was not so unusual. The political and religious aspects of the uprising had long ago been forgotten in the popular mind, replaced by the image, fostered by the hugely popular novels of Sir Walter Scott and R.L. Stevenson, of the Highlander as a romantic hero fighting a lost cause. John may also have felt that he was making amends, in a small way, for his family's desertion of the Stuart side after the unsuccessful rising in 1715, a change of allegiance without which they would never have achieved fame and fortune. It was an act of rebellion. By siding with the kilted rabble he was thumbing his nose at the stern redcoats who looked down from the walls of his grandfather's mansion. He was also giving a voice to the voiceless – ordinary men who had never before been allowed to speak for themselves.

But his espousal of the cause went much further than mere Romanticism: 'the Rising of 1745 was the natural reaction of the Jacobite clans and their sympathisers in the Highlands against what had been, since the coming of William of Orange in 1690, a calculated official genocidal campaign against the religion of many and the language of all Highlanders'. The charge of genocide was not going to win him friends in the academic establishment, nor was his named assault on respected authorities on the period. Nevertheless, his book attracted a few favourable reviews.[3]

If 1928 marked the start of a new academic interest for John, it also marked a further step closer to the disintegration of his family. When his parents and their four sons were together the strain was almost unbearable. John described the atmosphere: 'The family . . . only united in London or Paris – my father silent, my mother resentful, my brothers and I wishing we were in Scotland. What the situation needed was a shattering good row that might have cleared the air or at least led to a walk-out. But everyone was too polite and just sat hugging their resentments in silence and storing them up.'[4]

The boys were at a loss to know what was causing the tension between their father and mother, but at each vacation it had become more intractable. There was worse to come. John's younger brother Charles began to show the first symptoms of Hodgkin's disease, a cancer of the lymph system.[5] Since his irritation with Charles at school for his confidence and popularity, John had grown closer to his brother and gained respect for his strength of character and directness. If anyone could confront his parents and get to the bottom of the increasing rift between them, John felt it was Charles. He looked to him for the courage he himself lacked to demand answers, but Charles was growing progressively weaker and his illness was the cause of a new strain between his parents, who were already living apart. Duncan was unable to contribute to the cost of his son's medical treatment and Ethel took Charles on a tour of European health resorts, paying his doctors and hospital bills from her own allowance from the Waterbury family, effectively using her money to close her husband out.

John graduated with a pass degree in Rural Economy in 1929. No honours were awarded in the subject at the time, but he had been a diligent student despite the distraction of Gaelic and passed second or third out of 20 students. The end of his degree course left him more unsure than ever what he should do. Without any guidance from his parents and at the suggestion of his professor, he applied for a job with the chemicals company ICI to sell fertilisers and seeds. The job paid £3 a week and John went to London to be interviewed, but was rejected with the advice that he should get some practical farming experience to supplement his academic knowledge.

In order to do this he arranged to spend a year with Richard Tanner, who farmed his own land and managed neighbouring estates at Kingston Bagpuize, Berkshire,[6] not far from Oxford. John liked Tanner a lot, describing him as a good man and a splendid farmer, but he was not made to work. Instead he spent his time reading copies of the periodical *Revue Celtique*, a set of which he had bought from the Jesus College library, and occasionally organising cricket matches between Oxford teams and the village club, in which he played for the village. He also bought his first car – an eight-horsepower, two-cylinder air-cooled Rover, which had to be started with a hand crank. It was a museum piece even then, and he soon changed it for a second-hand Alvis. Despite the lack of practical farming work, it was an enjoyable year and a welcome break from the strains of his family, although he felt this again on a holiday to visit his mother at the villa she had bought near St Jean de Luz, south of Biarritz, close to the French border with Spain.

At the end of his year's farming placement, 'selling sulphate of ammonia to sceptical farmers for ICI' had become less attractive. At a loss to know what he should do with his life, he went back to Oxford and embarked on a postgraduate dissertation on the history of the Scottish agricultural township. He worked at it intermittently, splitting his time between Oxford, London and occasional returns to

Scotland, but his heart was not in it and work on his book about the Forty-Five took up most of his interest and time. The return to academia was, he later realised, a mistake. In a rare piece of introspection, he wrote in his notebook: 'Intellectual life was an escape from various emotional problems, the wrong kind of escape, for these were nettles which had to be grasped, not avoided.'[7]

His notebooks give few hints about what problems he was talking about, but we can guess that apart from the strains of his family life, at an age when many of his contemporaries had married or at least had women friends, he felt the lack of a relationship. Shyness and lack of opportunity kept him apart from other people and the succession of rented rooms he occupied were lonely. His contemporaries advised him that if he wanted to get on in life he should get a job in a prestigious company, join a fashionable army regiment or at least use the fact that his family was in *Burke's Landed Gentry* and *Who's Who* to get himself on the guest list of some society hostesses. But he did not have the confidence or the inclination to do any of these things.

His estrangement from his parents and his determination to stay as far away as possible from the forceful Aunt Olive probably saved him from an arranged 'dynastic marriage' to a suitable girl from the Argyll County set, but at the same time he had no one to guide him. He hardly spoke to his father, and his mother, who had no brothers and thus no experience of the young male world, was at the same time possessive and hypercritical of her sons. He was not going to confide in her. During a holiday at Inverneill he was invited by the Campbells of Crarae, who owned the neighbouring estate on Loch Fyne, for a cruise on their yacht *Susanne* to Dublin and the Hebrides. The trip was memorable for two reasons. It introduced him for the first time to the islands of Mull, Barra, South Uist, Lewis, Skye and Rum, but it also led to 'disastrous emotional consequences'. What these were or who might have been involved we do not know. The log book of the *Susanne* has long ago been lost. John wrote later: 'I at least obtained an interesting insight into the life of the real Establishment – but never made the grade, my own immaturity and lack of self-confidence being too great, but also I had a feeling against having to act the necessary part.'[8]

Apart from his lack of personal experience he also felt he lacked knowledge of real life outside the shelter of school and university.

During his year in France, one assistant master, whom John thought was more intelligent and sensible than his employer, had advised John to get some practical experience of work: 'go round the world before the mast – you could become a Cabinet Minister'. He was wrong about the Cabinet, but John recognised later that the sentiment had been right; he had been brought up in a narrow and protected environment and he lacked practical experience of people or problems.

Having rejected a second attempt to get a job at ICI, he still expected to follow the pattern of the generations and be asked by his father to manage Taynish. Despite his antipathy for the County he made some effort to fit in. Pressed by Aunt Olive, he had even joined the 'family regiment' – the 8th Argyll & Sutherland Highlanders – as a Territorial officer, a role for which he considered himself singularly unfitted. His father had ended the war with the rank of major and in peacetime had continued in a part-time role, later becoming the regiment's colonel, a rank John's grandfather had also held. In the regiment John rediscovered the rigid class system he had detested in the County. His brother officers were drawn from three distinct groups. Considering themselves at the top of the social – if not the military – order were the resident Argyll lairds. Next came the Anglo-Scots, well-off men with Argyllshire connections, but living in London. At the bottom of the heap were the local tradesmen or businessmen. 'The three types did not mix well',[9] John found.

The purpose of a territorial regiment was that, coming from the same area, the officers should know the men they were supposed to lead. But with Inverneill and Taynish increasingly being let to sporting tenants, John no longer had a permanent home in Argyll and was, in any case, spending most of his time in the south. As a first lieutenant, the most junior commissioned rank, he hardly knew the platoon he commanded and, anyway, felt he had no aptitude for the job. The training was completely inadequate and he felt they were being prepared to refight the 1914–18 war – or worse, the Boer War. Only once was an aircraft involved in their manoeuvres, and they never saw a tank. Nevertheless, he stuck it for nearly six years, resigning in indignation in 1933 only after, at a passing-out parade attended by his aunt, he heard the commanding officer remark that 'Miss Olive Campbell had given two nephews to the 8th'. His father, despite the family's long military tradition, had never pressed him to join the regiment and did not reproach him for resigning.

Another event in 1928 was to have a profound effect on John, although it was not apparent at the time. Since his grandfather's death in 1922, John's father, Duncan, had been increasingly occupied with tidying up the affairs of the estate. It was fairly clear there were debts to be settled, but John did not know the full extent of them. When he had reached the age of 21 he had expected to be taken into his father's confidence, but it had not happened. Now he discovered that it was his Aunt Olive, rather than himself, who had been made a trustee of the family settlement – the legal arrangement intended to provide for Duncan's brothers and sisters who had not inherited the Inverneill and Taynish estates. She would now be privy to the financial affairs of the family while John was kept in ignorance. To John this was more evidence of his father's lack of confidence in him. In fact Duncan was under enormous pressure. He had spent the six years following Old Inverneill's death sorting out his finances, but one fact was inescapable. The estates were losing money and Duncan's own earnings were not enough to meet the debts and outgoings. That year he took the decision to sell Taynish and began secretly to put the estate in order and search for a buyer.

It was another two years before the sale was complete and John learned about it only after the event. The news came as a shattering blow and deepened his unhappiness. He had lost his home – the place to which he had retreated when deprived of his parents' presence and affections, the place in which he had developed his love of landscape and wildlife and begun to learn Gaelic. It had given him interests that were to stay with him all his life, but now he could no longer return there. It was a severe emotional, as well as a physical loss. He felt he had also lost his career. He had believed he was training himself to take over the management of the estate, and its sale heightened his uncertainty about what he should do with his life.

All these things distressed him, but the deepest hurt came from his father's silence, and it was to overshadow the next 25 years. 'The fact that my father never took me into his confidence as heir made others suppose I was not considered capable of succession, something that aroused in me great resentment and influenced my thoughts, feelings and actions throughout much of my life,' he wrote.[10]

Without any explanation of the reasons, John assumed that the decision to sell Taynish was the result of his father's lack of faith in his abilities; he was deemed incompetent to manage the family land-holdings. He believed he now bore the mark of Cain: the County would know he was not up to the job. He felt deep remorse for the gold watch and cufflinks given to him by the estate tenants at his coming of age. He now knew they had been accepted under false pretences, he would never be their laird and never be able to repay the kindness they had shown him. Now he had no home. His parents lived separate lives, his father in Paris where he was working for IBM and his mother at St Jean de Luz. Inverneill was let every summer to shooting tenants and outside these times was occupied by his aunt, whose regime he refused to recognise. He had last slept in Inverneill House in 1928, when he had brought a group of Oxford friends for a reading holiday. It was 19 years before he was to sleep there again.

This was a very unhappy period for John, but the depth of his misery was yet to come. In 1932 Charles died at Merano in the Italian Tirol, a mountain resort with thermal springs where Ethel had taken him in the hope that the fresh air and hot mineral baths would ease his last months. John was devastated by his brother's death, but also bitter at his mother's possessiveness. In the 1930s Hodgkin's disease was still incurable and since there was nothing medically to be done, John felt his mother should have let Charles enjoy his last years in his own way. Even after death she could not let go. The body was taken across the Alps to Munich for cremation, but grief failed to heal the rift in the family. Duncan travelled to Germany for the service, but Ethel refused to see him. It was left to John to accompany her with Charles's remains on the steamer *Bremen* to New York. Ethel had decided that her son's ashes should be buried in the Waterbury family plot at Darien, Connecticut, rather than the Inverneill mausoleum, where his grandfather and ancestors were interred, and Duncan was unable to resist her.

Ethel saw herself as being among the elite of international society and she chose to sail on the *Bremen* because it was the latest word in luxury and speed. Launched only three years before, the ship had won the Blue Riband for the fastest crossing of the Atlantic on her maiden voyage, and then smashed her own record on the return trip. The rich and famous, such as Marlene Dietrich and Henry Ford, travelled on her, but, close to despair, John was in no mood to appreciate his fashionable surroundings. After the interment the family returned to Fairfield, the Waterbury family home, where John's grandmother Elizabeth, a perceptive and kindly woman and a widow since John Waterbury's death a few years previously, recognised that he needed a break from the constant demands of his mother. She gave John money and suggested he take a trip somewhere before the return voyage to Europe. He chose Nova Scotia, to visit the Gaelic-speaking descendants of the Scots dispossessed from the Highlands and Islands by the Clearances of the eighteenth and nineteenth centuries. As 'unwilling emigrants' they had been careful to preserve the Celtic oral traditions and music of the country they had left behind.

With no direct air services, it was a long journey and John endured two nights and a day on a train from Boston before he arrived at Sydney on Cape Breton Island.[11] He spent the next week seeking out the Gaelic-speaking descendants of emigrant Scots and he wrote 151 circulars, which he posted to Catholic priests requesting information for a survey of Gaelic in the area. At St Francis Xavier College, Antigonish – a Catholic university with a high proportion of Gaelic speakers among the academic priests – he met the Rev. P.J. Nicholson, professor of physics, a native Gaelic speaker whose ancestors came from Barra. It was the beginning of a lasting and important friendship. Everywhere he was treated with interest and kindness and he travelled back to New York via Quebec, Montreal and Toronto, determined to return.

# CHAPTER FOUR

# A Classless Society

On 4 August 1933 John Campbell took the steamer *Lochearn* to the Isle of Barra. He marked the date precisely and referred to it often.[1] It was a turning point in his life. He intended a three-week holiday – he was to stay for five years.

After the depression of the previous few years and the claustrophobia from the attentions of his mother and Aunt Olive, the island offered freedom and fresh air. From being lonely and finding it difficult to make relationships, he found himself meeting people and making lasting friendships almost as soon as he stepped off the boat. No one was concerned by his accent or his upbringing, they accepted him as he was.

The Hebrides – and Barra in particular – were not typical of the Highlands in culture, history or outlook. Rather than the rigid social hierarchy of Argyll, what John found was an almost classless community. Most people were either crofters (small farmers) or fishermen – often both – or the people who served them: shop and hotel keepers, doctors, priests and those who held official positions such as schoolteachers, post and pier masters. The social and economic gap between the professionals and the rest of the population was much narrower than on the mainland and people mixed easily together. Gaelic was the everyday language and only a handful of incomers did not speak it. The contrast with the Argyllshire County could not have been more marked.

The island had suffered under its share of feudal landlords, tyrannical absentees and enforced emigration, but had managed to shake off what John called the 'anglicising influence of the Big House'.[2] The last of the hereditary lairds, the MacNeills of Barra, had emigrated to the United States in the nineteenth century* and

* Although the title was revived in 1915 by an American claiming descent, he never lived on the island.

the Crofters' Act of 1886 had given small farmers security of tenure and rights to be able to resist the more outrageous demands of the proprietor. Land raids, when ex-servicemen returning from the First World War had claimed holdings for themselves, had broken up the last of the big farms and forced the government to buy out some of the larger estate holdings and redistribute the land to crofters.

Barra was coming to the end of a prolonged economic boom brought about by the success of the herring fishery which during its height employed 2,000 people, virtually the whole of the working population. It is hard now to imagine the importance of herring, but much of Europe depended on it as a staple food and the seas around Barra teemed with the fish. The industry dominated island life and Castlebay, the main town and port, was its centre. A 'small regiment of fish-curers . . . ran up temporary huts and bothies surrounded by piles of barrels destined for St Petersburg, Konigsburg, Danzig, Hamburg and Stettin. Daily catches amounted to many thousands of cran [the cran was the standard measure and consisted of four baskets, each having a capacity of about 1,000 herrings of average size]'.[3] The men worked on the fishing boats and were paid £5 and 5 per cent of the net earnings, plus a pound of strong black twist tobacco. The women worked in teams of three. Two did the gutting while the third packed and salted the herrings in the barrels, handling up to 100,000 herrings in a day.

After the First World War the herring industry began a long decline, but in the year John arrived the island still had 94 boats (23 under sail, the others motor-driven) employing over 100 men. It was a long way from the peak, but still enough to crowd the harbour at Castlebay and give the island a buzz of activity. Most of the rest of the population worked the land. The boom times may have passed, but in the economic recession of the 1920s and 1930s, the crofter/fishermen of Barra were happier and enjoyed more independence than the unemployed industrial workers of the cities.

John had moved back to Scotland at the beginning of 1933, partly to start work on what he hoped would be a second book and partly inspired by the growing interest in Scottish Nationalism. His former fellow Gaelic student, John Bannerman, had been instrumental in the formation of the National Party of Scotland the previous year and Lewis Spence, a folklorist, had contested the Midlothian by-election as a Nationalist a few years earlier. Nationalism appealed to John in a number of ways. There were its romantic links back to the Jacobite risings of the eighteenth century, but it was also a way of expressing the Scottishness he had missed in his education and upbringing. There was the added benefit that it outraged his Aunt Olive, a staunch Unionist.

His twin invitations to Barra could not have come from two more useful people. John MacPherson, universally known by his nickname as the Coddy, was not only providing John Campbell with accommodation in a guest house he ran at Northbay, but was to teach him Gaelic and help him achieve the *blas*, the fluency with the spoken language which would enable him to communicate easily with the native speakers. The Coddy would also provide invaluable contacts and information. He knew everyone in the islands, was an exceptional source of news and gossip and was one of the chief tradition bearers – the teller of innumerable stories from Barra's history and culture.[4] John immediately liked him and found in him, perhaps a little of the father's discipline he had lacked so far. In their lessons, when John stumbled over a phrase and retreated into English, the Coddy would hold up his hand to stop him: '*Abair siod fhathast, Iain.*' ('Say that again, John.').

They had first met in 1928, when John had landed briefly at Castlebay from the yacht *Susanne*. He had run into him again later the same year on a bus journey along the old road beside the shore of Loch Ness from Fort William to Inverness, where they were both going to attend a Mod (festival of Gaelic music), and the Coddy, who represented the northern half of Barra on the Inverness-shire county council, was also to attend a council meeting.

John described him as: 'rather short, thick-set and Napoleonic; he had an extremely fine-looking head and was quick of movement and of speech, whether in English or Gaelic'. Pictures of the Coddy show him often with an amused or mischievous look on his face. He had a ready wit and a renowned sense of humour and was well liked, gaining a second nickname in later life as 'the king of Barra'. He was also an entrepreneur, who put his people skills to good use. The *Oban Times* recalled: 'When cars came to the island he started a car- and motor-hiring business with considerable success [he had the first car ever imported into Barra, a model T. Ford]. As the tourists began to flock to the island he decided to build a boarding house, and this was the Coddy in his element and at his very best. He was the genial host, the great storyteller and the charming *fear-an-taighe*'.[5]★

The Coddy's house on Barra, although away from the main town, had an air, not of remoteness, but of a centre of activity and ideas. John remembered: 'The Coddy's personality and talents as a host brought him before long a large number of visitors, some of them distinguished ones . . . peers, politicians, officials, descendants of Barra, emigrants to Canada and the USA, scholars from Scotland, Norway and Gaelic Ireland, archaeologists, ornithologists, sportsmen and holiday-makers simply seeking change and a rest in the peaceful, unhurried atmosphere of pre-Second World War Barra, all made their way to the Coddy's, attracted by his vigorous personality and the kindness and hospitality of his wife and family.'[6]

Again the contrast with Argyll must have struck John. Instead of the weekend parties of lairds and colonels, whose conversation seldom strayed beyond shooting and complaining about the impoverished state of the gentry, the Coddy's fireside crackled with humour, debate and controversy. Here people from different backgrounds blended easily, anyone was welcome, but they had to leave their prejudices and social airs and graces at the door.

The two men were friends until the Coddy's death in 1955. He gave John not only a sense of the value and richness of the Gaelic tradition – from his own experience and by introducing him to other singers and storytellers – but also warned him of its fragility. It was overwhelmingly an oral tradition and even in the 1930s the language was under threat. If it was not recorded it would die out with the last of the native speakers.

If the Coddy seemed like a second father to John, Compton Mackenzie, although only seven years younger than the Coddy and three years younger than John's father, seemed more like an older brother. In 1933 he was 50 and, in contrast to later life when

★ *Fear-an-taighe* is literally 'man of the house', but a traditional ceilidh would have a *fear-an-taighe*, who would compère the event, make witty comments or tell stories.

television made his white hair and beard familiar, still had combed-back dark hair and the clean-shaven good looks of a matinée idol. He was already a prolific and successful author – his novel *Sinister Street* had won him critical acclaim and he had published more than a dozen books – but he also had a popular following and his portrait was included among the 20 best known British writers on a set of Wills' cigarette cards, part of the popular culture of the time. He was a friend of Scott Fitzgerald, Aldous Huxley, D.H. Lawrence, Somerset Maugham and Maxim Gorki. Younger and aspiring writers sought him out for advice and encouragement.

He was charismatic, with a reputation as a great talker and a patient listener and despite, like John, having been educated at public school and Oxford, mixed as easily with fishermen as he did with members of the House of Lords. He made friends quickly on Barra, not least with the Coddy, Ruaraidh MacNeil, a fisherman known as 'the Crookle', and the schoolteachers Annie Johnston and Neil Sinclair, known as 'Sgoilear Ruadh', the Red Scholar, a reference to his hair colour rather than his politics. With them all he shared a fondness for conversation, usually lubricated with whisky.

Mackenzie had been a man of boldness and action, serving with British intelligence in the First World War and writing a book about his experiences, which had led to prosecution under the Official Secrets Act. He was also an incurable romantic. The son of actor parents – and sometime actor himself – he had been born and educated in England but was eager to rediscover his Scottish ancestry. It was four generations since his family had left the Scottish Highlands for England and his grandfather had changed the family name from Mackenzie to Compton. The grandson, christened Edward Montague (Monty to his friends) Compton, revived the Mackenzie surname and with it his Scottish heritage. He joined the newly emergent Scottish nationalist movement and stood successfully in the election of Rector of Glasgow University on a Nationalist platform.

He was also a lover of islands and had lived successively on Capri, the Channel islands of Herm and Jethou, and Eilean Aigas, an island in the Beauly river in the Scottish Highlands. In 1925, on impulse, he bought the Shiants, a group of uninhabited isles in the Minch, which he seldom visited, but let the grazing to the MacSween family of Harris. D.H. Lawrence had written a short story '*The Man Who Loved Islands*', using him as a model. At the time he first met John Campbell, Mackenzie was working on a biography of Bonnie Prince Charlie and on a visit to the island of Eriskay, just north of Barra, where the prince had first set foot on Scottish soil in 1745, had become so overcome with the romance of the place that he bought the only property for sale – a wooden coastguard hut. It is unlikely he ever spent a night there.[7]

To help with his biography, John had sent Mackenzie the manuscript of *Highland Songs of the Forty-Five* and had received an invitation to Barra in return.

Like Mackenzie, John was also trying to reinvent himself as a Scotsman. He was acutely conscious of the fact that, although born in Scotland, he had spent most of his life in England, knew little of Scottish history, culture or customs and spoke with the accent of the English middle class. He landed in Barra in a kilt and wore it for a few days until he realised that no one else did. There was no tradition of kilt-wearing in the islands and the only people who did so were visiting lairds. Barra people were polite to visitors but, Mackenzie explained, if John wanted to gain their trust he had to be patient and not set himself apart. John stopped wearing his kilt, but there are several pictures of Mackenzie on Barra dressed in tartan.

Mackenzie was very different from John in temperament. His working timetable usually began after lunch and continued after dinner until late in the evening, after which he began conversations with his guests, sustained with whisky, which could last until five in the morning. He then slept until lunch, when the cycle began again. The Ulster poet Louis MacNeice tried to call on Mackenzie in 1937. 'His secretary told me that she could not say when he would get up, but that when he did get up he would be busy with his mail; Mr Mackenzie did most of his work at night; that was because it was creative; but if I left my address she would arrange that I should see him later. I passed out again over the doormat that said *Ceud Mile Fàilte*'.[8] (One hundred thousand welcomes.)

You could get away with this lifestyle without being thought eccentric only in Italy, Ireland or Barra, Mackenzie believed. 'In high summer nobody goes to bed until late because the pearly shimmer of the Hebridean midnight simply cannot be wasted in sleep. And in winter nobody goes to bed until late, because there is no point in getting up before the long protracted morning twilight has become full day.'[9] John found the exchanges and the stories around Mackenzie's hearth fascinating, but he could not last the pace into the small hours.[10]

Despite his relaxed schedule and chronic pain from sciatic neuritis, Mackenzie kept up a ferocious output of writing. He could command high fees and advances for his work, but he was always in debt and was forced to produce an endless stream of books and articles to fund his lifestyle and keep his creditors at bay. As soon as he got money, he spent it. John, by contrast, preferred to work in daylight and go to his bed early, he was cautious with his money and his willingness to unbend to strangers. The two built a lasting friendship on seemingly thin foundations – a shared interest in butterflies and moths, American mothers, Oxford and a need to express their Scottish identity. Each seemed to find in the other the qualities he himself lacked. John admired Mackenzie's confidence, fluency and decisiveness bordering on impulsiveness. Compton Mackenzie found in John steadfastness, a capacity for dogged hard work and unquestioning loyalty.

Within weeks of John's arrival Mackenzie involved him in a campaign. Barra fishermen worked the inshore waters of the Minch by drift netting and long-lining – traditional, low intensity forms of fishing suitable to small sailing or low-powered boats. Their vessels were no match for the steam trawlers from the English ports, particularly those from Fleetwood, Lancashire. Larger and much more powerful than the Barra boats, these dragged huge nets along the seabed of the Barra waters on their way home from the Icelandic fishing grounds. They took large quantities of fish, depriving the island boats of their catch, and landed them in their home port, taking away the work of the Barra fish processors too.

Technically the law forbade trawling within three miles of the coast, but it was not enforced and largely ignored. Mackenzie was incensed when he witnessed an English steam trawler working a mile offshore while a fishery protection cruiser carrying a government minister, was anchored in Castlebay and did nothing. He sent a telegram to the prime minister, but received a noncommittal reply from 10 Downing Street and decided to take action himself. He formed the Sea League, with himself as chairman and John as one of the secretaries. They produced a leaflet in Gaelic and English and distributed it around the island:

WHAT THE SEA LEAGUE STANDS FOR

The Sea League has been formed to demand the same protection for the livelihood of the crofter fisherman as is given to the sporting fishing of the landowners themselves.

Barra, Outer Hebrides 20th December 1933: objects of the Sea League are:

1. That the Minch between a line from Barra Head to Tiree and a line from the Butt of Lewis to Cape Wrath, shall be closed to trawlers, and that the fishing in this area shall be regulated to the benefit of the fishermen who live around it.

2. That the penalties for illegal trawling shall be increased, and the policing of the inshore waters made more efficient.

3. That the fines for illegal trawling shall be used for financing fishermen who have lost their gear through illegal trawling, or who want to commence inshore fishing for the first time.

Sea League intends to fight unceasingly for these objects.

JOIN THE SEA LEAGUE Subscription one shilling. Write (in Gaelic or English) to The Secretary, Northbay, Barra.[11]

Mackenzie and Campbell were amazed to discover that legislation from 1895 provided for protected fishery districts covering waters 14 miles from the coast for the benefit of local fishermen. A dozen had been established in England, from Cornwall to the Scottish Border on both east and west coasts, but no districts had ever been established in Scotland. They began a petition to Inverness-shire county council – the relevant authority – to set up such districts.

The two men toured Barra and the neighbouring islands of Eriskay and South Uist addressing meetings and collecting signatures. When everyone who caught, bought or sold fish signed the petition they extended the campaign further, to Benbecula, North Uist and Scalpay and received equally unanimous support. The movement caught the imagination of the islands. Ten-year-old Angus John MacQueen,★ remembered proudly wearing the badge of the Sea League at school in South Uist, enthused by the vision of life for the fishing community imparted by the headmaster, a Barra man. Outside the islands, however, progress was slower. The council spent years dithering over the issue and passed it to the Scottish Office, the outpost of government north of the border. John reported non-progress in *The Sea Leaguer*, a regular duplicated newsletter edited, produced and largely written by him: 'Slow Committeemen', July 1938; 'Still Waiting', December 1938. They waited a long time. It was 1964 before a fishery limit was established. John wrote then to Mackenzie: '31 years almost to the day after the first Sea League meeting at Castlebay our policy had been put into effect – at least one if not two generations too late.'[12]

The issue brought to the surface John's latent political feelings. 'Personally, I have never been more thoroughly convinced of the justice of any cause than I was of the Sea League,' he wrote later.[13] 'The islands were despised because they were poor, and they were poor because their economic interests in the greatest source of wealth accessible to them, the sea, had been sacrificed to those of the English trawling monopolies.' Decades ahead of his time, he also saw trawling as a threat to sustainability. Local boats using traditional methods had been fishing the Minch for countless generations. Industrial fishing was to virtually exhaust the fishery in two generations.

The campaign was vigorous and popular, but it had limited success. Penalties for illegal trawling were increased in 1934, but not enforced and eventually fishing all but died out in the islands. Nevertheless, the Sea League kept up its fight for the next five years and branched out into wider action, advocating economic development in the islands and supporting nationalist candidates in local elections. Prompted by John, a petition was sent to the Post Office to improve the islands' service and achieved some successes. In March 1939, *The Sea Leaguer* reported that letters between the

★ Later the Very Rev. Canon MacQueen, who wrote the foreword to a third edition of *The Book of Barra* in 2006.

islands of Canna and Barra, thirty-five miles apart, could be sorted on board ship, whereas previously they had been sent to Glasgow for sorting, adding ten days to the delivery time. There was also a demand to MacBraynes, the ferry company, for faster vessels, cheaper freight and livestock charges, and a special rate for married couples.

To raise political awareness in the island, John and Mackenzie decided to produce *The Book of Barra*, a collection of essays and historical documents intended to give the islanders a sense of their own history and heritage. Mackenzie, a convert to Catholicism, provided a chapter on Catholic Barra in which he contrasted the love of entertainment and the 'freedom from Sabbatarian taboos' of the southern Hebridean islands with the austere teetotal Presbyterian northern isles. But it was John who shouldered the bulk of the work, writing, commissioning, researching and editing the rest – tasks he threw himself into with energy and commitment. There were historical essays, original documents and articles on the folklore and place names of the island. All the contributors were unpaid – as was John – and all royalties were donated to the Sea League.

In 1934, Mackenzie finally sold the tenancy of Jethou, one of the smallest of the Channel Islands, which he had leased from the government but grown tired of after a few years. He used the money to build himself a large house overlooking the Traigh Mhòr, the vast cockle beach in the north of Barra which had also begun to serve as the runway for its airport. The laying of the foundations was celebrated with a party with dancing, whisky and Mackenzie sporting his kilt. John filmed the occasion and donated a silver dollar to bury beneath the house – a tribute to the author's American mother. It was completed a year later and named Suidheachan, literally 'the sitting down place', a fitting title for a building which quickly became the social and literary centre of Barra.

John accredited it with providing the island with the 'intellectual leadership and inspiration which the "Big House" should – but too often does not – give a Highland community.'[14] Perhaps he was thinking back to the Argyllshire Big Houses of his youth, which could never be accused of intellectual leadership or inspiration.

Mackenzie seems to have had less lofty ambitions. The builder had misread the plans and built the house the wrong way round, so the billiard room was the only one with a view over the sands. Mackenzie installed a full-sized table which became so popular that a new 'quickfire pool' game had to be invented to accommodate the numbers who wanted to play.

His memoirs tell of convivial evenings when large quantities of Scotch were downed by locals and visitors alike. John impressed Mackenzie with a unique feat of concentration during the games. 'He used to sit back on the narrow ledge in front of the bookshelves deep in one of the books without paying the least attention to the performance of his rivals. Then when the time came for him to play his ball the book would be put down on the ledge and his shot played, after which he would return to the book until his turn came to play again. In spite of his apparent complete remoteness from the game he would sometimes preserve his one life and scoop that penny pool.'[15]

Sharing the house with Compton Mackenzie was his secretary, Chrissie MacSween, a Gaelic speaker from Harris whose father had rented the grazing on the Shiants. Mackenzie was living apart from his wife Faith, although they remained close friends. He and Chrissie shared homes until Faith's death in 1960, when they married. The cost of the house – sited away from other buildings on the sandy neck joining the body of Barra to Eoligarry, its northern head – overran its budget and plunged Mackenzie into fresh debt. The Coddy bailed him out with a loan, which was repaid later – with borrowing from another friend.

★

Encouraged by Mackenzie, John was becoming more political and more radical in his ideas, particularly on the ownership and management of land, which he saw as central to the economic future of the Highlands and Islands. He was moving further and further away from the views of his family and the social class in which they moved, and now openly calling himself a Nationalist and demanding Home Rule and a Scottish Parliament.

In a joint letter to the magazine *Outlook*[16] the two men claimed:

As Scottish Nationalists, we are convinced that the evils from which the Highlands and Islands now suffer, and which have their roots in 150 years of misgovernment, can never be properly dealt with until they come under the direct attention of a Scottish Parliament that is concerned with the re-establishment of a Scottish peasantry. We know that the interests which are opposed to the radical legislation that would be necessary to destroy these evils are strengthened by being able to count upon the aid of English Conservatism. We know too that pressure of English business on the Westminster Parliament gives every opportunity for shelving problems which no Scottish Parliament could avoid facing immediately.

They called for limits on the amount of land that any individual or body could own, a sentiment which would have infuriated John's father who, even after the sale of Taynish, owned thousands of acres – land which one day would pass to John. The letter said there should be binding contracts between landowners and the state covering cultivation, development, management and residence, and limitation of the right of private property in wild animals and fish – a direct challenge to hunting, shooting and fishing. They demanded a development board for the north of Scotland, with substantial powers to acquire land and direct enterprise and transport. They wanted the nationalisation of steamship services, the closure of the Minch to trawlers, control and exploitation of water power in the Highlands and a knowledge of Gaelic to be compulsory for public servants in areas where the native language was spoken.

As a programme it went much further than John had ever done before in challenging the political establishment and the social class in which he had been born and brought up. He was soon to move from confrontation on the page to direct defiance in the courtroom.

When it was clear that his stay on Barra was more than a holiday, John arranged to have his car brought to the island. This was no easy undertaking since there were no roll-on roll-off ferries and the vehicle had to be carried on the deck of the *Lochearn* and unloaded onto the quay by derrick. He was one of the few people on the island to have a car and, like most other motorists, he resented having to pay road tax on an island which lacked proper metalled roads. In fact they were little more than cart tracks, built by charity labour during the potato famine of the 1840s and it was not merely the pot holes which took a heavy toll on suspension and tyres. There was a gap between roads in the north and south of the island, obliging motorists to drive on the wet salt sands of the Traigh Mhòr. To John it was another example of the way in which government ignored the needs of the islands, but expected them to pay their taxes anyway.

Following a familiar tale of ignored petitions to the county council to have the 12 miles of the island's roads put into a reasonable state of repair, the Barra car tax strike began on 1 January 1937. Led by Mackenzie and Campbell, with only one exception every car and lorry owner on the island joined the protest. Two priests, a doctor and even Dr Bartlett, an Englishman who had retired to the island and who was later lampooned by Mackenzie in his comic novel *Whisky Galore*, were involved. The group's legal adviser was Sir Alexander MacEwen, a county councillor and former provost of Inverness. They knew what they were doing was illegal, but they wanted their day in court.

In June, the 'Barra eleven' were duly arraigned before the sheriff at Lochmaddy in North Uist. They had paid their taxes before the hearing to emphasise the symbolic nature of their protest, but the sheriff was unimpressed. He stamped down hard on the strikers, imposing heavy fines with the alternative of prison – an embellishment to the sentence he had no right to make.

The affair provoked widespread publicity, with most of the press comment on the side of the Barra motorists, who felt emboldened enough to appeal. Motoring organisations started campaigns to raise funds for the costs and when the case reached the High Court the protesters got some redress. The judge rebuked the sheriff, reduced the fines to less than half and awarded the motorists costs against the county council. In *The Sea Leaguer* John claimed a moral victory. Compton Mackenzie, who had been singled out for criticism by one newspaper which described him as 'the Playboy of the Western World' felt especially vindicated when the following year the roads were repaired. The Playboy had won.[17]

The Sea League failed in its main objects, but it had a lasting effect on John. He learned from Compton Mackenzie how easy it was to move from thought to action, he gained confidence by having to speak in public and negotiate and he realised that cultural, environmental and economic development had to go together. He also acquired a lifelong scepticism of bureaucrats.

# CHAPTER FIVE

# A Bird Blown Off Course

There was an inevitability about the meeting of John and Margaret Fay Shaw; their paths and their interests had been intertwining for years. Several times they had been in the same place at the same time, but had not met until a wet night in 1934, when he took the *Lochearn* to South Uist to address a meeting of the Sea League. He had heard about the young American who was collecting songs and taking photographs and he hoped she might provide illustrations for his book. He might secretly have been longing for more than that.

Getting off the ship, he inquired at the Lochboisdale Hotel where Finlay Mackenzie, the manager, knew everything that was going on in the island. With the hotel only a few steps above the pier, it was the obvious place for passengers to wait for transport to their destination or to shelter from inclement weather. Hebrideans were seldom reluctant to pass the time of day. Mackenzie would certainly know the whereabouts of Margaret, but John probably did not expect to be told that she was in the hotel, playing the piano for pipe major John MacDonald, who was giving music lessons to local boys. The hotel manager introduced John in the formal style as 'Young Inverneill'.

Whether she lived up to John's expectations, we do not know. While she later described the meeting in her autobiography,[1] his notebooks are silent. The only public comment he made was in answer to a television interviewer 60 years later: 'As so often happens, we didn't take to each other at first, but we got to know each other and we were working in the same small world.'[2] Her initial impression of him was not good. He was gangly, shy and, she thought, conceited. He asked her to provide photographs, which she did despite being warned not to by a friend who told her that he knew John's kind: 'he'll never pay you anything'. It was good advice: she never got paid.

The courtship was slow and cool. They were an odd couple, he tall and introverted, she short and direct. Some months after their meeting, he invited her to spend a week with him on Barra but left her alone for hours on end while he chased butterflies with a net. Margaret 'found out in time that this is how he lives and enjoys and he expects you to do the same thing. Why walk along yacketing when there's really nothing much to say?' The following year, in March 1935, she took him home to Glenshaw to meet her sisters and aunts. John claimed later that he had gone to Pennsylvania with the intention of proposing, but he spent most of the time in his room, pounding his typewriter to finish his manuscript. When he did emerge it was to collect moth cocoons in the woods. Margaret agreed with her family that he did not appear to have much interest in her. No one was more surprised than she when, on his final day, he asked her to marry him.

Shyness may not have been the only reason for John's hesitant wooing of Margaret. His life to date had not given him much opportunity to meet or get to know women, and he had been caught between his own emotions and the attempts by his Aunt Olive to marry him off to a suitable girl from the Argyll County set. In efforts to find his own mate John had believed he had fallen in love at least twice, only to be rebuffed. Now nearing 30, he must have feared another rejection.

Margaret, too, had grown up without much experience of the opposite sex. She was born in 1903 – three years before John – into a family which bore superficial resemblances to John's own. Like the Campbells of Inverneill, the Shaws were substantial landowners, known and respected in their county. Their pedigree also went back to the eighteenth century, John Shaw, Margaret's great-great-grand-father, having arrived in Pennsylvania from Scotland in 1782. It was one of his four sons who chose the wooded valley close to Pittsburgh to build a substantial mansion – different in design and construction from Inverneill, being brick, with a square porch at the front – but at least equal in size and prestige. In a neat reversal of the Argyll practice, rather than the family taking their title from the land, the Shaws gave their name to the community which sprang up around the house, calling it Glenshaw. But there the similarities ended. Margaret's mother and father were loving and attentive parents, in contrast to John's who were often absent, and there was no doubt or shame about the source of the family wealth. The Shaws were iron and steel founders and Margaret's father managed the family mill in Pittsburgh, priding himself on knowing the name of every man who worked there.

Like John, Margaret grew up with nature and learned to name and value the plants and animals she found in the creek and on the hillsides around Glenshaw. She was the youngest of five sisters and used to the female company of her great aunts and Maria, the cook at the big house her great-grandfather had built. Maria's family, her son Louie, gardener and houseman, his wife Birdie, cook in Margaret's family home nearby, and their son Harry, were the descendants of slaves, but there was less social distance between them and the Shaws than if they had been a white family of servants in one of the great houses of Argyll. Harry, although closer in age to Biddy, Margaret's sister who was three years older, was Margaret's childhood play-fellow and attended the same elementary school as the Shaw girls.

Margaret's happy memories of her early childhood were brought to an abrupt end at the age of seven with the death of her mother. Her father, distraught, moved the family away from the 'woods, fields and freedom of Glenshaw' and from Louie, Birdie and Harry – her second family. Three years later her father died too. Her upbringing was now taken over by aunts, great-aunts and her sisters – particularly Martha, the next oldest to Biddy. The Shaw girls were noted beauties as well as being socially and academically able, attending the prestigious Bryn Mawr boarding school and later college. Little Margaret, short as well as young, was stunned by the loss of her parents. She did badly at school and suffered from low self-esteem. 'I was untidy and slow and called "dilatory" by my Great-Aunt Ellen, and had a mind that wandered. I was also plain.'[3] The only accomplishment she managed to pick up was the ability to play the piano, something she could do almost instinctively. She was given a few lessons by a church organist and later at school, but lacking other qualifications was not thought worthy of more formal musical education. In 1921, while John had left Scotland and was at Rugby receiving his secondary education, Margaret, now 18, was arriving at a boarding school in Helensburgh, near Glasgow. It seemed an extreme decision for the youngest and most fragile of the daughters to be sent across the Atlantic, where she knew no one and had only distant family and friends. It provoked fierce debate in the family between those who thought it would be the making of her and those who feared it would end in disaster. But Margaret, in perhaps the first demonstration of the adventurous spirit which was to stay with her all her long life, was thrilled at the prospect and relished the ocean crossing, the arrival in Glasgow (an industrial city which seemed as much home to her as Pittsburgh) and the new experiences of St Bride's School, high on a hill overlooking the busy River Clyde and on the road to Loch Lomond and the Highlands of Argyll.

She enjoyed her year. In most subjects she did no better than she had in America, but perhaps, 3,000 miles from Pennsylvania, she felt less overshadowed by the achievements of her sisters. St Bride's also provided an inspirational piano teacher who pushed her to play more demanding classics. At the end of the year concert she performed Chopin's First Prelude and the 'Butterfly' étude so well that she was presented by the headmistress with an inscribed copy of Kipling's *The Years Between*, the first and only school prize she ever received. It was something to show her sisters, but her year in Scotland also introduced her to another sort of music. She heard for the first time the bagpipes, played by a tinker who was begging for pennies, but more significantly the school was treated to a recital by Marjory Kennedy-Fraser, who had made a career of collecting Gaelic songs in the Hebrides and singing her own anglicised versions of them. The songs entranced Margaret, but at the same time she was aware that there must be more to them and determined that one day she would hear the originals.

After school in Scotland, Margaret returned to the US to study piano in New York. Her sister Kay was studying at the New York University Medical School and they both lived at the YWCA. The 'Roaring Twenties' in New York were a time of excitement and new ideas, but like John in Oxford a few years later, Margaret saw it from a distance. Her life consisted of music lessons and odd jobs to earn a little money. She too was painfully shy and would rather go hungry than enter the dining room on her own, but she pursued her interest in Gaelic, buying the first volume of Mrs Kennedy-Fraser's collected melodies, the St Columba Collection of Gaelic Songs and a

Gaelic grammar. Her chance to return to Scotland came with a student trip to Britain, which she made with a friend. The boat landed at Plymouth, the two girls took a train to Oxford and there hired bicycles, which they rode by way of the Cotswolds and the Lake District to Inverness, Kyle of Lochalsh and eventually to Skye, where Margaret was able again to hear the songs which had so caught her imagination, this time in the original by singers who spoke Gaelic as their first language.

Back in New York she planned and saved for the day she could return. She had tasted only a single rain-soaked day in the Outer Hebrides on a boat trip from Skye to Stornoway in Lewis, but she longed to visit the islands again. The opportunity came in the summer of 1926 when, with another friend and some money from a small legacy, she made a second trip, this time sailing to Glasgow, catching a train to Helensburgh and hiring bicycles there. The girls peddled up Loch Lomondside and on to Oban, where Margaret bought a practice chanter – the part of the bagpipes on which the melody is played.[4] After three days they took a ferry to Barra. Margaret described the landing in Castlebay in a letter to her sister Kay.[5] The town consisted almost entirely of low stone and thatch houses, some still without chimneys with the peat smoke rising through a hole in the roof. Everyone walking through the town greeted them, either in English or Gaelic. She watched the brown-sailed herring fleet leave the harbour in the evening as the setting sun turned the sea lavender and then purple. The morning revealed 50 boats already returned and unloading their catches of herring to be salted and packed.

She met the Coddy three years before John did, but was misled by the Barra accent into thinking his name was 'Hoddy'. She described him: 'in his under-shirt and suspenders [braces] and curly white hair and moustache'. Since the ferry to South Uist – where their bicycles were being sent – was a week away, the two girls accepted his offer to find them a boat which would sail them to Eriskay, the next island north. Margaret was enchanted: 'Nobody shall ever know how thrilled we were at that crossing. I hug myself now at the thought of it. There is so much white sand that the water is a brilliant blue and with the bright sun, I just waste the ink in attempting to describe the most beautiful place on earth.'

The boat was crewed by an old man who knew no English and a young man, Roderick, with whom she fell instantly in love:

> His appearance was in keeping with the scene – thank Heaven as also
> was the old man in his sea–jacket and cap with a visor – the young man
> was so tanned and his brown hair and eyebrows were burnt to a sort of
> copper colour. Like most of the islanders he had excellent features and
> blue eyes – then too, like most of the people in the district who learn
> English after Gaelic, he had the pleasantest speaking voice and the finest
> choice of words. I know no one who talks so delightfully, having the gift
> of both a soft, sort of soothing voice with perfect English and a way of
> describing a scene or telling a tale that would make any man think it
> could not be improved upon.[5]

The two-hour voyage passed too quickly and they were deposited on rocks and had to scramble with their bags to the shore, waving goodbye to 'the old gentleman with not a tooth in his head and the very excellent teeth of the irresistible Roderick'.

The contrast between travelling through the islands and the bustle of life in New York could not have been more marked. In a second letter to Kay a few days later[6] Margaret described the beauty of Eriskay – an island without roads – and the warmth of the people. As tourists – and American tourists at that – they were very rare creatures and treated with kindness and hospitality as well as curiosity. The schoolmistress put them up, they were taken to see the sights of the island and to visit the local celebrities – the priests and a woman reputed to have second sight, although she was not at home when they called. Margaret was keen to find the grave of Father Allan McDonald, who had been priest of the island, and a noted collector of folksong and folklore until his death in 1905, and about whom she had read a book.* They were sad to leave and their hosts 'would not let us pay a cent'.

The ferry journeys between islands were under sail, except between North Uist and Benbecula, where a cart took them across the ford. With the tide rising, the cart was flooded and the horse had to swim part of the distance. Margaret, trying to hold their bicycles

---

* *Father Allan's Island* by Amy Murray, an American musician who had collaborated with him in collecting songs in Eriskay.

upright and keep their luggage clear of the sea, was soaked. They travelled the length of the Outer Hebrides, from Barra to the Butt of Lewis, the most northerly point in the islands, but it was South Uist that appealed to her the most. Thirty years later she described the landscape which eventually drew her back.[7] The flat *machair*, on the west side of the island, grassland which is the best crofting land, and carpeted in summer with wild flowers, the air filled with the song of skylarks, the call of lapwing and corncrake; the east side of the island wild and boggy moorland rising to a line of high hills.

At the end of her month-long holiday, Margaret stayed in Europe, studying piano and music theory in Oxford, London and Paris – all cities where John was either living or visiting at this time, but their paths never crossed.

During her time in the islands she had begun to note down the words and music of songs, but she realised that classical forms were not adequate to understand Gaelic music, which used different scales, tonality and modes. She sought out musicians who could help her transcribe the music more accurately.[8] In Paris she was introduced to the famous teacher Nadia Boulanger, who took an interest in her notebook and encouraged Margaret to collect more songs. Later, on holiday in Dublin with her sister Biddy, she met Eileen Costello, a senator in the Irish Parliament, who had published a collection of 80 Gaelic folksongs in 1923.[9] She had been one of the first collectors of Irish songs to include the text and the music as well as translations and notes. Margaret was so inspired by the meeting that she stole some of Biddy's cash to buy the book, even though they were short of money.

Margaret's desire to become a pianist was being thwarted by rheumatism, which had started a few years earlier and been particularly bad in Oxford, where the cold, damp air had made her wrists stiff and painful. Back in New York extensive and expensive medical treatment had failed to cure her and a career in music seemed very distant. She confessed to one of her medical specialists that what she most wanted was to return to the Hebrides to learn Gaelic and collect songs. He urged her to do just that and, to the horror of many members of her family, she returned to South Uist. 'Of all the islands I'd visited there was something about South Uist that just won me; it was like falling in love; it was the island that I wanted to go back to.

Of course, I was not looking for *islands*: I was looking for a way to live my life.'[10]

Margaret wrote or recounted several versions of her arrival in South Uist, but never more lyrically than in her book *Folksongs and Folklore of South Uist*. There she described in detail the geography of the island, so different from that of the wooded valley in which she had grown up, and the lives of the people, which could not have been a greater contrast to those of the city dwellers amongst whom she had spent most of her adult life so far. After a few months living in lodgings in Lochboisdale she met the sisters Peigi and Mairi MacRae, who were to be close to her for the rest of their lives and beyond.

The MacRaes were typical of the working women of South Uist. Often these were widowed by the sea, or lived without their men, who were away on ships for months on end, returning in the spring to cut the seaweed and turn the ground. To an outsider the lives of the women must have seemed very hard, but they gave no impression of regarding their lot as unusual and appeared cheerful and contented. They farmed a croft in Glendale, which runs along the south side of Loch Boisdale. The house was on the north slope of Easival, one of the mountains which make up the spine of rock forming the eastern flank of the island and in winter the sun, which rises behind the hill, hardly reached it for weeks.

Their home had neither running water, sanitation nor electricity and was typical of the local dwellings, built of the stone which lay plentifully on the surface of the fields. It was constructed to a traditional design which had evolved as the best way to counter the harsh winter weather, being long and low with rounded ends and walls four feet thick under a roof of sods, topped with a thatch of rushes or straw. Originally it had been a *taigh dubh*, a 'black house', without a chimney or lining to the walls, where the mild, dark smoke from the peat fire was allowed to find a way out through a vent in the roof. But the MacRaes had improved it, putting in a fireplace at each end, lining and papering the walls and ceilings and painting the wooden door bright blue. The opening was barely five feet high, but it suited the sisters who, like Margaret, were short. They had equipped it with furniture and dishes made on the island, and in the corner was a spinning wheel and a basket of *rolagan*, wool from their own sheep waiting to be spun.

To Margaret the simple home exerted a magnetic attraction:

The view from Peigi's door was of the life of the island: the small figures
going about their crofts, the scholars crossing the hill to school, the
solitary figure with a staff herding cows, the boat being dragged ashore,
the brown sail on the loch, the smoke of the kelp fires on the sand dunes
in the west; overhead the long approach of the wild geese and swans.
One watched the shore to see the state of the tide, which governed the
time of work on the sea. The direction of the wind was always noted,
the shape of the clouds – as that strange cloud called *craobh* which
stretched like a narrow blanket from north to south above the hills and
gave the direction of the wind tomorrow. Winter nights brought an
amazing vision of stars. Northern lights, called by the Gaels *Fir-chlisne*,
men of the tricks, or the leaping, darting ones, appeared in long shafts of
white, green and reddish light to form ribbon-like folds on the centre of
the sky[11]

Peigi and Mairi kept a few sheep, a Highland cow called Dora, and
grew vegetables and winter feed for the animals on the five-acre
croft, working the hard ground with only primitive tools, like the
wooden *cas-chrom*, the foot plough. It did not provide them with a
living. Each had several part-time jobs to supplement their income
and at the time Margaret met them they were working in the
kitchen of their cousin, a prosperous farmer and businessman who
owned Boisdale House, a substantial stone mansion a mile or two
away. Mairi and her son Donald lived in the croft house; Peigi could
not afford to do so until she was old enough to receive a state
pension and she probably slept at Boisdale House. Immediately she
saw the croft house, Margaret asked the sisters if they would take her
as a lodger.

What was the attraction of this simple life only just above the
poverty line for this young American woman from a privileged background? Perhaps the new family with whom she was to spend five
years reminded her of Birdie, Harry and Louie, her parents' servants.
They expected nothing of her and accepted her at face value. Like
John in Barra a few years later, she could be herself here.

If she was looking for a way to live her life, the uncomplicated
existence of South Uist seemed to suit her. 'Peigi and Mairi had the

greatest wisdom, tolerance, cheer and courage and yet had so little. They were glad to have nice things, but they didn't expect them. They had enough food, and they took great pleasure in what they did possess. They had no envy.'[12] Yet on trips to visit her family, Margaret compared their happiness to families in Glenshaw caught by the Depression. The unemployed in America still had more than the working Hebrideans, yet the yearning for the things they had lost brought them to misery. 'They were lost, with no idea of how to cope. And they felt a terrible mortification,' she remembered.[13]

While John was reading and translating Gaelic songs in libraries, Margaret was hearing them for herself. Her quest to hear and learn more Gaelic songs could not have brought her to a better location. The house in Glendale resounded with song for much of the day and often the night as well. The economy of the croft depended on wool, and song was intricately entwined with each stage of processing it. 'In the summer Peigi would have washed and dyed the fleeces. Then she would card the wool, combing, cleaning and making it into *rolagan* for spinning in winter. Peigi was continually singing as she spun. The rhythm of her foot on the treadle brought forth the songs as naturally as her fingers turned the wool to yarn. When there was sufficient for a length of tweed we took it in a sack across the hill to Peigi Iain Bharraich, the weaver, who lived with her sister in a house just big enough to hold themselves and the loom.'[14]

The next stage of the process, the 'waulking' of the cloth to shrink it and make the dyes fast, is one of the great occasions of Gaelic singing. Margaret attended her first waulking, called *laudadh* in Gaelic, in Peigi's byre:

The planks that served as a bridge across the burn were made to serve as the table. A lantern hung from the rafters and shone down on the singers in their rough aprons, their heads tied in kerchiefs, their sleeves rolled high. The air was potent with the smell of hot [sheep's] urine, but no substitute will give the softness of texture nor set the colour, especially of indigo. When finished the tweed was thoroughly washed in a running stream and dried on the heather, exposed to the sun and wind for several days until perfectly clean.

The women kneaded and pushed the cloth round and round the table with song after song. The one who sang the verse line would give turns and grace notes to take in all the syllables, always in absolute time and with a rhythm that was marvellous to me. When it was thought to be sufficiently shrunk and the feel of the texture right, one would measure the length with her third finger. If not yet shrunk enough they would give it another song, always keeping it moist. When ready at last it was rolled up tightly and two women would face across it and, clapping the roll, would sing the *oran basaidh*, or clapping song, called in Glendale the *coileach*, in quick 2/4 time, which was for the purpose of finishing the *luadhadh*. The company would shout 'Give them the *coileach*!' for the words of these last songs are to a great extent extemporised and consist of witty and ribald remarks about the people present with reference to their actual or possible love affairs.

The singers then washed and changed, to gather with the other members of the party in the kitchen, where a dram was passed and tea with scones and cake. Then began the singing and dancing, with great hilarity. Those were days when a wearer could regard his homespun from the Hebrides with the thought of the songs and gaiety that went into the making of it.[15]

The long winter nights in the croft house provided Margaret with an immense number of songs and stories, folktales of the island told by the MacRaes and their neighbours, many of whom, like the four members of the Campbell family – Seonaidh, 'the bard', his brother Iain Clachair (the stone mason) and two of Iain's sons, were noted singers or storytellers. Seonaidh had never been taught to read or write, but he could recite any number of epic poems, word perfect every time, and was also a prolific poet and rhymer himself, sometimes composing amusing or satirical verses on the spot.

Mairi – usually known as Mairi Anndra (Mairi daughter of Andrew) – was keen to help, taking hours – and making others take hours – to ensure that Margaret had the words and the music down correctly. The words, it was stressed strongly, were as important as the music, and singers went to great pains to ensure that listeners could hear and understand the poetry of the songs clearly. 'With a tuning fork to find the key, I would struggle to write down what I heard. Then I was made to sing it and while the guest might from kindness smile – not Mairi Anndra. Her pride was in my getting it down as she knew I wanted – exactly as it was sung.'[16] In her time in South Uist Margaret noted down over 200 songs, but felt she had hardly scratched the surface.★

As well as songs and stories, Margaret collected proverbs and sayings and recipes for herbal cures, dyes, as well as local dishes and delicacies. She had also started taking photographs, using a large, Graflex camera, which weighed ten pounds, not counting the seventeen-inch lens and tripod. But she had willing subjects and achieved remarkable results, which even today stand out in technical quality as well as composition. She intended the pictures for the book she was planning, but was also able to sell several to magazines and newspapers. The high point – although it came after she had left South Uist – was an illustrated feature in *National Geographic Magazine*. The photographs have stood the test of time, but the prose, obviously extensively rewritten, has lost much of Margaret's simple and natural style and obvious love of the island.

Although she shared much of their lives, Margaret was aware that the little money she had coming from America, or from her occasional commissions, gave her a freedom which Peigi and Mairi could not enjoy. She could go to the Lochboisdale Hotel for a bath, or to wash her hair, or for Sunday lunch when she could eat vegetables – rare in the diet of the croft – although even these luxuries meant a nine-mile walk around the head of the loch or a boat trip, which in winter would invariably mean a soaking and on one occasion, when the boat's rudder was fouled by the rope tethering a lobster creel, led her to think she might not survive the crossing.

She helped out as much as she could. She wasn't much impressed by the Presbyterian church's request that she 'touch her rich friends'[17] for donations to the repairs to the manse (she had been brought up a Presbyterian, but she thought there were enough well-off people on the island to pay for that). Instead, she and the teachers put on a dance in the schoolhouse to 'get money for a hot drink at

---

★ She published 100 of them in *Folksongs and Folklore of South Uist* in 1955, but she and John Lorne Campbell went on to record ten times that number of Gaelic songs. Peigi MacRae, who visited Margaret frequently on Canna, recorded over 200 songs and stories on wire recorders. They are preserved in the Canna House archive.

lunchtime for the scholars who walk miles over the moor in terrible weather – half of them with too little breakfast and half a piece of scone for lunch'. Margaret paid for the refreshments and the piper, but entreated her sister Caroline not to show her letter to anyone who 'might get the idea I was trying to appear as Miss Give All'.[18] Later she paid for oranges for the children to give them vitamin C, and eventually she paid for the croft house to have running water and sanitation.

Margaret stayed on South Uist for 'four winters and six summers' until she met John and moved to Barra. She never lived on South Uist again, but in a real sense she never left it – returning frequently to visit her friends and inviting them to stay with her.

# CHAPTER SIX

# Recording a Vanishing Culture

John and Margaret were married in June 1935 in the manse of John's friend Calum MacLeod, minister of John Knox Presbyterian Church, Glasgow. Margaret's parents were dead, and none of her four sisters attended. She was given away by Fred Moir, an old family friend, by now a kindly man in his eighties with a soft white beard. He at least tried for a sense of occasion, hiring a limousine and buying Margaret white orchids to pin to her jacket. The only other guest was the minister's wife, Blanche, who provided the second witness. Neither of John's parents came, nor his two surviving brothers. At his insistence the service was in Gaelic and Fred Moir asked for a translation to ensure it was all legal. Margaret's Gaelic was not yet fluent and she was relieved that all she had to say was *tha* – 'yes'.

They honeymooned in the Norwegian Lofoten and Vesteraalen islands, where John wanted to study the favourable way in which the government treated local fishermen and island communities. In particular he was impressed that trawling was banned in the waters between the islands and the mainland, reserving the inshore fisheries for local boats. He was convinced that this was a major reason that Scandinavian islands had much larger populations than similar Scottish islands.

Afterwards they travelled across Europe so that Margaret could meet John's mother, who was spending the summer in Marienbad. When they returned to Scotland John exchanged his Hillman car and £30 for a boat, a stylish 38-foot motor launch with a lugsail at the stern, which he renamed *Gille Brighde*, literally the servant of St Bridget, and the Gaelic name for the wading bird known in English as the oyster catcher. The bird is black and white with a distinctive orange beak. He had the boat painted in the same colours – white superstructure and a narrow orange stripe around the black hull. They sailed her through the canals across Scotland and then, by way of the Clyde estuary, Loch Fyne and the Crinan Canal, across the Minch to Barra.

It was fine weather and a smooth journey, which encouraged John to decide that they could anchor the boat in Northbay and live on it as their first marital home. Despite being over six feet, John did not appear to find the boat restricting and was happy continuing to work on the *Book of Barra* in its tiny cabin. Margaret, however, found it cramped, especially the galley where, although less than five feet tall, she could not stand upright. It took serious storms, when the *Gille Brighde* dragged her anchor and narrowly avoided a collision, to persuade him to give up life on the sea and move ashore. After six weeks afloat, Margaret was relieved to have solid earth beneath her feet.

The Campbells set up home in a small cottage at Northbay let to them by the Coddy. It had previously been occupied by Compton Mackenzie, who described it in his memoirs: 'There was a sizeable sitting-room and kitchen on the ground floor with two bedrooms above. Although it was always called the Bungalow it really was not a bungalow. Chrissie [his secretary] had one bedroom above and the other was kept for guests. I myself slept in a tiny room off the sitting-room.'[1] The house was made of painted corrugated iron, lined inside with pitch pine boards. It had oil lamps rather than electricity and neither running water nor an inside lavatory. Margaret's sisters back in Pittsburgh were horrified, but it was luxury after five years in the thatched house in which she had been living in South Uist or the restricted quarters of the *Gille Brighde*. The couple made it comfortable, painting the walls, building bookcases and putting rugs on the floor. Margaret had used a $500 wedding gift from her uncle to buy a Steinway grand piano from Rae Macintosh's music shop in Edinburgh. It was shipped by 'puffer' from Glasgow and had to be manhandled into the living room. She filmed the last stages of its journey with her Kodak cine camera as the huge instrument, on its side and mounted on a trolley, was heaved by willing hands through the front door.

The first years of their marriage were spent visiting the islands and collecting Gaelic songs and stories in the Hebrides, the passion which they both shared. They had a sense that the heritage was both precious and fragile. It had to be recorded before it disappeared.

With the help of Annie Johnston, teacher at the Castlebay school and herself a singer, the Coddy and the Rev. John MacMillan, the Catholic priest at Northbay, they had been introduced to many singers and storytellers. They had no trouble in persuading people to perform for them, in fact as the word spread people would come to them, asking that their mothers or aunts be recorded. Annie Johnston would arrange ceilidhs when old women would vie with each other to sing. Many of the songs were completely new to John.

He could take down and translate the words and with Margaret's musical expertise he was able to capture the tunes, but he wanted to do more. He wanted to record their actual voices and particularly the accents and dialect words which would distinguish Barra songs from those of other islands or the mainland.

To do this he needed technology and he acquired it by sending away for an Ediphone recorder. This type of machine was not new; it had been introduced 30 years before by Thomas Edison and was in common use in businesses for dictation. But no one had ever used Ediphones for recording folksongs in the houses and workplaces of the singers and John was conscious that he was breaking new ground.

The device was primitive and cumbersome by today's standards. It had no electronics, the subject spoke or sang into a funnel connected by a flexible steel tube to the machine, where a steel needle cut a track in a rotating wax-covered cylinder. But it had a number of advantages. It was clockwork and portable – a valuable feature, since few homes in Barra or South Uist had electricity. It made an apparently permanent record,★ meaning that words and music could be transcribed later, rather than having to be done on the spot, when singers might have to be made to repeat phrases or whole songs, ruining the spontaneity. John started using his new acquisition with

★ John later found that the cylinders deteriorated as the wax hardened and was attacked by mould. Some became unplayable and it became essential to transcribe them. The work was done by several people including Margaret, Seamus Ennis and Calum MacLean, from the Irish Folklore Commission, and A. Martin Freeman. See J.L. Campbell, *Songs Remembered in Exile*, Aberdeen University Press, 1990, pp. 19–20. The machine John used is still in Canna House; although fairly compact it is extremely heavy. The surviving cylinders are on long-term loan to the British Library and are being digitised.

enthusiasm. Within a few months he had recorded 195 songs from 13 male and 17 female singers, most of the women persuaded to perform by Annie Johnston.[2]

John was building up a reputation in the islands as a man who cared about the people, their culture and their livelihoods. Several previous collectors had come to exploit what they found. He came to learn, to understand and to preserve. The *Book of Barra* was published in 1936 to critical esteem, even if sales were modest.

Yet it was not a completely happy time. Margaret's health was not good. Her rheumatism made the joints of her hands painful and limited her ability to play the piano, but there was more sadness to come. The couple's attempts to start a family ended in miscarriages – four in total. The experience must have been traumatic for Margaret, who was in her early 30s. Barra had only basic medical services. Eventually they had to accept that they would be childless, a misfortune they accepted with stoicism and spoke about only to their closest friends.

In the summer of 1937, to give Margaret a break, John took her to Nova Scotia. He was keen to revisit the people he had met on his first brief trip five years earlier, but also wanted to start a serious folksong collection. By taking his Ediphone to Nova Scotia he wanted to collect material and test his theory that despite being generations after the emigration by their ancestors from the Highlands and Islands of Scotland, the Gaels of this part of eastern Canada had preserved many of the same songs and stories and even had the same accents and used the same distinctive dialect words as their forebears. On his first trip John had travelled by train from Boston, a long and arduous journey that had left him without independent transport once he arrived. This time he and Margaret sailed to Quebec, taking with them John's new car, a Vauxhall. The drive across New Brunswick and Nova Scotia took them several days in the extreme heat of the Canadian summer. Their British car, particularly its 'flipper' indicators which popped out of the side each time John wanted to turn, caused great interest, much to John's irritation and Margaret's amusement. Eastern Nova Scotia had largely been populated in the eighteenth and nineteenth centuries by immigrants from Scotland – many of them Gaelic-speaking Catholics – who displaced the indigenous population and early French settlers. The first migrants had left Scotland voluntarily, attracted by the promises of escaping the virtual serfdom they suffered as 'tenants at will' of the big landlords in Scotland – the 'will' being exercised by the landlord rather than the tenant. They were often lured away by emigration agents, who were paid commission by shipping companies, and promised fresh starts on fertile land with financial bounties once they arrived in the New World. These promises often failed to materialise.

The success of the kelp industry meant that at first landowners were reluctant to lose them and did what they could to thwart the exodus. Tenants and employees were obliged to collect, dry and burn kelp for the important minerals it contained. It was arduous and unpleasant work. For this Roderick MacNeill of Barra paid his tenants £2 5s (£2.25) a ton. Transporting it to the markets in Liverpool cost him another £1 5s (£1.25), but there he could sell it for as much as £22 a ton. With a profit margin this fat, landowners in the Western Highlands and Islands grew rich, built extravagant houses and lived lifestyles even beyond their considerable means.[3]

But by the 1820s the kelp boom was over and prices scarcely covered the cost of production. Landlords looked to other ways to maintain their incomes. Clearing their tenants from their crofts and turning vast estates over to large-scale sheep farming seemed to be the answer. In Barra a second Roderick MacNeill had also to contend with over-generous settlements to friends and relatives made in his father's will. His efforts to force his tenants to make up the shortfall in his income by working harder for less money and paying ever increasing burdens led to poverty and famine for many, but did not prevent his financial ruin in 1837. The solution, according to his trustee in bankruptcy, was the enforced transportation of two thirds of the Barra population to North America.[4]

Similar stories could be told of numerous other islands and mainland estates. Sometimes whole communities with their clergymen arrived in Nova Scotia together. They had to create new lives for themselves from scratch, not only founding settlements where none existed, but bringing previously uncultivated land into production, which often, in the thickly wooded hills of Nova Scotia, meant felling and clearing forests. They brought with them their language and culture, calling their new villages Lochaber, Moidart, Keppoch, Arisaig, Strathglass and Inverness.[5]

Many of the emigrants from Barra ended up on Cape Breton Island, which John had visited in 1932. Now a bridge connects it to the mainland of Canada, but in 1937 John and Margaret had to take a ferry across the Gut of Canso. If the familiar place names had led them to expect a landscape similar to the bare hills of Scotland, they were disappointed. 'For miles and miles we passed through dense forest, where a white farmhouse showed from time to time in the middle of a few cleared fields. Sometimes these farmhouses appeared empty and deserted, with conifers springing up again on the fields which had once been laboriously cleared for tillage. The forest seemed to be alive and to hold the country in its grip, intense, malignant, ever ready to reclaim as its own the land that had once been won from it. Vast areas seemed entirely unoccupied.'[6]

John revisited old acquaintances, such as Jonathan MacKinnon, who had edited *Mac Talla*, a weekly Gaelic newspaper that, although it had long since stopped publishing, had enjoyed a longer life than any other unsubsidised Gaelic journal anywhere. MacKinnon explained why parts of the country looked abandoned and why Gaelic culture was under threat in Nova Scotia as it was in Scotland. A secondary wave of emigration had taken people from the east to the newly opened western provinces of Canada. 'Now some of these people are beginning to come back, especially from Saskatchewan, which has been badly hit by drought. But even so, Cape Breton is three parts empty. Land can be bought for next to nothing here. The churches have not got a quarter of the population they were built to hold.'[7]

Wherever they went John and Margaret asked for songs which had been composed in Scotland – they were also invited to attend a *luadhadh*, a waulking of the tweed, like the ones they had witnessed in Barra and South Uist. In Cape Breton it was known as a 'milling frolic'. They recognised some of the songs and the process of waulking the cloth was the same, but there were distinctive differences. It was men, rather than women, who worked the tweed and the occasion was much more festive than it might have been in Scotland. The evening opened with speeches and humorous anecdotes told by a man 'in excellent Harris Gaelic', and when the milling or waulking began many of the audience linked hands and swung their arms to the music while joining in the chorus. Another incongruous note was struck by the young people present who 'leaned back against the wall of the hall chewing gum.'[8]

John and Margaret stayed six weeks in Cape Breton and used forty-three wax cylinders recording ninety-five traditional songs and ballads, two games, seven local songs and three original songs sung by their composer. Before they left, John persuaded Jonathan MacKinnon to introduce him to the chief of the Micmac Indians. The Micmacs once occupied much of the maritime provinces of Canada and parts of Quebec and Newfoundland, but by 1937 had been reduced in number to around 4,000. Their chief, Gabriel Syllibuy, related in the Micmac language the story his grandfather had told of the coming of the first Scottish settlers. He also brought singers who sang plain-song hymns, having been converted to Christianity by French priests in the eighteenth century.

John was keen to re-establish his contacts with St Francis Xavier College (St FX) at Antigonish, on the Nova Scotia mainland. The Gaelic, mostly Catholic, communities of the Western Highlands and Islands had always prized education highly but only gained influence over their own schools after the Crofters' Act of 1886 gave them a majority on local school boards, which had previously been dominated by representatives of their absentee English-speaking Protestant landlords.[9] It was natural that they would want to found higher education institutions and unsurprising that since so many of them had been driven from their homeland, they should do so in their new communities.

St Francis Xavier College⋆ was founded in 1855, although classes had been held elsewhere for the previous two years. Its impetus came from the Catholic Church, which was anxious to ensure a supply of educated young men for the priesthood, but from the beginning it had sought to give its students a good general education. John renewed his friendship with the Rev. P.J. Nicholson, known throughout the college as 'Doc Pat', whom he had met on his first trip five years before. His ancestors had emigrated from Barra and he was a cousin of Annie Johnston. Despite being a scientist and having been born and brought up in Cape Breton, he could speak and write Gaelic fluently, edited a Gaelic column in the local newspaper and

⋆ Now St Francis Xavier University

had a deep knowledge and interest in the language and its culture. He greatly encouraged John and gave him introductions to many local singers and storytellers.

While in Antigonish, John and Margaret also linked up with Angus McIntosh, a young Scottish scholar whom John had first met on Barra. Although his main interest was middle English, he had moved to the Hebrides to learn Gaelic. Now studying at Harvard, he met them at St FX.

John had another reason for wanting to visit the college. Touring Cape Breton he had come across co-operatives – creameries, saw-mills, fish and lobster canneries, credit unions – owned and managed collectively by local families. Their aim was to increase prosperity, reduce the island's dependence on imported goods and foods and combat depopulation by providing jobs for young people. When he talked to the workers a common thread emerged; they had been helped and encouraged by the Extension Department of St FX. He sought out the department's director, Dr Moses Coady, and was profoundly impressed by what he was told.

Coady was a very unusual man – a Catholic priest, educator, idealist and trade unionist. His views, expressed at length in his book *Masters of their own Destiny*,[10] were a blend of the power of self-help, radical politics and hard business sense. The road he advocated was not an easy one:

> In addition to their daily occupations, the people must put in extra work on a program of study and enlightenment in order that they may create the institutions that will enable them to obtain control of the instruments of production. Building the new society is as much their business as digging coal, catching fish, or planting seed. If they do not bestir themselves to bring it about, no one else will. The only hope of democracy is that enough noble, independent, energetic souls may be found who are prepared to work overtime, without pay. Such a sacrifice is not necessary in a dictatorship – it is not even permitted. In a dictatorial system, all the directing energy comes from the top. In a democracy, it is the privilege of the people to work overtime in their own interests – the creation of a new society where all men are free.[11]

Coady told John that the department's primary role was educational, running study groups and self-help classes, but they had quickly learned that if their work were to have any lasting benefit they had to have an economic development role as well. '[We] would go into some fishing village or farming community known to be backward and depressed – in debt to the local merchants, exploited by middlemen and so on. We would hold a mass meeting and tell the people what things were really holding them back; it was surprising how often these things were not clearly realised. We would tell them of what had been done by people like themselves by co-operative effort to better their conditions. Eventually we would get the people into a neutral state of mind in which they would be at least prepared to give our plans fair-minded consideration.'[12]

The Antigonish Movement, as it had become known, had only been going for less than ten years, but its success had been profound. Coady told John that there were 90 credit unions in Nova Scotia, 35 co-operative canning factories, 25 co-operative stores. There were 30,000 people involved in 1,400 education groups and the movement was growing all the time. 'We have yet to find a community so down and out and broken-spirited that it cannot respond to our teaching,' he added. It was a message of hope and John went away fired with enthusiasm for what co-operation might do for the Hebrides.

The Campbells travelled home via Boston and Pittsburgh, to visit Margaret's family, and Washington, where they were put up in the Martinique Hotel by *National Geographic* magazine, which had offered to publish an article illustrated by Margaret's photographs of the Scottish islands. They also lectured to members of the National Geographic Society and showed Margaret's ciné films. They left after three days, well pleased with Margaret's $350 fee and $50 expenses. In New York they stopped to spend some of the money. John bought the latest in technology to replace their primitive and heavy Ediphone. The Presto J6 recorder, an electronic system which cut 16-inch disks, would produce better-quality sound and more durable recordings, but also needed large batteries.

Back in Barra, John was still fired with what he had learned in Canada. He published a special 'Nova Scotian Number' of *The Sea Leaguer*[13] in which he described in enthusiastic detail the Antigonish Movement, its educational study groups and visits to co-operative ventures. He urged a similar approach in Scotland, particularly recommending a co-operative lobster-canning factory in Barra, but he also drew a general lesson: 'Granted that at present in Scotland we are hampered by administrative sloth and red tape and various kinds of feudalistic survivals from which the Nova Scotians are happily free, it still remains the truth that this kind of education is necessary to produce in the Highlands an independent-minded, well-informed younger generation who will not tolerate things their forefathers had to put up with.'[14]

He returned to the theme a year later, when with Sir Alexander MacEwen, the lawyer and Nationalist politician who had represented the Barra road tax strikers, he wrote a strident pamphlet: *Act Now for the Highlands and Islands*.[15] John described it as a 'call to action' and advocated 'land and sea training centres, schools for smallholders, continuation classes, study clubs and generally to encourage the study of co-operative methods'.

As a manifesto for the development of the north of Scotland, it was ahead of its time. As well as his Nova Scotian experience, John also drew on what he had learned in Norway on his honeymoon. He repeated the demands of the Sea League for the setting-up of inshore fishery zones reserved for local boats, but also repeated the call made in his letter with Compton Mackenzie three years earlier, for the establishment of a Highland Development Board with a ten-year plan. Ferry fares should be regulated so that they were the same as rail fares for an equivalent journey, married couples should only have to pay 1 ½ times the adult fare, mail should be sorted on ship to end the nonsense of letters for neighbouring islands having to be transported to a mainland sorting office and then be sent back again.

The booklet was a mixture of the visionary and the practical. It called for land resettlement schemes, the revival of the kelp industry and the encouragement of rural industries and tourism. Every island should have a pier, where passengers and livestock could board without having to be transferred by small boat; there should be waiting rooms where passengers – who might have to walk miles and then have to wait hours for delayed ferries – could shelter from bad weather; there should be better Third Class accommodation – or better still only one class on ferry services. The booklet read like an election address – and perhaps that was how it was intended.

# CHAPTER SEVEN

# Absent Neighbours

John's political ideas were still in a formative stage, but he was beginning to realise that the ownership and control of land were fundamental to economic development and that without the creation of jobs and prosperity it would be impossible to retain populations in the islands and remote mainland communities. This would spell the end of their unique language and culture. He could learn a lot from his research into the history of the islands, but to bring it up to date all he had to do was look around him for examples of the ownership of vast estates and the dead hand of absentee landlords. To the east of Barra and the Uists, between the Outer Isles and the mainland, the Small Isles of Canna, Rum, Eigg and Muck provided graphic illustrations.

In the late eighteenth century these islands formed part of the estates of the MacDonalds of Clanranald, a powerful clan which owned vast areas of the West Highlands and whole islands in the Inner and Outer Hebrides. In the Jacobite risings they had sided firmly with the Stuarts, fighting for the Old Pretender in 1715 at the Battle of Sheriffmuir, where their chief, or captain, was killed. They fought again for Bonnie Prince Charlie at the battles of Prestonpans, Falkirk and Culloden in 1745–46. But then their chiefs underwent a remarkable political and cultural transformation, and less than two generations later their captain had been absorbed into the English establishment. Reginald George MacDonald, born in 1788, succeeded to the title at the age of six. He was educated at Eton and moved into the upper reaches of London society. In 1812 he married Lady Caroline Anne Edgecombe, daughter of the second Earl of Mount Edgecombe. He also became Member of Parliament for the rotten borough of Plympton, Devon, which had only forty voters returning two MPs and was in the gift of his father-in-law.

The fashionable lifestyle MacDonald was leading did not come cheaply, but his Highland and Island estates were producing a substantial income and for a time he could afford it. The Napoleonic Wars, which limited imports of potash, pushed up the price of kelp to over £20 a ton – and Clanranald's estates were producing 1,000 tons a year. But the war ended in 1815 and the kelp price collapsed, sinking to £3 a ton, hardly more than the cost of labour to gather it from the beaches and the transport costs to get it to the potash factories. MacDonald's spending, however, did not decline and his debts reached the colossal figure of £74,000.[1] The trustees of his estates saw only one way out; they started to sell land. In 1813 the estates of Lochans, Dalilea, Eilean Shona and Muck were sold. In 1826 Arisaig and Bornish in South Uist went and a year later Eigg and Canna.[2]

The Isle of Rum had changed hands several times between Clanranald and the MacLeans of Coll, and in the first half of the nineteenth century saw some of the worst scenes of forced evictions, with the native population emigrating to Nova Scotia and elsewhere in Canada. It was bought in 1845 by Lord Salisbury, who wanted to add a Scottish sporting estate to his English properties. His enthusiasm lasted 18 years and in 1863 he sold it to Captain Farquhar Campbell, who also owned land in Mull, where his attempts to prosecute his tenants for alleged small thefts of firewood did not endear him to the inhabitants.[3] Although he owned the island until his death in 1886, he did not visit it very often and let the shooting to a succession of rich sportsmen, the last of whom, the prosperous Lancashire industrialist John Bullough, bought it in 1888. Bullough built houses to shelter his shooting guests and planted trees, but he was mostly concerned with building up the sporting value of the estate, introducing deer and game birds. When he died, aged only 53 in 1891, Rum passed into the ownership of his son, George.

At six feet eight inches tall, George Bullough was almost literally, as well as metaphorically, larger than life. One of his first acts as proprietor was to lay his father's body to rest in an octagonal stone mausoleum at Harris, a remote part of the island. According to John Love, Rum's definitive historian: 'The passage running into the cliff behind was lined with enamelled tiles and mosaics. Legend has it that one of Sir George Bullough's less tactful guests was moved to comment how it reminded him of a public lavatory in Waterloo Station.'[4] Sir George appears to have taken the comment to heart, because he later removed the coffin and had the tomb blown up.

His taste for extravagant building was still intact though. He demolished the lodge house and built his fantasy. The architects were Leeming & Leeming, who had designed the Admiralty Buildings on Horse Guards Parade. Red sandstone blocks already cut to size were brought from Arran, 150 miles away.

'Construction began with a hundred or so masons and craftsmen being imported from Lancashire. Bullough apparently insisted that they all wore kilts, with local tradition adding how the reluctant workforce had to be sweetened with a bonus on top of their wages because of the blood-thirsty midges! No expense was spared. The two-storeyed building was of a striking castellated design, surrounded by a covered colonnade where Sir George could take his early morning constitutional dryshod. The household was awoken at 8 a.m. by Neil Shaw playing "Johnnie Cope" on his pipes,' reported John Love. 'The four corners of the building were offset with small turrets which inside provided small dressing rooms for the upstairs bedchambers. Above the main door a large crenellated tower was topped with a tall turret, embellishments which strove to justify its claim to the title "Kinloch Castle".'

The castle boasted all modern conveniences, including lights powered by one of Britain's first hydro-electric schemes. It would be decades before the estate workers would have electricity in their homes. The sumptuously furnished building boasted the last word in entertainment – an 'orchestrion', an electrically driven barrel organ with pipes and percussion which could play a selection of popular hits of the day, as well as classical pieces such as the *Ride of the Valkyries* and the *William Tell Overture*. Sir George's imagination was not confined to the interior. 'Rich soils were shipped from Ayrshire as the basis for his lavish gardens, rockeries and lawns. A small golf course and bowling green were laid out, even a racquets court. Two hundred yards of heated glasshouses nurtured every fashionable hothouse fruit: grapes, peaches, nectarines and figs. In its heyday Kinloch Castle required forty staff, no less than fourteen of them gardeners.'[5]

The Bulloughs were absentee landlords of exactly the kind John

Lorne Campbell believed were stifling progress in the islands. The elaborate and expensive 'improvements' to Rum were enjoyed by the Bullough family and their guests for no more than three months each year, the remainder of the time being spent in London, the Continent or the Bulloughs' other estate in Perthshire. This was no classless society like Barra; estate workers on Rum were little better than serfs and were expected to get off the road and hide when they saw someone from the 'castle' approaching. The days of wine and roses, however, did not last forever. The economic depression of the 1930s reduced Sir George's income; the heated greenhouses were abandoned and the vintage champagne in the castle's cellars was sent to London for auction. Sir George died in 1939, but his widow and children continued to visit the island occasionally to shoot.* He was interred in a granite sarcophagus next to his father in a new mausoleum built, not in the style of a public lavatory, but of a Greek temple. In 1967 Lady Bullough joined them there.

The history of another of the Small Isles was no less troubled. When the profligate Clanranald sold Eigg in 1827, the buyer was Dr Hugh Macpherson, professor of Hebrew and Greek at King's College, Aberdeen. By the standards of the day, he was not a rich man, but he was able to pay £15,000 for the island and to keep it until his death. Although he was always an absentee landlord he had the reputation of being fair and compassionate and when the potato famine hit the island in 1846 his lawyer was able to put up a stout defence against official charges of inaction to alleviate the suffering of his tenants. He had bought meal and other supplies costing £150 to distribute to the population and forgone rent from the smaller farmers. But the lawyer added a qualification which summed up the prevailing attitude: 'The moral obligation of a landowner in such cases must have a limit. A proprietor cannot be required to supply subsistence to a redundant population who remain at home and sit idle rather than migrate where they can earn a fair day's wage for a fair day's work.'[6]

Macpherson died in 1854 leaving the island to his daughters, the oldest of whom, Isabella, lived on Eigg and exercised a benevolent maternalism over her tenants and workers. The island changed hands

* Rum was gifted to the Nature Conservancy Council (now Scottish Natural Heritage) in 1950.

again in 1896, when it was bought by Lawrence Thomson MacEwen (who also styled himself Robert Lawrie Thomson), a self-made businessman and sometime adventurer, journalist and arms dealer. He also bought the neighbouring smaller island of Muck at the same time and contemplated moving the entire population of Eigg to Muck to leave the larger island as a deer farm for shooting – on a similar pattern to Rum. The Crofters' Act had, however, given his tenants security and rather than forcing them to go, he had to resort to persuading and cajoling them to give up their crofts in favour of other holdings in the north of the island where, it was said, he would not have to see the poor people.[7] Thomson became sentimentally attached to the island, although he was not permanently resident and left the day-to-day management to his factor. He died in 1913 and was buried on Castle Island, close to Eigg pier.

At the end of the First World War John MacEwan, Thomson's nephew, decided to sell Eigg, although he kept Muck and continued to farm there. The new buyer was Sir William Petersen, an arrogant and vain bully. 'Everyone was made to feel the brunt of his temper and, unfortunately, his temper was in proportion to his size. He was a huge bear of a man and boasted about it as a sign of his Viking ancestry. Acts of generosity were offset by arbitrariness and excessive control', comments the island's historian, Camille Dressler.[8] The lodge house built by Thomson had burnt down and, perhaps with an eye to the over-grand mock castle built by the Bulloughs on neighbouring Rum, Petersen decided to build his own folly. Not for him, however, the London architects, imported craftsmen and pre-cut sandstone. The large mansion he commissioned had a keep, battlements, a turret and a flagpole displaying his standard, but it was 'a flimsy timber-framed construction reinforced with steel, the walls made out of chicken wire and plaster'. When fire broke out five years later the entire construction burned to the ground.

Sir William's finances proved to be as insubstantial as his home. He died in Canada in 1925 deeply in debt. His embalmed body was brought back to Eigg in a glass-topped coffin and the islanders were invited to pay their respects.

The next owner of the island had a superficial similarity to Petersen in that he was a shipowner, and in fact he had first seen the island when visiting as a guest at one of Petersen's shooting parties. There, however, the similarity ended. Sir Walter Runciman had inherited a huge fortune from his father and, despite his ability and willingness to spend money on improvements on Eigg, was not extravagant or spendthrift. He viewed the island not as a status symbol, but as a respite from his day job, which was being a Liberal MP and later a cabinet minister in the national government led by Ramsay MacDonald. He was a keen shot, but also a bird watcher. With his wife Hilda – a practical and likeable woman and also a sometime Liberal MP – he invested in the island with a view to making it self-supporting. He rebuilt the lodge, this time in a less ostentatious and more lasting style and brought what historian Camille Dressler describes as a 'golden age' to Eigg.

The new monied proprietors brought investment to the islands and sometimes lasting improvements, such as postal services and telegraph lines. But the effect of their ownership was to make the populations almost entirely dependent on the proprietor for their livelihoods. To be dismissed usually meant losing your home along with your job and having to leave the island. Independent enterprise was not encouraged and sometimes actively stamped out. It was a precarious and uncertain existence. Islands turned into playgrounds were dependent on the whim or the fortunes of the owner. Local customs and traditions were suppressed in favour of the laird's notion of what Highland estate workers should wear and how they should act. English was favoured over the native Gaelic and, with rare exceptions, the more pious proprietors built Protestant churches even though most of the populations were Catholic. It was not a firm foundation on which to build a sustainable future.

# CHAPTER EIGHT

# The Isle of Canna

Even if he had not landed on it, John would have known Canna, the fourth of the Small Isles, because the *Lochmor* and *Lochearn* called there on some of their runs between the Outer Isles and the mainland ports. Tied up at the pier, he would have had ample time to survey the green, sheltered bay, the grandeur of Canna's cliffs and the fertile pastures. He would probably also pass the time of day with the Gaelic-speaking farm workers as they loaded or unloaded livestock or supplies. The Canna estate sold cattle, sheep and vegetables on Barra and South Uist and there was some inter-marriage between the farmworkers and crofters of Canna and the outer islands.

According to one myth, the name 'Canna' derives from the Gaelic words for 'the island lying across'.[1] Other possible origins are from the Early Irish 'wolf-whelp', Old Norse 'knee-shaped', or another possibility from Gaelic 'little whale or porpoise'.[2] In truth, no one knows where the name comes from,[3] it may owe its origins to Gaelic or to Norse – Gaels and Norsemen both lived there at some time. But, even if the etymology is doubtful, the phrase 'lying across' fairly describes the island's situation. At four and a half miles long by one mile wide it has the same elongated shape as its larger neighbours in the Outer Hebrides, but unlike them it is orientated east–west, rather than north–south. It lies 'across' the Minch rather than along it.

This is of more than passing importance. When the wind swings round from the prevailing westerly and blows from the Arctic, it strikes Canna on its north face, 600-foot cliffs of granite which form a vast collar turned up against the chill. The lower, gentler, fertile pastures sloping down from the cliffs to the sea on the south side are thus protected from the worst of the cold and face the sun. That is not the only way in which geography and geology has been kind to the island. Canna has one of the best natural harbours in the

Hebrides, deep water protected on one side by a promontory of rock jutting out from the main settlement of Coroghon and on the other by Sanday, Canna's satellite island. Even at the lowest tides, when it is possible to walk from Canna to Sanday across the sands, there is enough depth of water for the harbour to remain navigable.

The first sight of Canna when approaching from the mainland by sea leads you to think that 'whale' might not be a bad description either. Its outline suggests, not a small mammal, but a vast creature floating on the surface, its head formed at the east end by Compass Hill and Carn a'Ghaill, the highest point at 688 feet (210 metres). As the eye travels west the outline slopes down to the low pastures at Tarbet, before rising steeply again to the tail at Garrisdale. As you approach the island and can make out more detail, you see that Canna is made of basalt and its exposed cliffs on the south side have weathered to form ranks of hexagonal columns, huge organ pipes like those around Fingal's Cave on the island of Staffa and the Giant's Causeway on the Antrim coast. Closer still and you see green fields separated by grey stone walls and belts of trees, planted to provide shelter from the winds.

Canna is a captivating isle and in 1937 it captured the imagination of T. Ratcliffe Barnett, a Minister in the Free Church of Scotland turned travel writer. In his book *Highland Harvest,* he described the varied scenery of the island. 'You can climb the heather hills, wander over moors, stand on beetling cliffs, walk among fields, sit among the fruits and flowers of gardens enclosed, or listen to the wind in the trees. If you leave the meadows and climb to the top of the highest hill you will look upon a panorama of sea and land scarcely to be surpassed. In the west you see Barra, Eriskay, South Uist, Benbecula and North Uist. Northwards Skye fills the horizon from Neist Point to the Point of Sleat. Eastwards lies the mainland from Knoydart to Ardnamurchan, with Rhum, Mull, Coll and Tiree floating in the summer seas. Due south lies the rocky isle of Heisker, with the lighthouse which sends its powerful flash across nine miles of sea right into your bedroom window.'[4]

With its natural advantages it is no surprise that Canna has been home to men and women for thousands of years, as its rich store of archaeological sites testifies. Dwellings and artefacts from the Neolithic and Bronze ages have been discovered, along with many later finds. The island was a base for monks and nuns from the monastery on Iona, who spread Christianity to the islands, and it passed through the ownership of powerful clan chiefs, nobles and prelates. It was for a time the home of one of the most famous Gaelic scholars and bards.

Canna had been leased from Clanranald since the late eighteenth century by the MacNeill family – Hector[5] and, after his death, his son Donald, who bought the island for £9,000 when it came on the market. Hector and Donald appear to have been prudent tenants and generous landlords, living on and farming the island, building houses and improving the farm. But Donald was 60 when he bought Canna, unmarried and apparently without an heir. He had also acquired the property at a time when the kelp industry – which provided an important supplementary income – was starting to decline. He appears to have done his best to rectify the succession problem despite his age, fathering at least a daughter and two sons, although who their mother or mothers was or were is a mystery – he never married. He died aged 79 in 1848 leaving the island to his eldest son, also Donald, a teenage schoolboy.

Donald Junior's ownership of the island was ill-starred from the beginning. His illegitimacy meant that his father's will was invalid under Scots law and a lengthy court process was necessary before it could be proved. A second problem was that he had not lived very long on the island – having been sent to stay with relatives on the mainland while attending school – and he knew nothing about farming. He tried to make up for his shortcomings by becoming apprenticed to a farmer in the Scottish Borders, but he was a naïve and vulnerable young man who badly missed a father's guidance. Despite being already engaged to a girl living on Canna, he managed to entangle himself, or was deliberately ensnared, with two other women. The mess was sorted out in court, with Donald MacNeill the poorer.

He married the Canna girl – Isabella – and they had five children. He built Canna House for her, a fine stone three-storey mansion overlooking the harbour, far grander than any existing house on the island and a step up – geographically as well as socially – from the smaller and altogether more humble dwelling on the shore which had been the laird's house up until then. But his stewardship of the island was not a happy one. His expenditure always outstripped his income and he sought credit from friends, neighbours and suppliers near and far. He appears constantly to have been in debt and borrowing more and more money. With agriculture in decline and harvests poor, the island could not support its relatively large population any more than it could support its owner's lifestyle.

There had been voluntary emigration from Canna during his father's time, but Donald Junior's ownership saw the first compulsory Clearances, which were now becoming commonplace in the Western Highlands and Islands. The most brutal acts were seldom carried out by the proprietors themselves, but by agents, factors (estate managers) or tenants who had rented the land already occupied by crofters or landless cottars for grazing. Large-scale sheep farming was more profitable for landlords than the rents they could obtain and, until legislation gave them some security of tenure, the crofters had no legal right to resist.

The story of John MacLean, a sheep farmer from Moidart on the Scottish mainland, who rented the grazing at Keill, Canna, was typical. He employed the starving crofters he had displaced to build walls between his newly created fields – they can still be seen on the island today. He paid them, not in money, but in meal, which he bought from the government's Relief Fund.[6] People who had once been self-sufficient – albeit at a level little above subsistence – were now dependent on handouts, and meagre handouts at that.

The population of the island, which was 255 in 1841, halved over the next 20 years and halved again by the 1930s. It is not surprising that many islanders opted to leave on the ships provided by the landlord's agents. An uncertain future on the other side of the Atlantic was better than certain starvation and virtual slavery at home. Some would have stayed, but had no choice. They were compelled out of their homes and onto the ships chartered to take them away. John Lorne Campbell met some of their descendants in Nova Scotia. There is a tradition on Canna that as Donald MacNeill stood in 1851 watching his tenants and farm workers boarding the boat to take them into exile, an old woman turned and cursed him: *'Thig an latha fhathast gum fag sibh Canaidh cho bochd ruinn fhin.'*[7] 'The day will yet come that you'll leave Canna as poor as ourselves.'

It was 30 years before the old woman's curse on Donald MacNeill was realised, but realised it was. By the winter of 1881–82 the proprietor of Canna was finding it increasingly hard to keep his creditors at bay. The Canna file at the offices of his solicitors, Messrs J. & F.J. Martin at 122 George Street, Edinburgh was bulging with demands from all over Scotland.[8] The Scottish Amicable Life Assurance Society was pressing for payment of interest of £330 9s 5d on its outstanding mortgage on the island. Lawyers from Edinburgh, Glasgow and Greenock were persistent in their attempts to get replies to their requests for some explanation why their clients had not been paid the sums owed to them. The firm of Sproat & Cameron were particularly anxious, having 'several claims on our hands against Mr MacNeill and some of the parties have been pressing us to charge and poind* with a view to bringing matters to a point'. The Rev. John Sinclair, the Church of Scotland minister for the Small Isles, wrote from his manse on Eigg complaining at the non-arrival of his stipend, which had gone unpaid for another half-year, bringing the total arrears to £84 16s 5d. Perhaps more threateningly, the Collector of the Queen's taxes wrote from Oban to demand payment of £21 16s 10d and, having received no satisfactory reply, put the matter in the hands of the Edinburgh Office of the Inland Revenue, which threatened 'the unpleasant necessity of proceeding to recover by warrant'.

To escape his burden MacNeill put Canna up for sale in 1880 and authorised his solicitors to accept offers over £17,000 for the land, with the stock and equipment to be purchased at valuation, or at £23,500 for the whole lot. He advertised it in *The Field*, the *Glasgow Herald* and *Land*, 'a journal for all interested in landed and house property', but paid none of the bills and the entreating letters from the three magazines asking for payment were added by the clerk at Martin's to the fat file of creditors. However, the advertisement produced some potential purchasers and the Edinburgh lawyers Murray, Beith and Murray sent a valuer to the island on behalf of one of their clients. Among others registering interest was Mr Robert Thom, a West of Scotland-based timber merchant and shipowner. But interest waned and one by one those who had considered bidding either withdrew or made offers which MacNeill rejected. Mr Thom's solicitors wrote to say that he was going abroad

---

* Seize property

and might be away for three months and so would not be making an offer. If the island was unsold on his return he might consider making a bid.

By the spring of 1882 the clamour from MacNeill's creditors was growing and he again advertised Canna for sale. One of those who responded was a Robert Kerr, who wrote to J. and F.J. Martin in April explaining that he was not enquiring the price on his own behalf, but for 'a gentleman who is at present in America'. It seems likely that the gentleman in question was Robert Thom.

Thom was a remarkable man. Born in 1826 in Glasgow he trained as an analytical chemist, but at the age of 22, in search for adventure, he and a friend joined the crew of a sailing ship bound from the Clyde to Montevideo in Uruguay. There was a crew of 15, and the young Thom experienced almost every aspect of seamanship. When they arrived at their destination they found that Montevideo was at war with Buenos Aires, its nearest neighbour across the Rio de la Plata. The war does not appear to have inhibited trade, for the bay was full of ships, nor did it stop the young men going ashore and meeting local people, especially girls. For Thom and his companion it provided some diversion from the tedium of watches: through their telescopes, they were able to follow the fighting from the top of the mast of their ship.

But it was on the voyage home that the biggest excitement was to come. The cargo of wool caught fire and with the wooden vessel ablaze the crew was forced to abandon ship. Thom, who was suffering badly from scurvy by this time, determined to die on the ship to give his crewmates more chance of survival, but his friend leapt back aboard and threw him into the boat. They drifted for two weeks before reaching the Dutch colony of Suriname in Central America, where Thom recovered in hospital.[9] His near death did not deter him either from travel or adventure and he went on to establish enterprises in the Americas and back home in Glasgow, including a carpet-making business and a trading company, Thom & Cameron. At the time of his interest in Canna, Robert Thom was already a rich man and a substantial landowner, having bought the estate of Barremman on Gareloch, 40 miles from Glasgow, where he had a reputation as an improving and considerate landlord.[10]

Thom bought the island in the summer of 1882, paying the very full price of £23,500,* but the sale was not straightforward. Having given more than the asking price for land, stock, boats and other equipment and furniture and fittings in the houses he was dismayed to find on his arrival in July that cattle, wool and other items had been removed and sold by MacNeill. Thom's solicitors started pressing for recompense but the row grew bitter and personal, with Thom at one stage telling MacNeill's son that he regretted having parted with the money and if another purchaser could be found he would be willing to hand the island over. MacNeill claimed that some of the sheep belonged to his servants and tenants and household furniture and other items to his children. 'I am determined that I will not leave the house until I get everything I ask delivered over to my son,' he wrote to his lawyers.

But the sale had to go through and a short time later MacNeill was admitting he was 'entirely at Mr Thom's mercy . . . he may turn me out any time now'. In August MacNeill's creditors met in Glasgow. It became clear that, despite achieving his price for the island, he could not meet all his debts in full. The island was mortgaged to the extent of £18,500[11] and by the time all the debts were settled a year later, ordinary creditors had to settle for a little over half of what they were owed.[12] The old woman's prophecy had come true: MacNeill left Canna as poor as the people he had expelled.

Thom was a keen shot and his interest in Canna seems mainly to have been for the usual rich man's reason, as a sporting estate. He appears to have visited the island often, and made improvements including in 1892 building the first pier in the Small Isles, enabling ferries and cargo boats to dock, rather than having to load and unload into small boats in the bay. It also led to Canna's having a part in the booming herring fishery, until Mallaig, with its rail connection, took the trade away. Thom also replaced the watermill, built in Donald MacNeill's time, with a more efficient steam-driven grain mill and established a smithy, so that farm machinery could be repaired on the island. Many of the farm workers living on Sanday were owed wages at the time of the sale of the island and MacNeill, unable to pay them, gave them crofting rights to land instead. Notwithstanding this arrangement, Robert Thom helped them to

* Over £1.1 million at 2010 prices

improve their houses. He established new herds, first pedigree Highlands and later Galloways, and began planting trees to provide shelter and timber. Although a Presbyterian himself, he respected the religion of his tenants and workers and in 1886 allowed the wife of the Marquess of Bute to build a substantial square Catholic chapel on Sanday, dedicated to the English king St Edward the Confessor.[13]

But Barremman, his mainland estate from where he could visit his businesses in Glasgow, with a little over two hours' travel by steamer and train, remained his home. Thom had five daughters, but only one son, Allan Gilmour Thom, born in 1870. In 1896 Allan married Mary Johannan Cameron in St Giles' Cathedral, Edinburgh. She was a Skye woman, whose family home was Talisker House, on the island's west coast, and well used to Hebridean life. Some time after their wedding they decided to buy out Allan's sisters' interest in Canna, go to live on the island and become active farmers. In 1905 a new house was built for them on the slope of the hill above the harbour, with fine views over Sanday to the mountains of Rum. It was named Tighard – 'High House' in Gaelic. Robert Thom died in Barremman in 1911 and Allan marked his passing by building a Presbyterian church on the road to Canna pier. Compared to St Edward's, which faces it across the harbour, it is a modest but attractive building, made of stone and modelled on the early Celtic churches at Glendalough in Ireland.

Allan Thom did not have the wealth of his father, which had been divided among six beneficiaries and further depleted when Allan bought his sisters' share of Canna. He saw himself as a farmer rather than a rich landowner, and worked the land alongside his employees. Nevertheless, he still had an income independent of his earnings from Canna as a result of his shareholding and directorship of Thom & Cameron, the family firm, and he was able to send his sons away to private schools. Alan Cameron Thom, born in December 1896, was deaf from birth, the result it was believed of a botched forceps delivery. He was sent to a special school for the deaf in Northampton. His brother, Robert Victor Gilmour Thom, born three years later, was sent to Fettes, the prestigious Edinburgh public school.

During school holidays both Thom sons returned to Canna and Alan's diary makes it clear that they took their share of physical

labour in the fields and, when the weather was poor, did maintenance work on farm equipment, boats or net mending. They
supplemented the farm income with sea fishing for cod, haddock,
herring, flounders, whiting and lythe as well as lobsters and mussels.

They also shot birds – snipe, woodcock and curlew, occasionally
geese – and rabbits, a major pest on the island, which they also
trapped using ferrets and sent to the mainland for sale. During the
lambing season they shot crows and gulls to stop them preying on
the newborns. Robert was called up in February 1918, joined the
Argyll & Sutherland Highlanders and fought on the Western Front
in the last battles of the First World War. When he returned he
worked for a while on one of his mother's family's farms on Skye
before moving to Canna, where he steadily took over more of the
management of the farm from his father and eventually also the
directorship of the family business.

The Thoms' relationship with their workers and tenants was very
different from that of the Bulloughs on neighbouring Rum. They
worked alongside them, but also shared their social life. Each New
Year, Alan Thom, the son, recorded in his diaries, they attended the
island's Hogmanay party, dancing in turn with all the ladies and
sometimes ending the evening with a firework display. There are
accounts of social visits by Mrs Thom to the wives or widows in the
more remote cottages. Although they worshipped in the new
Presbyterian church, the visiting Catholic priest was always entertained at the Big House, to tea, dinner or an overnight stay. When
Robert Thom travelled around the Small Isles collecting names for a
petition to the General Assembly of the Church of Scotland for the
removal of an unpopular minister (described by Camille Dressler
in her history of Eigg as 'an Irishman with a penchant for cider'[14]),
he was careful to specify that the replacement should be Gaelic-
speaking.

Allan Thom died in November 1934 after 18 months of suffering
from cancer of the throat. He was buried beside the church he had
built to commemorate his father. His sons and widow continued
to live on the island, but Mrs Thom was becoming increasingly
debilitated by arthritis and Robert, in his mid 30s and unmarried,
began to question his own future in a place where it was not easy to
meet potential brides. In 1938 his brother Alan became engaged to

Jessie Cassells, whom he had met through mutual friends. She was also deaf, but had studied art in Glasgow. They determined that after their wedding they would live near her family in Hamilton. The prospect of being left alone on Canna, particularly with another war looming, did not appeal to Robert and, with his mother and brother's agreement, he put the island up for sale. A prolonged agricultural recession since the First World War had reduced land values substantially since his grandfather had bought the island, but he still hoped to achieve enough to allow the family to resettle on the mainland.

# CHAPTER NINE

# Into Ownership

When John arrived back from Canada in early 1938 he learned that he was about to receive his share of a $200,000 trust left to him and his brothers by his American grandmother, Elizabeth Waterbury.[1] The news was a surprise, since his mother had never indicated that her sons would inherit anything directly from her family, preferring to allow them to believe that anything they received would be what she chose to leave them. With Charles dead, the money would be split three ways, giving John $67,000, which he calculated would be worth around £13,000* at the prevailing exchange rate. The money had become payable when he reached the age of 30 in October 1936, but legal formalities took over a year to complete. For the first time he had the prospect of capital, and he knew exactly what he wanted to do with it.

Since his father's sale of Taynish John had had no expectation that he would one day be asked to take on the management of Inverneill. He had convinced himself that his father had disposed of the estate because he lacked confidence in his eldest son's ability and John had even toyed with the idea of renouncing his inheritance over the family's remaining property in favour of his youngest brother George (Colin having emigrated to the United States). Buying land of his own would give him a place to live, a career and an opportunity to prove to himself, his family and the Argyll County set that he was not the incompetent they believed him to be. It might also enable him to put into practice some of his ideas about land ownership.

He began to look for a farm and considered the Treshnish estate on the west coast of the Isle of Mull, which also included several small islands. It was said to be in poor condition, but the asking price

* About £400,000 in 2010 money.

of £3,000 would be well within his means and he took it seriously enough to discuss it with Donald MacCallum, the auctioneer at Oban, who had a lot of experience of local property. John and Margaret also went to see Killundine House, on the mainland opposite Mull, but although the house was on the market the estate had already been sold to the Forestry Commission.

Then in March the Coddy gave John the startling news that the Isle of Canna was for sale and would shortly be going on the market.

The Coddy was enthusiastic, describing the island as the finest in the Hebrides, with good grazing, fine houses and a deep and sheltered natural harbour. It also had regular transport connections to the Outer Hebrides. He made it seem 'like a Garden of Eden', but John was sceptical. Canna was more than three times the size of Treshnish and he didn't believe he could afford it. Nevertheless, he talked to Compton Mackenzie about it a few days later and – predictably, given his passion for islands – Mackenzie was full of enthusiasm. He was also able to add some information: through a contact in the London office of John D. Wood & Co., who were acting as sub-agents for Knight Frank & Rutley in trying to sell the island, he found out that the asking price was £9,000, 'not open to offer'. The price was lower than John had expected, but this further dampened his interest. In addition to the asking price, he would have to purchase the livestock and farm equipment at a price agreed by professional valuers, have something left to invest in the farm and money to live on. Add up all that, plus professional fees for surveyors, auctioneers and lawyers, and he did not think he had enough money.

Mackenzie, however, was not daunted. He was engaged in writing *The Windsor Tapestry*, a hagiography of the Duke of Windsor, who had abdicated as King Edward VIII the year before. He saw the duke, now living mostly abroad, as a 'king over the water', through the same rose-tinted spectacles as he regarded Bonnie Prince Charlie: a rightful monarch displaced by a conspiracy of the political establishment against the will of the people. In his book he described listening to the duke's abdication broadcast while at Suidheachan, looking across 'eight miles of sea to that white beach of Eriskay, whereon Prince Charles Edward had landed all but nine of two hundred years before to win back his father's kingdom'.[2]

The duke still had many supporters and *Time* magazine described a dinner held by some of them:

> The Octavians, several hundred Britishers who have banded together to perpetuate the memory of the Duke as Edward VIII, were determined to accord the [duke's 44th birth]day more formal recognition. Some 250 members, largely middle-aged men and women, crowded into a second-rate restaurant in London's Holborn district for a commemorative dinner and dance. From the French Riviera, where he is summering with the Duchess, the Duke sent greetings. High spot of the evening was the tearful speech of sallow-faced, hollow-eyed novelist Compton Mackenzie, whose plans for a pro-Edward book, *The Windsor Tapestry*, were quashed by the duke himself. 'We want him back!' wailed Author Mackenzie. 'We don't want to send greetings to France. We want to send them to Fort Belvedere [the duke's former residence outside London]. The country needs him, for he is the greatest influence for the peace of Europe.[3]

Overlooking the duke's alleged German sympathies and his marriage to a divorced woman, Mackenzie was convinced that his book – no longer an authorised biography, since the duke had refused his blessing – would still be a bestseller. His publisher had contracted to serialise part of it in the *Sunday Pictorial*, for the considerable fee of £5,000. Mackenzie would receive half on publication and on this basis he had no hesitation in telling John that he would come in on the purchase: they would buy the island together, with Mackenzie occupying Canna House, the large, handsome stone building overlooking the harbour, while John and Margaret lived at Tighard, the later house on the hill above, built by the Thoms, with magnificent views over Canna and Sanday to the cliffs of Rum.

John still had doubts, but the idea had been planted in his mind and it started to grow. Two days later he was in Edinburgh visiting Margaret. She had had an operation – perhaps after the last of her miscarriages – and was having to take a lengthy convalescence in a private nursing home, which she hated. He told her that Canna was for sale. The following day he telephoned Sir Alexander MacEwen, the lawyer and Nationalist politician, who was to be his co-author in *Act Now for the Highlands and Islands*. They shared views on the ownership of large estates and MacEwen added another dimension to the plan sketched out by Mackenzie. The Department of Agriculture for Scotland had been buying land for crofts for landless families from the Outer Islands as part of the land resettlement programme. John could sell part of Canna to the government to accommodate people from Barra, Eriskay and South Uist, recouping much of his outlay and increasing the population at the same time. MacEwen offered to use his influence with the Scottish Office to make this happen. Fresh from his visits to the co-operatives of Nova Scotia, the idea of doing a little to reverse the Highland Clearances and improve the economic sustainability of the island appealed to John.

There was also another driver. He wanted to keep the island out of the hands of an absentee landlord who would turn Canna into a rich man's playground, a sporting estate where the rights of inhabitants came a poor second to the pastimes of the laird. With the examples of Rum and Eigg, he believed this was a real possibility. His fears were heightened by reading the sale document from John D. Wood.

Canna had never been used as a shooting estate, but the agents did their best to talk up its sporting potential, mentioning the snipe and woodcock, the wildfowl and the 'rick pigeons'. There were no game birds on the island, but that did not daunt the estate agent's copy writer: 'It is known that pheasants would do well and grouse and partridge should not be difficult to establish.' The island has no major rivers and no lochs, so the lack of freshwater fishing was passed over quickly, but it was emphasised that the proprietor had the salmon fishing rights round the shores and claimed that 'sea fishing is quite above average for the West Coast'. The climate was praised as being 'drier than that of Skye' and 'owing to the formation of Canna the cold north winds blow over the top of it and it faces the sun all day long'. After praising the views, the author added another bonus: 'The island is almost immune from tourists and hikers.'

Within a day or two the plan hatched between John and Compton Mackenzie had been formalised and elaborated in detail. Since Mackenzie's earnings from *The Windsor Tapestry* would not materialise in time, John would buy the island and sell Mackenzie the mansion house and as much land as the rest of his money would buy. John would then rent back the grazing on this land. The two would jointly employ a gardener for their two houses, with Mackenzie meeting two thirds of the cost and John the remainder. The estate burdens – rates and other costs – would be apportioned between them. The scheme did not stop there. The two men also planned a political future for John. With the help of votes from grateful families resettled on Canna, he would become elected as the councillor for the Small Isles on the Inverness-shire county council. From this springboard he would fight a Highland parliamentary constituency as a Liberal Home Rule candidate.

With the comfort of the promise of Mackenzie's money and the prospect of selling land to the government, John arranged to visit the island, contacting Robert Thom, who was handling the sale on behalf of the family. The response was not as welcoming as he had hoped and he guessed that the family was not united in wanting the sale. Robert, John believed, was being obstructive from the start.

When John telephoned to arrange a visit he was told that because of Mrs Thom's poor health it was impossible to put anyone up for the night. This meant that the property had to be inspected in a day – impossible for an island the size of Canna, with hardly any roads and no motorised transport. It also meant that John could not use the ferry. To get there and back in a day and allow enough time ashore he would have to charter a vessel – extra expense and inconvenience.

Nevertheless, he was not deterred. On the morning of 4 April, less than two weeks after he had first heard from the Coddy that the island was for sale, John, with lawyer Robert MacEwen, son of Sir Alexander, and Donald MacCallum the auctioneer, were boarding a hired boat in Mallaig harbour. The portents were not good. The day was squally, the sea was rough and off the Point of Sleat, less than a quarter of the way to their destination, the engine of the launch broke down. By the time repairs had been made and they reached Canna pier, half the day was gone. The party had lunch with the Thoms and John was surprised to find Mrs Thom in apparently good health.* With the sea still rough and a four-hour return journey ahead of them, the party left in the late afternoon, having only had a cursory look at the land and the livestock. MacCallum thought that

* Alan Thom's diary records that she was in bed a few days later.

both were in reasonable condition, but since Robert Thom was unable – or unwilling – to provide numbers of cattle and sheep, he was not able to calculate how much John might have to pay for them.

The next few days were hectic for John as he travelled first to Edinburgh, then to London and fired off telegrams to Mackenzie, asking him to confirm his participation, to Thom, demanding livestock numbers and to MacCallum, asking for an estimate of the value of the 'live and dead stock' – buildings and equipment. All three replies were equivocal. He had visited the island for one afternoon only and did not even know how many cattle and sheep he was buying. Nevertheless two days later on 8 April he made an offer of £9,000 for the island, plus the stock and contents of the houses at valuation. He made his way to Edinburgh, where he again visited Margaret and then returned to their home on Barra.

After a late start, 13 April proved to be a long day. He left the house at Northbay at 11 a.m. on his boat. He had sold the *Gille Brighde*, which was showing her age and had been damaged by storms so that the hull leaked. He and Margaret had fond memories of sailing the islands in her, but John had realised that her sleek lines were not the most practical. Hearing that John MacNeil, a local fisherman, was returning to Barra, John made an arrangement with him. Together they would buy a more robust vessel which MacNeil could use to net herring when John Campbell did not need it. They bought the fishing boat *Assure* from an owner in the east coast of Scotland and MacNeil sailed her through the Caledonian Canal and across the Minch. She was 40 feet long, 14 feet in the beam and had a draught of 7 feet. With a 26/28 hp Kelvin paraffin engine she was a practical boat able to withstand rougher weather. After repainting, John re-registered her in Castlebay under the new name *Noamh Antonai*.*

On 13 April their destination was Mingulay, a small, rocky island 15 miles away to the south. The day was cloudy and overcast, but the sea was calm, there were only light winds coming from the north-west and visibility was good. The two-hour voyage would take them down the jagged east coast of Barra, west of the island of Vatersay and the rocky outcrops of Sandray and Pabbay.

---

* St Antony

Mingulay had not had a permanent population for 30 years. It was a remote and rugged island, with formidable 600-foot cliffs falling sheer to the sea on its west side. There was good grazing for sheep, but very little else and the islanders endured a hard existence. In 1908 most of the population of 135 decided to change their fate, deserted their homes and settled themselves elsewhere, some taking part in the famous Vatersay land raids, seizing crofts on their neighbouring island from the absentee landlord.

They had left behind a complete village, with houses, a school and a church and each summer shepherds returned to graze their flocks on the rich pastures and bring life again to the ghostly village. John had urgent business to conduct with one of these men, but there were no telephones on Mingulay and he was too impatient to wait days or even weeks for an exchange of letters. As soon as they landed in their leaking dinghy, he sought out Ronald MacIntosh and offered him the job of farm manager of Canna – a post which strictly he was as yet in no position to guarantee. Nevertheless, the offer was accepted and John made the journey back to Northbay.

When he returned to the bungalow at 6.30 p.m. he had been planning a solitary dinner and an early night, but two telegrams waiting for him persuaded him otherwise. One was from MacEwen, saying that his offer for the island had been accepted. The other was from his mother offering help with the cost. Elation and adrenaline swept away the exertions of the day and the exhaustion of the last three weeks. He determined to go as quickly as possible to Fort William and then on to Edinburgh to visit Margaret.

The logical course would have been to wait for the next sailing of the *Lochearn* from Castlebay to Lochboisdale and there transfer to its sister ship the *Lochmor* for the journey to Mallaig. But John was in no mood to delay. After his hurried meal and a brief talk with Compton Mackenzie he persuaded MacNeil to take out the *Noamh Antonai* again to make an evening voyage to South Uist. It was nearly full moon and gaps in the cloud would have given them some light. They made good time and arrived at 11 p.m., giving John enough time to call on Finlay Mackenzie at the Lochboisdale Hotel before catching the night sailing for the mainland. The hotelkeeper was pleased to hear John's news and 'filled me up well – too well', John recorded in his diary. He arrived in Mallaig the following morning, tired after a night on the ship's benches and probably hungover, and caught the first train for Fort William.

After lunch with his lawyers, he went to the offices of Stewart Rule & Co., solicitors, and signed a document which was to define the course of the rest of his and Margaret's lives. The legal agreement brought him 'the Island of Canna and adjacent islands including the Islands of Sanday, Humla and Heisker, salmon fishings, so long as they belong to the First Parties [the trustees of the late Allan Thom] and all parts and pertinents connected therewith including all heritable fittings and fixtures including grates and threshing mill and oil engine in the houses and premises belonging to the First Parties.'

In fact John's haste to complete the purchase and his anxiety that he might be beaten by a rich outsider were misplaced. Alan Thom's diary makes clear that the island attracted much less interest than they had hoped. On 3 April he had written: 'Mr Wolton from London is coming to spend three days with us and we hope we shall like him and that things may be satisfactorily arranged that he may buy Canna. He is a Yorkshireman and a sportsman.' John Campbell visited the following day, but Alan Thom believed 'that probably he will not purchase'. A week later the two Thom brothers waited a little sceptically on the pier for Mr Wolton to step off the ferry – but they waited in vain. He failed to show and there is no indication in the diaries that they had any alternative buyer in prospect. If they were disappointed, it did not last long. They heard the same day that John had decided to bid and less than a week later the sale was completed at their asking price.

The business in Fort William completed, John caught a train for Edinburgh to visit his wife, but he was not at ease and her condition was not the only thing preying on his mind. The adrenaline had worn off and fatigue had taken over. He began to turn over in his thoughts what he had just done and he was not sure what her reaction would be. Not for the first time in his life he felt that he had acted impulsively and in Margaret's absence his old lack of confidence in his abilities and judgement resurfaced. His brittle outer shell – which Margaret had at first mistaken for conceit – concealed shyness and self-doubt.

He had taken a bold step, but he was already questioning whether he had made the right decision. He knew he had been headstrong, but had he thought through the consequences properly? Should he have gone to his father first to ask his advice? Had he given enough consideration to the alternatives? The Treshnish estate would have been cheaper, had he dismissed it too hastily? Did he have enough money behind him to make his new venture work? He had his long journey to Margaret's bedside to turn these things over repeatedly in his mind and by the time he reached the Scottish capital he had not resolved them. He arrived in the convalescent home long-faced and looking serious: 'I've bought the island of Canna,' he blurted out.

Her reply was characteristic: immediate and positive. 'How wonderful,' she said.

Margaret's reassurance and, probably, a night's sleep, helped his mood, but he did not stay long in Edinburgh. He wrote to Ronald MacIntosh confirming the job offer and setting out the terms: MacIntosh was to supervise the shepherds and oversee the field work. John would keep the accounts. Then he was off to Oxford to discuss the purchase with his old agriculture professor, James Watson, and with his bank manager, but he did not stay long there either. The following day he was in Paris asking his mother for a loan of £5,000. The next week saw him back in Oxford before returning to Edinburgh.

Somewhere in this hectic itinerary he received 'a bitter letter' from his Aunt Olive reproaching him for wasting his resources on Canna when he could have used the money to buy back Taynish. Apparently the estate had been put up for sale three years earlier when the man who had bought it from John's father was killed in a car accident. No one had thought to inform John and in any case at that time he did not know he was about to inherit money from his grandmother. The tone of Olive's letter provoked an equally strong response from John and the two did not speak or write to each other again for many years. John's father, however, did not criticise him and later visited Canna, telling his son that he was pleased he had found an estate he liked.

★

At the beginning of May John again visited Canna, this time crossing on the ferry and staying with the Thoms. He spent the next three days looking over the island and meeting his new employees, but if he thought that his problems were over he did not know that 700 miles away in London events were in train which would unravel the neat plan he had agreed with Compton Mackenzie.

The *Sunday Pictorial* had traditionally been a right-wing newspaper, but its circulation, which reached 2,500,000 in the mid-1920s, had been falling steadily. By 1938 its sale was half the peak · figure and its publishers, Associated Newspapers, decided to act. Cecil King, newly promoted as director of the paper and a member of the Harmsworth family which controlled the company, took the bold step of sacking the editor. His chosen replacement was a brilliant 25-year-old Welshman, Hugh Cudlipp, who was to go on to be one of the most successful of London editors and publishers. Between them King and Cudlipp completely remodelled the paper, changing its political outlook and giving it a brash and strident new character.

In particular Cudlipp decided not to go ahead with the serialisation of *The Windsor Tapestry*. Mackenzie, meanwhile, was in his house in Barra, fighting sciatic pain to complete the book and oblivious to the changes which were about to be made. So, too, were his publishers, who sent galley proofs of each chapter to the *Sunday Pictorial* as they received them from Scotland. The news hit Mackenzie as he got off an aircraft at Edinburgh airport and was handed a copy of the *Sunday Pictorial* for 22 May. He described his reaction in his memoirs.

Here is that front page of the dirtiest evacuation of journalism within my experience. I might have been excused for supposing that the Fleet river carrying the sewage of London was again flowing down Fleet Street. It began with a headline of letters 2 ½ inches high:

THE DUKE

Below this was a double headline of letters 1 ½ inches high:

APPALLING BOOK[4]

The rest of the front page attacked the book and Mackenzie in vigorous style, with a signed editorial by Cudlipp declaring: 'Today this newspaper takes a course unprecedented in the British Press. Today this newspaper denounces a book which six months ago it acquired the right to publish.' Mackenzie was furious and his anger increased the following Sunday when the *Pictorial* returned to the subject, publishing the results of a poll which claimed that 91 per cent of their readers supported their stance, with only 9 per cent siding with Compton Mackenzie. The paper called on Mackenzie's publishers not to allow the book into print.

As far as John was concerned, the row meant that Mackenzie would be unable to complete his part of the bargain they had made. The arrangement had always been contingent on the serialisation of *The Windsor Tapestry* bringing in £2,500. Now that money would not be available, Mackenzie could not buy Canna House and would not come to live on the island alongside John and Margaret. John had lost a big part of his financing plans, but also a collaborator in the venture to repopulate Canna and help to turn the economic tide in the Hebrides. He would also have less contact with the man who had done so much to bring him out of his shell and would lose the intellectual stimulus that Mackenzie's house parties had provided.

It was a crushing blow, but it was too late to back out now. He had signed the sale agreement and was to take possession of the island on 29 May, the day of the *Pictorial*'s second attack. He did not blame his friend and always believed that Mackenzie had been done a grievous wrong, describing the events in his notebook nearly 40 years later as 'an outstanding low in gutter journalism'.

The truth, however, may be more complicated. On its first front page, the *Sunday Pictorial* had also printed a photograph of a cheque for £5,000 drawn on the bank of Coutts & Co. and made out to Compton Mackenzie. It was signed by two directors of the newspaper company, one being Cecil King himself. The caption read: 'Despatched last night, the cheque that ends a deal which a section of Mackenzie's book made inglorious.' Mackenzie denied having received the cheque, but a week later the *Pictorial* was again claiming that the cheque had been sent. In any case the book was not dead. A short time later Mackenzie signed a deal with the rival *Sunday Dispatch* to serialise chapters of *The Windsor Tapestry*. The price was £1,000, of which his share, after paying his publisher and agent, would be £450. With the controversy whipped up by the *Sunday Pictorial* the serialisation went well and the *Dispatch*'s circulation rose.

Later, in July1938, the book itself was published in Britain and the United States and did well enough to merit a reprint after the war.

When Mackenzie had written to his wife Faith on 13 April 1938 to tell her about John's offer for Canna, he made no mention of the plan he had made with him, nor the possibility that he might go to live in Canna House: 'Inverneill' (MacKenzie always referred to John as 'Young Inverneill,' a title John never used himself) 'has put in an offer for the island of Canna. If he gets it, it means he will be able to feed quite 40 people when we have the war this hopeless government of ours will land us in. It is a charming island four miles long by one – same configuration as the Shiants. It is in the middle of the upheaval a million years ago which begins at the Faroes and ends at the Giant's Causeway. South slope and marvellous soil. Small population is Catholic. Attractive church built by the Butes, with an £80 a year endowment. The price is £9,000 with stock at valuation, about another £4,000 . . .'[5]

Whether shortage of money was really the cause of Compton Mackenzie's not participating in the purchase is open to question. A few months before, in the autumn of 1937, he had been captivated by an advertisement for Woodbine Cottage in Hampstead's Vale of Health:

By the summit of the Heath, Whitestone Pond and Spaniards Road, A most unique and genuine Period Cottage, in quiet and very secluded Countrified Surroundings. Small Old-World garden. Freehold Price £2,500.[6]

His memoirs make it clear that he saw the serialisation rights of *The Windsor Tapestry* being committed to the purchase of the cottage. He made an offer of £2,250 and it was accepted.

# CHAPTER TEN

# *Into Debt*

John was keeping up his punishing schedule, shuttling between Edinburgh, where he visited Margaret and brought her up to date on progress with the purchase, and Canna and Barra, where he had to pack up his and Margaret's possessions and hire more staff. On 10 May he again took the *Noamh Antonai* to Mingulay to see Ronald MacIntosh, but found him in very poor spirits and suffering from a hernia. John had hoped to take him back with him to help with the valuation of livestock on Canna and supervising the shearing of sheep, but MacIntosh could not be persuaded off the island.[1]

The task of valuing the livestock was still to be done and John's valuers still had no exact idea of numbers. In late May they made another visit to Canna to carry out the task for themselves, only to be met at the jetty by Robert Thom, who informed them that he was not prepared to ask his employees to handle the sheep valuation. MacCallum, the auctioneer, had come prepared: 'That is quite all right Mr Thom, we have brought our own men to do that.' The process began that evening with the valuation of implements, horses and pigs and continued for three more days, with the two flocks of sheep – Cheviots and Blackfaces – cattle, pigs, poultry and odds and ends including hay in the haystacks and manure in heaps.

John was annoyed to find himself obliged, under the agreement he had signed, to pay for various small amounts of wood, paint, petrol and fishing gear, most of which he thought unusable and which Thom was hardly likely to have removed from the island if John had been able to refuse to buy them. At the beginning of June a new team of valuers from Wylie & Lochhead of Glasgow arrived to assess the furniture in the houses. By the time the process was complete, John found that he had to pay £5,601 for the farm stock and a further £536 for the furniture, garden tools and miscellaneous other items on top of the £9,000 he had already committed to buy the island. When he added in fees, legal expenses, stamp duty and other costs the total came to over £15,600.★

It was more than he had, but somehow he had to find this money, plus working capital for the farm and something for him and Margaret to live on. He wrote to his mother asking for an interest-free loan for a third of the total, but the response was less than encouraging. She refused to lend him anything, but offered to give him £1,000. He had to accept, but her offer was of little immediate use. The money arrived in irregular instalments which, when John added them up some time later, came to a little over £900. There was a further blow when he tried to realise his inheritance from the Waterbury trust. It was not in cash, but in various securities invested in US and Canadian companies with which his American grand-father had been associated. They could not be immediately liqui-dated and when he started to sell them, the amount he could raise quickly was much less than the £13,000 he had hoped for.

With his mother's contribution and his share sales he scraped together £9,000 – not nearly enough. He was faced with the stark realisation that he was going to fall well short of the purchase price, let alone having a reserve for investing in the farm and living expenses.

Sir Alexander McEwen again came up with a solution. Through clients of his law firm he placed four bonds secured on the island and raised a loan of £5,000 for John at 4½ per cent interest. The National Bank of Scotland in Inverness – probably again through MacEwen's intervention, since John did not have an account there – also provided an overdraft of up to £1,500 at the same rate, against the collateral of John's life assurance policies and some of the Waterbury securities which he had not yet been able to sell. This borrowing just enabled him to meet his obligations, but he im-mediately had to draw down all but £38 of his overdraft facility, leaving him little headroom.

This was the first time in his life that he had been in debt and the strain of it weighed heavily. The only chance he had of paying it off was to make a success of Canna, but he had never been a practical farmer and he had never had to manage other people. And he would

★ About £575,000 in 2010 money.

have to face these challenges alone for several months; Margaret's prolonged stay in hospital and then convalescence in Edinburgh meant she was not able to join him until August.

Although the Thoms were still in residence on the island, John was now owner and manager of the farm and he got his first taste of day-to-day farming. His diary notes sheep shearing on 8 June. Mac-Callum, the auctioneer, had to provide men to supervise the work because Ronald MacIntosh, John's choice as head shepherd, had not arrived. This added to the expense. But two days later he was sending twenty-one sheep and six pigs to market, bringing in £39 7s 6d and £9 15s respectively – his first farming income. The next day a calf was sent to Barra and fetched £2 5s, but it was not all on the credit side of his ledger. Eighty tons of coal arrived, costing him £1 15s 6d per ton, a reminder that on an island many essentials have to be shipped in at extra cost. Farming Canna was not going to be as straightforward as he had observed it in the gentle countryside around Oxford.

Another reminder of the fragility of island life came a few days later. Hector MacLeod, a crofter on Sanday, died and John attended his funeral, the first of many. The island had a population of 38, but many of them were old people. Years later John added a sad note to this entry: 'No one has lived in his house since.'

The island had a rent roll of nearly £400, the rents for crofts and tied cottages being assessed and fixed by an independent board under agricultural legislation. But John received little of this, since, as proprietor, he was the occupier of the most expensive properties, the farm, Canna House and its associated buildings and Tighard, which he kept for friends and occasional paying visitors. There were also burdens to pay. There was annual land tax of £3 15s, and feu duty of £5 19s 5d to the Crown, which was the feudal landlord under the system of property tenure in Scotland at that time. Rates (local land tax) were around £40, however he received a rebate from the council of nearly £30 to pay for the upkeep of the roads on Canna. His attempt to get the county council to pay for road reconstruction failed. The last burden, which John paid 'not with any particular enthusiasm', was £31 15s a year towards the stipend of a Church of Scotland minister for the Small Isles, who had no congregation on Canna. John was an Episcopalian and the crofters and farm workers were Catholic.

John's mother arrived from Paris in the middle of all this and stayed for a week. John never sought more of his mother's company than he could help and probably didn't welcome her visit, although she did offer to buy curtains for Canna House and later an album of fabric samples arrived from a smart firm of London decorators.[2] Alan, with whom John got on quite well, was the first of the Thom family to leave in the third week of June with Mrs Thom following a few days later, but, much to John's annoyance, Robert stayed on in Tighard. The two had virtually stopped speaking despite having remaining details of the purchase to settle. When John believed Thom had gone back on a verbal agreement about the cost of the furniture in Tighard he sent him a note rather than walk the few hundred yards up the hill from Canna House to talk face to face. Robert Thom left at the end of June without saying goodbye to John and handed the keys to a maid.*

Meanwhile John and Margaret's belongings were still arriving from Barra, brought by John MacNeil and his son Roderick in the *Noamh Antonai*. The Steinway grand piano was carefully removed from the corrugated iron house in Northbay and installed in the much grander drawing room of Canna House, where it remains today. In a mark of what John called 'deThomification' he took an old upright piano which had been left in the house – assessed by Wylie & Lochhead as worth nothing – down to the shore and burnt it. But later Margaret discovered a John Broadwood square piano dated 1835 in the attic and had it restored. It too is still in Canna House.

The description of the Thoms given in John's notebooks is undoubtedly coloured by his disputes with Robert over details of the purchase agreement. Four decades later he was able to take a more measured view. In his history of Canna he wrote with approval of their ownership of the island and the improvements they made to the homes of the crofters and employees, the farm and the

---

* Robert Thom's daughter, Mrs Johanna Frampton, believes that one source of animosity might have been that John was a Campbell and the Thoms, on their mother's side, were MacDonalds. 'My father was born in 1899 when the '45 and the Glencoe massacre were not that long ago.' Perhaps to prove his Jacobite credentials, John sent Robert Thom a copy of his book *Highland Songs of the Forty-Five*.

environment by beginning the planting of shelter-belt trees.[3] Robert, by this time living in Cornwall, helped John with information.

The summer of 1938 was warm and dry, ideal for haymaking, shearing and sheep dipping. John bought two swarms of bees – the first on Canna – and arranged for an expert from the Glasgow University Biological Society to install them in their hives. By late August he was collecting his own honey. Ronald MacIntosh had now recovered from his hernia and arrived in July with the MacNeils on the *Noamh Antonai* and John MacNeil stayed to do farm work and painting and joinery. But he cut his knee with an axe and John Campbell again had a demonstration of how island life was going to be different. The nearest doctor was on Eigg and had no boat of his own. A visiting fishing boat volunteered to go to collect him, but although it was 4.30 p.m. when the accident occurred, it was midnight before the doctor arrived to treat the wound. John protested to the Scottish Department of Health about the lack of transport and an inspector from the health department was sent to investigate but ironically, bad weather kept him storm-bound in Mallaig. MacNeil does not seem to have been permanently injured – two weeks later he was painting the library at Canna House to cover 'hideous red wallpaper'.

There were other improvements to be made. John had an outside lavatory for use by farm workers constructed in the bothy, a low stone building at the water's edge – another first for Canna. Near the end of August Professor Watson arrived from Oxford with his wife to offer John advice, at least on the theory of Hebridean farming, if not its practice.

Margaret landed on Canna on 29 August. The weather was fine and she was pleasantly surprised by what she found. There was a proper pier, which she appears not to have expected (none of the other Small Isles possessed one and passengers had to climb down from the ferry into small boats to reach the shore).[4] She liked the gardens and the fine views over Canna harbour to Sanday and the cliffs of Rum, but the house itself she thought had a melancholy air, 'as though the home of sick Brontës'.[5] Immediately she set about clearing out rusty, damp, motheaten or woodworm-infested furnishings. The island had no electricity. 'There were only candles and lamps. The bench in the kitchen hall held all the lamps and you had to trim the wicks and clean the shades and watch you didn't turn them up too high. The Thoms had maids for this chore, but I was well accustomed from Barra.' Oil lamps were replaced with bottled gas a few years later, but it was over a decade before Canna had electricity.

Some things in the house rather intrigued her. The baths in the two bathrooms were made of wood, rather than iron and she rather liked the fact that they were warm when you sat down in them. She wanted to keep them, but they were too far rotted. She did, however, manage to preserve a wooden sit-in steam bath bought for the first Mrs Thom. It is still there. In September a plumber arrived to install modern WCs and bathrooms.

There were stuffed birds in glass cases all over the house; British birds like a raven, which was blue with mould, and exotics, which were probably picked up by old Robert Thom during his travels. An albatross had lost one of its glass eyes and many of its feathers. There was also a seal in a case in the front hall which, Margaret claimed 'presented a study of the moth, from the larvae to the little moths themselves'.[6] The stuffed creatures were removed from their cases and taken by wheelbarrow down to the shore to be burnt. A greenhouse was made of the glass.

The responsibility of owning the island and the worry of the debt were taking their toll on John's mood, probably heightened by fatigue. He was a big man, young and fit, but he had never before had to do physical work and his regime was now one of relentless long days. Like many other farms in the West Highlands and the Hebrides, Canna had no tractor or motorised implements of any sort. What machinery there was had to be powered by hand or by horse. John worked in the fields alongside his men. Fred Pattison, a grandson of Fred Moir who had given Margaret away at their wedding, worked on the island for three summers as a schoolboy. He remembers eight-hour days, scything or stooking corn or back-breaking bending to pick potatoes.

John sent his first large consignment of lambs to market. He had arranged for the coastal freighter *Dunara Castle* to transport them, had been instructed to have the animals ready for loading and had gone to a lot of trouble to ensure that they were waiting in pens on the quay. But the ship arrived on Sunday afternoon and the crew, strict Presbyterians, refused to load them on the Sabbath. The work could not start until after midnight and it was 1 a.m. on Monday before the ferry left Canna. On its voyage to Glasgow the vessel picked up other sheep from other islands, so that there was great overcrowding and some confusion as to which sheep belonged to whom. John was told the paint marks – which distinguished Canna sheep from others – had been changed during Sunday evening (when the lambs were still on Canna).

He began to think someone was deliberately trying to make his life harder by switching paint marks. 'It was not difficult to surmise the author of this outrage,' John noted, although not recording who it might have been. The presence of Robert Thom on the quayside when they docked in Glasgow on Tuesday morning aroused his suspicions, although it is difficult to see how he could have interfered. The big lesson for John, however, was to come. Sheep prices had slumped during 1938 and after deducting the freight cost, commission and other expenses he received only £301 for nearly 400 animals, much less than he had hoped. John's paranoia about someone trying to thwart his efforts on Canna continued. On 11 October a Galloway cow was lost over the steep cliffs at the west end of the island. John wrote in his notebook: 'Sabotage?'

Life continued, however, and despite occasional setbacks and bad weather he was learning the practical day-to-day realities of Hebridean farming and starting to apply Oxford theory to a real estate. It was not all work. He and Margaret crossed the Minch to Barra for John MacNeil's wedding. Sir Alexander MacEwen came to stay and they discussed starting a Folk High School in Tighard. There must have been a mild spell in October, because John noted: 'a primrose, strawberry and sea pink in bloom'. On 1 November they held a big Hallowe'en party and later that month John started the first of a series of tree plantings: six cherry, two crab apples in the garden, twenty-six birches on the brae and four mountain ash (rowans) and four poplars at various gates.

The first part of John's plan with Compton Mackenzie – buying the island together – had never materialised. Now a second part – John's political career – was also to get off to a less than auspicious start. Despite the lack of grateful resettled families on Canna, John managed to get supporters to have himself nominated as a candidate for the Small Isles in the county council elections, but that was nearly as far as it got.

On the day his letter containing the nomination papers was to be collected bad storms hit the island. The ferry could not reach the pier and left without picking up the post. With the deadline approaching, John had to hire a motorboat to come out from Mallaig to collect the papers, then a car to get them to Fort William on time. There was more bad weather on election day in December and when he tried to reach Fort William and then Inverness for the count he had to contend with torrential cloudbursts which flooded the road and caused landslips. When the result was announced he might have wished he had not made the journey. Commander William Mac-Ewen, the owner of Muck, received 38 votes. John received 28. That appears to have been the end of his political aspirations. There is no further reference in his notebooks to trying for elected office.

The end of his first year on Canna, however, ended well. He began work with Sir Alexander MacEwen on *Act Now for the Highlands and Islands*, he made his first trip to Heisker, the tiny island he had bought along with Canna and Sanday, and was shown over the lighthouse. On the way back he was surprised to see the outer islands covered in snow, although there was no snow on the Inner Isles. The health board inspector finally managed to reach the islands to make his report on the need for a dedicated boat for the doctor and John and Margaret held their first Christmas party on the island with Allan MacIsaac, one of the Sanday crofters, taking the role of Father Christmas. Midnight mass was celebrated for the first time in 15 or 20 years and on Christmas Day the Campbells entertained the visiting Catholic priest, friends Neil Sinclair and Annie Johnston from Barra, and Peigi MacRae, Margaret's former landlady from South Uist.

CHAPTER ELEVEN

# *War and Hard Times*

The holiday spirit did not last long and the next few years were to bring John to the lowest point of his life and several times to regret his impetuosity in buying Canna. He was increasingly finding that practical farming, particularly on an exposed, remote island, was not as easy as he had imagined. Nor were his management skills or character judgements always up to the job. He had not only to earn his own living, but also to provide for a whole community, and his life so far had not prepared him for either role.

Gaelic was still the everyday language of Canna and several of the old people were proficient singers and storytellers. John and Margaret held weekly ceilidhs in their house to record them. Yet despite their ability to speak Gaelic, the crofters and farmworkers saw the new proprietors as the laird and his lady. They might occasionally be invited into the Big House or find the laird working in the field alongside them, but that was no different from life under the Thoms. This was not the classless society of Barra and whatever fantasies John may have harboured about Canna becoming a workers' co-operative on the Nova Scotian model were soon abandoned. The island's inhabitants had known nothing but the master–servant relationship and, without a Moses Coady and his evangelists from the St Francis Xavier Extension Department to prepare the ground, expecting them suddenly to develop entrepreneurial ambitions and skills was unrealistic.

Another factor which John could not ignore – although he tried to – was that war was coming. By the beginning of 1939 many people, including Compton Mackenzie who had a very jaundiced view of the abilities of Prime Minister Neville Chamberlain, saw war as inevitable. Since his rise to power in Germany, Hitler had steadily broken each of the terms of the Treaty of Versailles which had ended the First World War. By annexing Austria and part of Czechoslovakia, re-arming his military and reoccupying the western territories which had been taken away from Germany in 1919, the Nazi leader pushed Britain and France into making more and more concessions. A growing body of opinion in Britain saw that Hitler could never be satisfied, but John clung to the belief that Chamberlain would avoid conflict by continuing his appeasement policy.

When it became obvious that Britain would go to war John decided not to fight. As a farmer he was in a reserved occupation and not liable to be called up. He could, however, have voluntarily rejoined the 'family regiment', the Argyll & Sutherland Highlanders, but to do so meant either hiring a manager to run the farm in his absence, which he could not afford, or leaving Margaret on her own to do the job – and she had no farming experience. He quickly rejected the idea, but he worried that he would be thought a coward and that the Argyll County Set would think he had bought Canna merely to escape having to fight. Margaret later joked that John would have failed a medical because of his 'pigeon toes'. He had been a Territorial officer with several years' service and had he wanted could have expected to be commissioned again – even in an administrative role. The truth may be that he had not enjoyed being in the army and lacked the confidence to lead. Even the 'Anglo-Scots' and the Argyll gentry, whom he despised, could affect an officer's swagger, which he could not.

Politically he was now a long way from the attitudes of his family and he justified his action to himself in political terms. He later wrote in his notebook:

> I felt strongly that the Highlanders had too often put their loyalty unreservedly at the disposal of Westminster Governments, which in peace time had promptly forgotten their services, and had in times past tolerated the evictions and clearances which had torn thousands from their homes and had shown subsequent neglect which resulted in the Highlands and Islands being the poorest and most backward part of the country. I stayed where I was, glad I might be able to do something constructive when so many others were involved in destruction.[1]

Of his three brothers, Charles was dead, Colin permanently resident in the United States and George, who had read engineering at

Cambridge, was engaged on war work. Thus the military tradition of John's branch of the Campbells of Inverneill maintained by his father and grandfather came to an end. The Second World War was the first major conflict for over a century in which they had not participated. The rift between John and his Aunt Olive was complete by now so it is unlikely that she said anything to him, although given her closeness to the regiment and the Argyll gentry she would not have approved. Despite his own military history, John's father did not reproach him.

The outbreak of war on 3 September 1939 did not even merit a line in the *Annals of Canna*, John's account of his purchase and early years on the island, but he could not shut the conflict out of his mind for long. At the end of November, during a terrific storm, a body was washed up on the beach at Sanday. A police inspector and the doctor were called from Mallaig to inspect the corpse, which was identified by the name written on his oilskin as C.H. Bridges, captain of the trawler *William Humphries*, one of the first victims of the German submarine war. The unarmed boat, with a second trawler, the *Sulby*, was fishing near Rathlin Island, off the coast of Northern Ireland, when they were shelled and sunk by U-boat 33. All 13 crew were lost and the body of Captain Humphries had drifted 250 miles before washing up on the sand. He was buried a few days later in the Catholic churchyard on Canna.★

The Minch was a major sea route for Allied shipping heading for the North Atlantic, and U-boats prowled the waters laying mines and looking for easy targets. Explosions from merchant ships being torpedoed or from British destroyers hunting submarines were often heard on Canna and the men took to walking the beaches early in the morning to conceal any bodies which might be washed ashore before the women were up. Margaret describes in her memoirs one particularly poignant scene, a rocky cove on Sanday filled with the bobbing caps of naval ratings. They were from the crew of HMS *Curacoa*, a light cruiser which had been accidentally rammed and sliced in two by the liner *Queen Mary*, which was serving as a troopship. Three quarters of her crew of 430 were lost. Occasionally

★ U-33 sank 11 Allied ships before being sunk herself in the Clyde estuary in February 1940. Rotors recovered from her 'Enigma' encoding machine helped to crack the German naval codes.

submarines or mines were spotted off Canna, but attempts to report them to the Admiralty were hampered by wartime restrictions on the use of telephones and telegrams.

John was especially irritated by the bureaucracy. At the outbreak of war the whole of the Highlands and Islands had been declared a 'protected area', and the inhabitants had to obtain a 'Certificate of Residence'. Visitors had to get military permits to enter the area and letters, telephone calls and telegrams were censored. John wrote to Compton Mackenzie about one incident when Margaret had attempted to send a telegram to the doctor on Eigg asking him to come to a woman who was unwell. She was told that the message would be delayed because it had to go first to Glasgow to be passed by the censor. When John tried to get precise details so that he could register a complaint he was refused information. 'The Canna post-mistress is now dithering with fright at the idea of having divulged an official secret,' he wrote.[2] A few weeks later he wrote again: 'The proposed new Defence Regulations . . . destroy the entire moral basis of British propaganda in this war and would be a most dangerous weapon in the hands of unscrupulous and vindictive politicians. After them we would only need a secret police to approximate to a Nazi state ourselves and, by then, what moral cause shall we be fighting for?'[3]

The war brought hardship to Canna. Many of the adult men were away in the army, or the Royal or Merchant Navy, leaving old men, women, children and John and Margaret to shoulder the hard work on the farm. But in several ways the community was better off than city dwellers, or even those on mainland farms. There was plenty to eat. The rationing of eggs and milk, butter and cream did not apply on islands, there were potatoes and vegetables, fish and occasionally a sheep would 'go missing'. Obtaining flour was a problem, but one morning the island awoke to find the shores strewn with sacks of Canadian flour from a torpedoed merchant ship. Margaret had yeast from a Glasgow baker and made bread, rolls and cinnamon buns.

And there were a few lighter moments. At the end of October 1940 one of the shepherds at Tarbet was alarmed to find eight cold, wet and exhausted men knocking on his door at dawn. His fear that they were the start of a German invasion was unfounded. They were from a naval tanker, the *Attendant*, which had run aground on the rocks off the north coast of Canna. The skipper and crew had abandoned ship and taken to the lifeboat for an uncomfortable night in the storm, although had they waited for low tide they could have walked ashore.

They were put up in Canna House where, John recorded, 'they ate the cupboard bare', but there were compensations. Margaret was later paid £25 for the board and lodging and on the first night John noted 'some of the gentry from Sanday raided the vessel and removed food, mirrors, clocks, crockery, cutlery etc'. Such bounty from the sea was not thought to be theft by Hebrideans. A year later a much more famous stranding happened on the rocks off Eriskay when the SS *Politician*, a cargo ship bound from Liverpool for Jamaica and New Orleans carrying 260,000 bottles of whisky was wrecked. The incident provided the story for Compton Mackenzie's most successful novel, *Whisky Galore*, and the thousands of cases of Scotch 'liberated' from the vessel were dispersed all over the islands. Mackenzie himself gratefully received a supply at his home on Barra, a few bottles found their way to the South Uist home of Peigi and Mairi MacRae, where they were concealed in the straw bedding of Dora the cow. Despite John's disapproving tone at the raiding of the *Attendant*, a few bottles from the *Politician* even made their way to his study in Canna House.*

The *Attendant* remained fixed on the rocks for five months and several Admiralty experts declared her 'unsalvable'. In March 1941 mines were spotted floating by the ship and a minesweeper, the *Bridport*, had to be summoned to destroy them. Her visit provided a welcome diversion for Canna. Margaret, a life-long chain smoker, went aboard and bartered potatoes and vegetables for 500 cigarettes and Donald MacDonald, one of the farmworkers, exchanged a collie pup for 320 fags. In spite of more sightings of submarines and mines, a spell of good weather enabled a salvage ship to refloat the *Attendant* two weeks later.

The war made farming much more difficult, but it was not the main cause of John's difficulties: his inexperience was to count much more against him. Things started to go wrong and he was slow to

* *Whisky Galore* was later adapted as a film, with small parts played by Mackenzie himself and the Coddy. Two full bottles from the '*Polly*' are still in John's desk in Canna House.

spot them and slow to put them right. Without expertise of his own he had to rely on others and as he was soon to discover, his judgement was flawed. He had been advised when he took on Canna that, while local men made good workers, they should not be relied on as managers or foremen; islanders would not accept their neighbours or relatives giving them orders. He therefore passed over local men and brought in outsiders to fill the responsible positions. It took him a decade to realise that this had been bad advice.

Although Canna was a mixed farm, with cattle, sheep, pigs and growing potatoes and vegetables for home use and sale, the two flocks – Blackface and Cheviots – were the mainstay of the island economy. Their management was entrusted to Ronald MacIntosh, the Mingulay shepherd whom John had gone to such lengths to entice to Canna. In late 1939 John started to notice discrepancies in the number of sheep he thought should have been sold or should still be on the island and the numbers accounted for by MacIntosh. A confrontation failed to resolve the difference and led to MacIntosh declaring he would resign at Martinmas – 11 November, less than two weeks away. Such short notice would have left John to manage the sheep and the shepherds, some of whom had been recruited by MacIntosh himself. He refused to accept the resignation, but MacIntosh, although he agreed to stay, stepped down as foreman.

There were problems with other staff too. John called them together and, perhaps ill-advisedly, threatened that unless morale and the standard of work improved he would put the whole island down to grass and sack most of the staff, keeping only two shepherds. Unsurprisingly his speech failed to have the desired effect; problems persisted and, as he recorded later, 'the winter dragged on in an atmosphere of very bad feeling'.

There were personal problems between some of the new people John had brought to the island and the existing inhabitants, but also he felt that some of the staff had not transferred their allegiance from the Thoms to himself and Margaret. He was still young – 33 in October 1939 – and believed that loyalty should have come with the purchase agreement, rather than being earned. Margaret seems to have dealt with similar problems in a more direct way. Faced with a dairy maid who refused to clean the dairy, and a milk supply which was much less than she knew should be produced, she took matters into her own hands – literally. She may not have grown up on a farm, but she had learned to milk a cow from Peigi and Mairi on South Uist. She whitewashed the dairy and took one of the cows, Lettie, home with her and placed it in a stable near the house. It provided a reliable supply of milk, cream and butter.

The MacIntosh problem was not so easily solved. He was still unhappy, and in February 1940 again gave notice, this time declaring he intended to marry Mary Macdonald, a girl Margaret had brought from Barra to help in Canna House. Relations between John and Ronald MacIntosh did not improve and the shepherd left the island in April with Mary, who was now obviously pregnant. John spent the next few months travelling around Scotland fruitlessly interviewing shepherds, who were either unsuitable, or could not persuade their wives to move to Canna.

By the summer the depletion of the flocks became obvious. Not only were the numbers lower than John thought they should be, but the 'tupping', when the rams are put with the ewes to breed the next season's stock of lambs for sale, had not been properly managed so there were fewer lambs to fatten and sell. Record books had been destroyed and ewes had not been properly marked, making it impossible to keep an accurate count or know the age of the sheep. This would have repercussions for years to come as the estate produced fewer lambs for sale each season. As John began to quantify the problem a shock arrived by post: a claim of unfair dismissal from Ronald MacIntosh. John immediately prepared a defence and a counter-claim alleging mismanagement of the flocks.

The case came before the sheriff in Fort William in October. His judgement, which arrived a few weeks later, dismissed MacIntosh's claim and awarded costs against him. John's defence had rested on the bad management of the sheep, but in part of the judgement, which seems archaic and unduly harsh today, the sheriff also found that the proven (indeed admitted) 'course of immoral conduct' between MacIntosh and Mary Macdonald was also sufficient grounds for dismissal. Mary had complained in her evidence that she had been badly treated, but the sheriff appears to have believed Margaret that her insistence that Mary go to the mainland to have her child was in her own best interests. With her experience of miscarriages and knowing how long it could take to bring a doctor to Canna, Margaret had obvious sympathy for the girl, who had worked for her since 1935.

The end of the court case, however, did not solve the sheep problem. Donald MacCallum, who had given evidence for John at the hearing, was brought to Canna to oversee the proper ear-marking of the sheep, supervise the tupping and the following spring to manage the lambing. He had recommended buying extra ewes to rebuild the flocks, but a combination of bad luck, poor stock selection and a bitterly cold winter with heavy snow (John had to use skis to get about the island), meant that many of the new animals died. It took several years to overcome the problems and it was not until 1947 that Canna earned an adequate return on the flock. In the meantime the island suffered a considerable loss of revenue and extra expense. There were other problems too. Cliff-top fences on the island were in a poor state of repair; the Thoms had lacked the capital to renew them and now so did John. He had bought 38 cattle to fatten and resell. Used to fields with fences around them rather than an island farm, four were lost over cliffs and the remainder were eventually sold for £2 each less than he had paid for them.

John also lost some allies. John MacNeil, his friend and former boat partner from Northbay, Barra, gave up his croft on Sanday and took a job as an engineer on a fishing boat. Towards the end of the war Charles MacArthur, described by John as 'the best man on Sanday' died and a year later Donald MacLean★ died aged 49 of heart and kidney problems. They were, said John, 'our two best boatmen. This was a grievous loss to our small, decreasing and already 'mentally' in-bred community. Meanwhile all offers made to the Department of Agriculture for Scotland of land for settlers from the outer islands were spurned.'[4]

He felt the mental pressure of being responsible for the island, but he had also been doing hard physical work for the first time in his life and was constantly tired. In moments of despair, he thought of giving up the island and seeking a job in the Allied Military Government. He tried to keep up his Gaelic in the vain hope that he might find some alternative employment that way, but the strain of running the farm, the constant losses and the worry of the debt he

★ John wrote 'Donald MacKinnon', but this appears to be a mistake.

had taken on in order to buy Canna took a heavy toll on his health. He had no means of paying off the mortgages except making a financial success of the farm – and it was anything but a success.

At the end of 1944, while on a visit to Barra, he collapsed. He booked himself into a nursing home in Edinburgh for the winter, but when he returned home in May 1945, just as the war in Europe ended, he still felt 'fit for nothing' and did not join in the VE Day celebrations. The summer was bright and warm, but he could not enjoy it and in August he collapsed again. He felt he had to get off the island and he left Canna to take refuge in Oxford with his former tutor, where he spent ten months 'in a state of complete mental and physical exhaustion'.

While in Oxford, Margaret told friends later, he received 'psychotherapy' from a psychiatrist who was also a Catholic. The therapy appears to have included counselling and advice that John should think more of others and, in particular, think of his duty of care. This may have been when he started to think about the relationship between landowner and tenant and to idealise a Highland form of 'noblesse oblige' in which the laird recognises not only his rights, but also his responsibilities. If it existed in the Highlands it had been largely obliterated by the Clearances and John himself more often wrote about the wrongs Highland proprietors did to the conditions and the culture of their workers and tenants than he did about the responsibilities they shouldered on their tenants' behalf. But it was a concept that was to recur in his writing and to shape his relationship with Canna.

John's departure left Margaret to manage the farm. She knew little about farming and had to rely on others for advice – although she had picked up some practical skills on South Uist and in fact had been doing farm work long before John ever got his hands dirty for the first time. She surprised the Canna people by her ability to cut and stook corn, skin rabbits and care for orphaned lambs in her kitchen – at one time she had 13 and they all survived.[5] She could not match John for farming knowledge, but she had determination and strength out of all proportion to her size. In adversity her own shyness and self-doubt were overcome. She was, she declared, 'made of Pittsburgh steel' and it was her stubbornness during this period which kept the community together and saved the farm.

However, when John returned from his long absence he was not pleased with all her innovations. Urged on by the Canna farm-workers, she reinstated the herd of Highland cattle originally established by the Thoms. Large, long-coated beasts with wide horns, they are emblematic of the Highlands and able to survive on poor hill land in all weathers, but they gain weight slowly and have largely been displaced on commercial farms by faster growing breeds. Margaret bought three heifers from South Uist and an elderly bull from the Isle of Kerrera, off Oban. John was dismissive, describing them as 'bred for bone, horn and hair'.* He was even more annoyed that Margaret had allowed 'Big Hector' (Eachann Mòr) who had taken over some of the farm supervision from his father Angus MacDonald (Aonghus Eachainn), to plough up several fields of grass to plant for corn. They had previously grown cocks-foot, a grass which made good hay for winter feed. After cultivation, John complained, all they produced were daisies and thistles.

John's mentor in Gaelic, John Fraser, who had spent part of the war with his wife living in Tighard, died in 1945. His chair, the Jesus Professorship of Celtic, was advertised by Oxford University the following year and John made a half-hearted application. Despite his publications and pioneering work in the islands and Nova Scotia in recording spoken Gaelic, he had no formal academic qualifications in the subject and would have been temperamentally unsuited to the politics of academic life. He expected the rejection, but was still unsettled when it came, suffering headaches and 'lassitude'. At the end of 1946 he and Margaret went to the United States for the first time since 1937. It was the break he needed and he found a different world with a different perspective. He took the opportunity to visit Nova Scotia and St Francis Xavier University where after a period of instruction he was received into the Catholic Church in St Ninian's Cathedral, Antigonish.

John's conversion to Catholicism can be seen as a final step in his need to 'belong'. The one line in his notebook – written in Gaelic, although the rest of the text is in English – gives no explanation and in the only other reference to religion at the start of his tenure on Canna he describes himself as an Episcopalian. He wrote a rather

---

* He eventually acknowledged that the Highland herd was a success and he took delight in giving the calves Gaelic names.

confused account a few years later in which he seemed to attribute his decision partly to his dislike of the Protestant, centralised British state and partly to his rejection of the Theory of Evolution, although he does admit to an 'aesthetic sympathy' for Catholicism growing from his interest in Gaelic and the Hebrides.[6]

He was virtually estranged from his family and had rejected the landed society in which he had grown up. He appears to have kept up with none of his contemporaries from school or Oxford. Adopting the religion of the islanders who had accepted him for what he was, among whom he felt most at home and whose language and culture he had been at pains to learn was a final step in 'joining' them. As time went on his religion became a great source of comfort and strength to him and he was fortunate to know some exceptional priests, both in Scotland and Nova Scotia, who helped and guided him. He would take a mischievous delight in displaying his tribalism by talking to non-Catholic friends about 'us Papists', and became a vocal convert to the Jacobite cause – perhaps in atonement for the fact that his own ancestors had fought against Bonnie Prince Charlie and against the people he had sought to defend in his first book, *Highland Songs of the Forty-Five*. A few years later Margaret was also received in the Catholic faith, although she continued to insist on the Protestant hymns she had sung in her youth in Pennsylvania being sung in the Catholic chapel on Canna – much to the confusion of the rest of the population. Charles Wesley's *Christ the Lord is risen today* was a favourite.

When he arrived home from Canada, John received an unsolicited offer to buy Canna. He might have been tempted to take it had the prospective buyer come up with a reasonable price, but the £10,000 offered would only just have cleared his debts and left him little or nothing to finance a fresh start somewhere else. It would also have been an admission of defeat, acknowledging that perhaps the rumours among the Argyll gentry had been right, he was incapable of managing an estate. John countered with a price of £15,000, but the offer was withdrawn.

# CHAPTER TWELVE

# Turning the Tide

Despite John's troubles, the work that he and Margaret were doing in Gaelic and conservation on Canna, in trying to run the island as a sustainable community rather than as a sporting estate or rich man's playground, was attracting some attention. The young poet and folklorist Hamish Henderson, newly demobbed from the army, arrived on Canna in 1946 and was so impressed by his visit that he dedicated his Fifth Elegy to John.

Another visitor in the same year was Gavin Maxwell, who had not yet achieved fame as a naturalist and author of *Ring of Bright Water*, but was attempting (unsuccessfully) to run a shark fishery from the nearby island of Soay. He arrived in his boat *Sea Leopard* with John Hillaby, a journalist from *Picture Post*, who later described the visit.

> So we went ashore at Canna to have dinner at the grand house of the bonnet-laird and his wife, friends of Gavin by the name of John Lorne Campbell, a Gaelic scholar and lepidopterist, and his wife Margaret. It was a remarkable dinner. There was a tremendous tradition of ancient ceremonial, and a tremendous amount of whisky consumed – especially by Gavin who was always popping up to give Gaelic toasts, though he didn't know any Gaelic. The wife had 'the sight' and with hazel twigs and salt she exorcised boggarts and banshees that plagued their sheep and cattle. And there was a lot of talk about sea monsters, pixies and things like that.[1]

The references to Margaret having 'the sight' and to banishing boggarts and banshees may owe more to the whisky consumed than to fact, but despite the apparent disorder of the evening, Gavin Maxwell became a friend of the Campbells until his death from cancer in 1969. He also brought his lover, the poet and academic Kathleen Raine, to Canna and at one time or another John and Margaret nursed both Gavin and Kathleen through the hurts of that tempestuous relationship – made more difficult by Maxwell's homosexuality. After Maxwell's death, Kathleen Raine continued to be a frequent visitor and correspondent of Margaret's until her own death in 2003, and wrote several poems about or inspired by Canna. She also brought others to the island, including the painter Winifred Nicholson, who came with Raine in 1950 and returned the following year with her son Jake. They stayed with the Campbells in Canna House, a visit extended by the stormy weather which prevented her from going out but not from painting. She produced two canvases, *Equinox* and *Isle of Canna* from looking out of the window.[2]

Music was always being played in Canna House, with Margaret playing from her extensive library, particularly her favourites, Mozart, Schubert and Beethoven. Any visitor who was proficient enough was pressed into playing duets: Fred Pattison, returning for holiday visits after his wartime stints of farm work, played with her, as did Faith, Compton Mackenzie's estranged wife. Sometimes John joined in, playing the flute or French horn.

John's health continued to be poor and his energy levels were not helped by an operation for varicose veins, which also hindered his ability to climb Canna's hills and supervise the management of sheep and cattle. In 1949 he made a trip to the Uists and Barra to record Gaelic storytellers. He was pleased with the results, which preserved a little more of a vanishing heritage, but the expedition left him exhausted and further increased his overdraft.

Finance was still a major worry. The losses from the farm meant that the overdrafts on his personal account, which he had kept since his student days in the Westminster Bank Oxford branch, and the estate account in the National Bank of Scotland in Mallaig, were constantly rising and were well above the limits which his tolerant bank managers had set. Livestock prices were improving, but Canna was still paying for the mistakes of the past decade.

John had wanted to renew fences, field drains and farm buildings, modernise the workers' houses and cottages and mechanise the farm, buying the first tractor and motorised implements – all things the Thoms had lacked the capital to do. But he too was short of funds and these things had to be put off. With the farm continuing to lose money, his main source of income was a small trust left to him by his American grandfather to which he had become entitled in 1942. It consisted of 137 shares in International Business Machines (IBM), which paid dividends by issuing new stock rather than in cash, meaning that John had periodically to sell shares to placate the banks.

In 1949 he was on the point of deciding that he could not afford to keep Canna any longer, when fortune smiled on him in two unexpected ways. In America the price of IBM shares leapt as the company moved away from mechanical calculating machines, took the first steps into electronics and began to benefit from computing contracts with the US government and military. At home the Chancellor, Sir Stafford Cripps, announced a 30 per cent devaluation of the pound against the dollar. John's potential income was now worth more and on the strength of it he was able to increase his overdrafts again. He would be in debt for many years yet and the prospect of paying off the mortgages he had shouldered to buy the island was remote, but any threat of the banks refusing him further credit receded.

John now had cash, but not energy or stamina and, much to her irritation, he had not been impressed by Margaret's farming decisions in his absence. In 1950 he decided that the solution was to hire a factor – an estate manager to run the island for him and bring to it the practical hands-on experience he lacked. It was a bold decision, given his previous erratic record of choosing suitable or able employees.

After some searching he chose Major J.P. Michael, a Gaelic-speaker from Strontian, a small village in Argyll. John, so astute and ruthless in nosing out frauds and charlatans in print, was much more trusting in face-to-face encounters and the 'Major's' credentials, which he accepted without question, impressed him. Michael claimed to have an estate background and a good war record and he looked the part, dressing in smart trews and a deerstalker hat. In fact the Army List for the years 1945–50, the official record of all officers in the British Army, contains no Major Michael and the few officers with the same surname have different initials and lesser ranks. Not for the first or the last time John was taken in by a good appearance and a plausible manner.

John gave Major Michael Tighard to live in – a large and imposing house suitable for the rank of factor – and for a while things seemed to go according to plan. The major got on well with the Gaelic speakers on the island, but it was not long before he fell out with some of the more recently appointed staff, a few of whom saw the opportunity to make mischief at the expense of the new boss, spreading rumours and gossip. Far from handing over responsibility, John now found himself trying to patch up quarrels and eventually to accept resignations from some of the men he had recently hired.

To John, in his enfeebled state, the cause of the constant unrest seemed obvious: 'I regret to say there is a hard core of complacency, conceit and ill-will which has plagued the island for I don't know how many years,' he wrote. 'It is manifest in a feeling which may be summed up as "I don't care what happens as long as I get my money out of the place" and by a nature which derives greater satisfaction from disaster than from accomplishment. The very best of farmers might well have been driven out of the place by it.'[3]

His answer was not to do things differently, but to do more of the same – a lot more. 'Nothing will cure it except a wholesale immigration of fresh blood. I have tried to secure this by attempting to persuade the DOAS [Department of Agriculture for Scotland] to buy part of Canna for land settlement, but I have been met with frigid indifference by the bureaucrats of Edinburgh. Yet if this evil spirit could be exorcised the island could be happy and prosperous. I don't know how it is so deeply ingrained in the people. Strangers coming here catch the infection.'

John's mood was not improved by awful autumn weather which lasted from August to late October, making harvest and general farm work difficult and deepening the mood of gloom. A shepherd who had fallen out with Major Michael left the island, followed shortly afterwards by a cattleman whose son had lost two fingers in an accident with a turnip cutter.

To give themselves a break, John and Margaret spent Christmas and New Year in Rome, but the last leg of their return journey wiped out any benefit the holiday might have given them. The train from Glasgow to Mallaig was trapped by snowdrifts on the bleak and remote Rannoch Moor. For 24 hours the passengers, without water or heating, huddled around a stove in the restaurant car awaiting rescue. John, still fragile, could not cope. He locked himself in the lavatory with a book and refused to come out until rescue arrived. Margaret was exasperated, but it was a clear indication that he had not yet recovered from his breakdown. When they got back to

Canna, Major Michael, who had been supposed to look after Canna House in their absence, had returned to Tighard, leaving their home cold and unwelcoming.

Margaret was now very worried over John's mental state and if he left the house at night to check on the farm she would follow him with a torch to make sure he was not planning to throw himself off the cliffs.

Employment problems persisted throughout 1950 and into the following year. Major Michael hired a shepherd who proved to be totally inadequate for the job and had to be fired and Margaret hired a cook-housekeeper from London who lasted only a week before quitting and demanding her return fare. Then suspicions began to arise about 'the Major' himself. He asked for – and was given – an advance on his salary, but it was not until several weeks later that John discovered that his factor had been helping himself to the estate bank account and by the time he had asked for his advance was already overdrawn on the entire year's salary. There were more problems with expenses for 'the Major' to attend cattle sales on the outer islands and the mainland. A visit by John to Tighard revealed that Michael had ordered improvements and embellishments to the house which had been paid for by signing cheques on the estate bank account.

Matters came to a head when Michael left the island to take his pregnant wife to Inverness. John took the opportunity to go through the estate books and records, but that did not take long since nothing had been kept up to date and it was unclear what had been spent and what had been earned. John cancelled Michael's authority to sign cheques, but the damage had already been done. An offer to 'straighten things out' did not resolve matters. Robert MacEwen, John's lawyer, was summoned to Canna to confront 'the Major', who admitted his debt and offered to pay it off at £1 per week. He was dismissed.

The episode preyed heavily on John's mind and he mentioned it frequently in letters to friends.

After a most unpleasant fortnight the offender left on the 28th of June. Examination of the estate shows he must have cost us nearly a thousand pounds between embezzlement, neglect and unauthorised expenditure – mostly on his own house – for which many of the bills have not yet come in. He is now reported to be in the West Highland Hotel at

Mallaig entertaining all and sundry to drinks and stories of how badly I have treated him. He is said to be getting a job with Lord Brockett! I have just had a letter from the Ministry of Labour indicating he had made a fraudulent claim for unemployment benefit! Some fellow! We felt very sorry for his wife; but she is obviously going to have to choose between leaving him and acquiescing in his lies and frauds.

Canna Estate is now embarrassed to an extent that is probably greater than its market value and if I want to keep it I shall have to remain in full charge and give up any thoughts of collecting more folklore, except on a very small scale.[4]

By a strange coincidence John and Margaret next met Michael six months later, travelling by first-class railway sleeper to London. John feared that the debt repayments would cease and Michael did leave Britain for Rhodesia.* For a while he kept up the repayments, but eventually they stopped, leaving the last £150 to be written off. Margaret told friends later that they had come close to losing the island. The additional expense at a time when their debts were mounting was almost the last straw and left John demoralised, but 'the Major's' departure had come just in time to prevent several Canna natives from deserting the island. In particular the Mac-Kinnon family had been on the point of leaving after repeated disagreements with Michael.

John tried to put on a brave face. Warner and Ann Berthoff, friends of Margaret's sister who made the first of many visits in 1950, found him reserved, but got no inkling of the financial worries he was facing. Around this time he found a confidant and mentor in Fr John MacLean, a native of the Isle of Barra, who had been appointed parish priest of the Small Isles in 1948. Fr MacLean preached in Gaelic in the Catholic church on Sanday and was always entertained in Canna House. John valued his company and his friendship and respected his opinions. He was soon to leave these islands to take over the parish of Bornish, South Uist, but before he left he helped John to regain his confidence and strength. Margaret took a telling picture of the two men sitting on two baulks of timber – the priest open and reassuring, John with his face clouded and concerned.

* Now Zimbabwe

Fr MacLean also gave John one crucial piece of practical advice. He persuaded him that the solution to his problems on Canna was not to go on repeating his mistakes, but to reverse them – not to continue searching for outsiders to fill the vital jobs, but to trust the islanders themselves.

John acted on the recommendation and appointed 'Big Hector' MacDonald as working manager and shepherd of the Cheviot flock. Hector had been born on Canna in 1901 and had started to work on the farm as soon as he left school at the age of 14. A large, imposing man, he was physically strong and respected in the islands for his knowledge of cattle and sheep. He was also a fine singer of Gaelic songs and an accomplished piper. He became a trusted employee and friend to John at precisely the time he needed both, but they sometimes looked an odd couple. At livestock sales Hector, smartly dressed, would often be mistaken for the laird, while John, in a worn tweed jacket and a shapeless black beret he had acquired on a visit to the Basque country, was taken for a farm worker.

Hector's nephews were employed under him. Ian MacKinnon was made shepherd of the Blackface flock and his brother Angus, who had recently left school, became a tractorman. Later, a third brother, 'Wee Hector', also joined the farm staff. Jessie MacKinnon took over the dairy and she and her family moved into The Square, one of the two-storey farmhouses. Norah Boyle, who had come from Donegal with her brother to do temporary work on the island, began to help Margaret in the house and, a few years later, married Ian MacKinnon. The only outsider to arrive was Miss Sheila Lockett, whom John had met when she had been staying in the Coddy's guest house on Barra. A trained secretary, she had impressed John by offering to take down the Coddy's innumerable stories in shorthand. He offered her a job on Canna, partly as his secretary and partly to keep the accounts, which he determined were never to be allowed to be neglected again.

John had now done what he had been told by 'experts' in 1938 he should never do; he had put Gaelic-speaking islanders into the key positions on the island. It was a while before he would realise it, but in doing so he had broken the evil spell. Canna would from now on be a more harmonious and prosperous place.

At the end of the war John had bought a three-quarter size billiard table from a nearby commando training camp at Knoydart which was being disbanded. He installed it in the 'morning room' – the single-storey extension off the dining room of Canna House, which henceforth became the 'billiard room'. The Saturday 'penny pool' evenings at which all were welcome were a reflection of the events Compton Mackenzie had hosted on Barra, but with three important differences: Margaret served tea and scones rather than whisky – she told Angus McIntosh they could not afford beer – games were played for tokens (first farthings, then Cypriot piastres and latterly French francs) rather than money and, unlike nights in Suidheachan which could continue until dawn, the Canna House parties ended in time for the laird to have an early night and the farm workers and their families to continue the festivities – with alcohol – at the farmhouse at the Square. John was meticulous in keeping scores, at first just the totals, but then calculating averages. The championship for each season was determined by the highest average.

★

John's relationship with his mother had been deteriorating since the death of his brother Charles. In 1929 John's parents' marriage had all but broken down and his mother had moved out of the Villa Dupont in the fashionable 16th arrondissement of Paris where she had lived with John's father and bought the Villa Italiena in the Basque village of Guéthary, between Biarritz and St Jean de Luz on the French side of the Spanish border. It was large and comfortable, although she did not spend all her time there, living a sybaritic life touring European resorts, staying in the best hotels or the homes of her wide circle of society friends. Europe in the 1930s was not yet divided by war or the Iron Curtain and Ethel Campbell ranged over the Continent as far as Istanbul.

Occasionally she would descend on John for holidays or family conferences, usually summoning him to Inverness or Fort William. She was always very generous, bringing elaborate and expensive gifts, but he quickly tired of her conversation, her possessiveness and her fussiness. In the best hotels, she would order a Pimms cocktail, without the customary trimmings of cucumber, orange and sprigs of mint or borage, but, inevitably, it would be brought with fruit and greenery and have to be sent back. She would order sandwiches, but demand that any cress was removed.

John, never a patient man, suffered in silence. She was, he wrote later, a rich woman with too little to do. He found her self-absorbed and went to extraordinary lengths to avoid speaking to her. After he bought the island, John refused to have a telephone installed in Canna House in case he was caught unawares by one of her long calls. The telephone was connected in the bothy, below the house on the shore. When John felt mentally prepared to talk to his mother, he walked down and returned her call.

The divorce when it came was by mutual agreement on the grounds of separation, but there was a dispute over the jurisdiction under which the hearing should be held. Ethel wanted the divorce to be under French law, which demanded a shorter period of separation, but Duncan's Scottish landholding prevented him from being considered a French resident, even though he had been living in Paris while working for IBM. Ethel suggested they could get over this by at least nominally making over the estates to John, but Duncan would not hear of it, preferring to wait the longer period demanded by Scots law. At the time, John did not understand the significance of his father's stubbornness and saw it as confirmation that he was not considered a fit person to inherit.

After the fall of France to the Nazis in 1940, Ethel had abandoned her villa and moved to England, where she spent the war alternating between the 'season' in genteel Cheltenham and the Park Lane Hotel in London, which had 'American-style' en-suite bathrooms, still a rarity in Britain. Throughout the war she made infrequent visits to her sons, John and George. The task of securing her French house and moving her furniture and valuables out of the reach of the Nazis and into safe storage was left to Saturnino Sagarzazu, a Basque who had worked for Mrs Campbell since she had moved into the area. Close in age to John and his brothers, he quickly became their friend. Whenever they had to visit their mother, an evening's drinking out with Saturnino came as a welcome relief from her company.

John had first met him in 1930 and invited him to stay with him in Oxford while he had been a student there. In 1933 the two had toured the Spanish Basque country, with John, who had welcomed the declaration of the Spanish Republic, becoming increasingly concerned about the way in which political dissent on the left and the regional independence of the Basques and the Catalans, who had enthusiastically supported the new government, were being suppressed by the Soviet-backed communists. The two men had even been rivals for the affections of Vicenta Bueno, a beautiful Basque girl who was a pianist but also taught French. Although John lost out to Saturnino, who later married her, it was not enough to spoil the friendship.

During the war Saturnino became part of the underground movement helping Allied soldiers and resistance fighters fleeing the Nazis, taking them by fishing boat or across the Pyrenees from France to Spain, from where they could reach neutral Portugal. But economically, times were tough. The Basque region suffered badly throughout the Spanish civil war, the Second World War and the economic depression in the north which followed under Franco's dictatorship. Ethel Campbell never returned to the villa in Guéthary and her possessions stayed in storage for more than 30 years until retrieved by John and his brother George.

It always rankled with John that his mother had never paid Saturnino for saving her belongings, nor any of the Basque fishermen he had enlisted to help him move furniture and other items. They were allies in time of war, she said, they should not expect payment – and in any case they were nothing more than common smugglers. As soon as he could, John returned to Spain, found the men and paid them.

John's mother had never spoken to her sons about their eventual inheritance. What small legacies John had received from his American grandparents had come as a surprise to him, usually in the form of a letter from New York lawyers. In the late 1940s – probably from the same source – he discovered that his mother was living on the income from a family trust set up by her father, but she had no access to the capital, which was to pass on her death to her sons. They were, in the jargon of the time, 'Remainder Men'. Ethel was in good health,* but John was advised that he could raise money immediately by, in effect, borrowing against his share of his eventual inheritance.

The debts he had incurred to buy Canna weighed heavily on him

---

* She died in 1967 aged 86.

Inverneill House: John thought that the newer, square block on the right added by his grandfather had a damp, haunted air and would not sleep there without the traditional Highland talismans against evil: Bible, rowan wood and a cold-steel knife or dirk. (Copyright © National Trust for Scotland)

Duncan Campbell, John's father, and John's grandfather, 'Old Inverneill', whose loss of the family fortune was kept secret for 50 years. (Copyright © National Trust for Scotland)

John with his mother, 1912.
(Copyright © National Trust for Scotland)

John with his brother Tearlach. (Copyright © National Trust for Scotland)

Taynish House, where John grew up. In the woods and meadows of the estate he learned his love of wildlife and began his butterfly collection. (Copyright © National Trust for Scotland)

Old Inverneill prepares to lead his grandchildren to church. John, as the oldest, is in front. The woman on the right may be the 'hell-fire Calvinist', Miss Martin.

LEFT. John at prep school: 'a barbaric society, with its cliques and bullying and terrifying authority.' (Copyright © National Trust for Scotland)

BELOW LEFT. John in his late teens. He learned to play most wind instruments at Rugby, but felt himself lacking in confidence and maturity. (Copyright © National Trust for Scotland)

BELOW RIGHT. Olive Campbell, John's aunt, organised his twenty-first birthday party at which John spoke his first words of Gaelic in public. His mother and father were separated, and neither attended. (Copyright © National Trust for Scotland)

ABOVE LEFT. On Barra John found an almost classless society – in contrast to the rigid social hierarchy of Argyll. (Copyright © National Trust for Scotland)

ABOVE RIGHT. The Coddy, uncrowned King of Barra, was a mentor to John and helped him perfect his Gaelic. (Copyright © National Trust for Scotland)

RIGHT. The Barra schoolteacher Annie Johnston was recorded by John and introduced him to other Gaelic singers and storytellers. (Copyright © National Trust for Scotland)

LEFT. Margaret Fay Shaw had been living on South Uist for five years when John met her. No one was more surprised than she when he asked her to marry him. (Copyright © National Trust for Scotland)

BELOW. John and Margaret's first married home at Northbay, Barra. John is fishing on the shore. (Copyright © National Trust for Scotland)

With money from an uncle, Margaret bought a Steinway grand piano and had it installed in the living room. (Copyright © National Trust for Scotland)

The house had no electricity, running water or inside lavatory. Margaret's sisters were horrified, but they made it very comfortable. (Copyright © National Trust for Scotland)

ohn and Margaret in Nova Scotia in 1937. (Copyright © National Trust for Scotland)

Canna in 1938. When John bought the island it was unmechanised. All farmwork had to be done by men or horses. (Copyright © National Trust for Scotland)

Ploughing in 1938. (Copyright © National Trust for Scotland)

One of the first jobs was to remove dozens of stuffed animals and birds, many of which were rotting. (Copyright © National Trust for Scotland)

Most of the stuffed creatures were burned on the shore. (Copyright © National Trust for Scotland)

LEFT. John and his father, who never reproached him for buying Canna nor for refusing to fight in the war. (Copyright © National Trust for Scotland)

MIDDLE LEFT. Fr John MacLean helped John during his recovery from a nervous breakdown. He also persuaded him to trust the islanders more. (Copyright © National Trust for Scotland)

BELOW. The christening of 'wee' Hector MacKinnon. John is second from left. (Copyright © National Trust for Scotland)

ABOVE LEFT. John with members of the Folklore Institute of Scotland: (left to right) John, Duncan MacDonald, the South Uist storyteller, unknown, and Rev. T.M. Murchison. (Copyright © National Trust for Scotland)

ABOVE RIGHT. Big Hector, the farm manager. His dapper dress sometime meant that he was mistaken at sales for the laird, while John was taken for the farmhand. (Copyright © National Trust for Scotland)

RIGHT. Sheila Lockett (left) and John (right in pith helmet) lend a hand with the haymaking. (Copyright © National Trust for Scotland)

John entertains Roland Svensson, Sheila Lockett and a visiting priest during a picnic (Copyright © National Trust for Scotland)

Regular visitors to Canna: John's Basque friend Saturnino Sagarzazu. (Copyright © National Trust for Scotland)

Roland Svensson was one of several artists to visit Canna, and draw inspiration from it. (Copyright © National Trust for Scotland)

Margaret with Saturnino's daughters, Maria Carmen (left) and Magdalena. (Copyright © National Trust for Scotland)

ABOVE. After Saturnino's death, John gave Maria Carmen away at her wedding. (Copyright © National Trust for Scotland)

RIGHT. John and Frank Collinson in 1969 with the first of their three volumes of Hebridean folksongs.

BELOW RIGHT. Dr Morton Boyd, director of the Nature Conservancy Council, became a friend and ally in conserving Canna's wildlife. (Copyright © National Trust for Scotland)

John was a regular visitor to Compton Mackenzie's house in the south of France. (Copyright © National Trust for Scotland)

John (sitting, right) and Lord Wemyss sign the agreement transferring Canna to the National Trust for Scotland in 1981. Standing: Jamie Stormonth Darling (middle), the Trust's director, and (right) Brian Lang, secretary of the National Heritage Fund. (Copyright © Ray Perman)

Ian MacKinnon (front left) with his family, John and Lester Borley, Director of the National Trust for Scotland (left, second row). Winnie MacKinnon (behind Borley) and Geraldine MacKinnon (middle, front row) still live on the island, as does their mother Nora (right, partially hidden by her son Patrick). Ian's early death drove a wedge between the Trust and the islanders. (Copyright © National Trust for Scotland)

John and Margaret in 1989. (Copyright © National Trust for Scotland)

Shelia Lockett, Magda Sagarzazu and John, with Patchin, Margaret's dog.

The Canna Advisory Group: (from left) Hugh Cheape, Neil Fraser, Margaret, John and William Gillies.

John on Canna in 1991, aged 85 and still wearing an appropriate hat for every occasion. (Copyright © National Trust for Scotland)

John's grave on Canna, surrounded by bluebells in a wood planted planted by himself and Saturnino. (Copyright © National Trust for Scotland)

and not seeing any eventual means of paying them off had been a major cause of his breakdown. He had counted on the farm earning enough to pay off its own purchase price, but he knew now that it could never do so – the best he could hope for was that it would break even, but until now it had not even made enough money to pay the interest on his borrowings. Some of the first bonds that his lawyers had placed with their clients in 1938 had had to be repaid, but the only means of doing this was by raising fresh loans. In the meantime John's overdrafts were rising.

The prospect of paying off some of the loans, reducing his overdrafts and having some working capital to do the things on the farm which he knew needed to be done was too good an opportunity to miss. He raised £6,500 on the strength of his prospective inheritance, which was enough to repay some of the debts and make improvements, such as installing electric light and inside lavatories in farm cottages and croft houses, renewing fencing and field drains and buying tractors and machinery.

The cash did not remove his money problems and John was to be in debt for the next 15 years. In 1958 the Highland regional manager of the National Bank of Scotland was writing, in a courteous tone which present-day bank communications have abandoned, to point out that John's overdraft in the Mallaig branch was £6,776 12s 8d, well above the £6,000 limit. Three years later, John was writing to the manager of the Westminster Bank in Oxford to assure him that his overdraft, secured against IBM shares, was safe as long as the share price kept rising.[5]

But now he at least knew he would eventually be able to repay his borrowings and he could keep his bankers at bay by pointing out that IBM shares left to him by his American grandfather were steadily and dependably increasing in value. Money was never easy and he had to fight battles with the tax inspector, who suspected that the farm was deliberately run at a loss to shelter some hidden source of income, but the mental strain of living under debt was considerably lightened.

# CHAPTER THIRTEEN

# A Voice for the Voiceless

James Hamilton Delargy – always known by the Irish form of his first name as Seamus – was born in 1899 in Cushendall, where Glen Ariff, largest and most famous of the nine glens of Antrim, meets the sea at Ireland's north-east coast. His family were seafarers and his father, a captain, built the house in stages when he returned from distant voyages. In the strongly Protestant province of Ulster, the area was predominantly Catholic and, although the Delargys used English, Irish Gaelic was still spoken among the old people. Seamus acquired a life-long love of folktales from the village barber (also the local boat builder and farrier), who promised a story if the young boy would not cry while his red hair was cut.[1]

After his father's death, Mrs Delargy moved the family to Dublin and put her boys into Castleknock College, where Seamus learned Irish and developed a passion for collecting and preserving the language that was to stay with him through university and for the rest of his life. As a young man he visited the Gaelic-speaking Irish islands of Rathlin and Aran, Donegal in the west and the Scottish Hebrides. He also returned to his birthplace to write down stories from the last native speakers. In a newly independent Irish republic, Delargy could combine an academic career with a quest to preserve and popularise the ancient traditions and language of his country. He found generous and willing support in his university and from the government, which in 1935 funded an Irish Folklore Commission, with Delargy as its head.

It was from the commission in June 1936 that Seamus Delargy wrote to John Lorne Campbell, who was then still living in Barra. He praised John's efforts and invited him to Ireland to see the commission and to visit the some of the Irish-speaking areas where its staff were collecting. John was unable to accept the offer, but the two men started a correspondence which was to last for 20 years. The letter came out of the blue and was a warm endorsement of the pioneering work John had been doing, but which had failed to attract any official recognition in his own country, still less any financial support on the scale that the Irish were devoting to the preservation of their traditional culture.

That year John had published *Orain Ghaidhlig le Seonaidh Caimbeul,* the *Gaelic Songs of Shony Campbell,* a South Lochboisdale bard who had been a neighbour of Margaret's when she lived in South Uist. Two years later he produced *Sia Sgialachdan, Six Gaelic Stories* from South Uist and Barra. No commercial publisher was interested and he had to pay for the small-run booklets himself. Following the Irish example he had bought his first recorder, the Ediphone, which he used on Barra and in Nova Scotia, but unlike the Irish Commission, he received no help with the cost. Appeals to British or Scottish organisations for help with funding were ignored and when he offered copies of his recordings to libraries and universities none were prepared to accept them, even as a gift.[2]

Other men may have been put off, but John was being driven by a passion which did not rely on commercial success or official recognition to keep it fuelled. He wanted to record a heritage which he feared might not last much longer, but also to right some wrongs. Hebrideans, he felt, had too often been exploited by others for their own recognition or gain; he wanted to give them a chance to speak for themselves. Delargy gave him practical and moral support when no one else would and after the war he sent members of his staff to the Outer Hebrides to continue the work of collecting and to work on Canna on transcriptions of songs John and Margaret had recorded. One of them was Calum Maclean, who had been born on the island of Raasay, one of five remarkable brothers – Sorley Maclean became a distinguished Gaelic poet and scholar, another brother became a headmaster and two became doctors. Calum graduated with a First in Celtic Studies from the University of Edinburgh, then moved to Dublin for his postgraduate degree.

In 1947, inspired again by Ireland, John and a few friends and supporters founded the Folklore Institute of Scotland (FIOS). Delargy attended the inaugural meeting in Edinburgh and pledged the full support of the Irish Folklore Commission, which he promised would continue to collect songs and stories in the Highlands and Islands until such time as the Scottish Institute was able to take over. It would then gift the new organisation copies of all its Scottish material.

John was elected president. 'High-sounding name,' he wrote a few months later, 'but its professed aims have not been realised yet owing to the difficulty of finding a good secretary.' This deficiency was remedied when the young Hebridean academic and poet Derick Thomson took on the post.

The new institute's intention was to promote and support the study of folklore in Scotland and to publish texts, recordings and a journal. It acquired several recording machines and began to record songs from Gaelic singers living in Glasgow. Although several academics became founder members, there was no official support from the universities and certainly no hope of state funding similar to that enjoyed by the Irish Commission. The government seemed completely indifferent, or on occasion actually hostile, to the Gaelic language. The Folklore Institute was a small start at trying to change this attitude and at least John now had a position which appeared to give him some standing in the folklore community.

In the same year he helped to establish the Barra Folklore Committee. This, with funding from royalties from *The Book of Barra* and a small grant from Inverness-shire county council, recorded 200 songs and stories, several published as *Folksongs from Barra*, a booklet and gramophone records. By now John, always keen to keep up with the latest technology, was using a Webster wire recorder, which he had ordered from the US only to have it impounded by the British Customs & Excise for six months. When he finally retrieved it he used the machine to capture songs and stories from Angus MacLellan, a remarkable bard and storyteller from South Uist, and lent it to Canon Ewan MacInnes, in Barra, who held ceilidhs in his home. The quality of the recording was good and a spool of wire could record half an hour of speech or music on each side, but the Webster needed mains electricity. In South Uist only the hospital and one or two private houses and buildings had power, so John had to invite reciters to the

Lochboisdale Hotel for sessions.[3] The task in front of the new Scottish Institute was urgent. Calum Maclean, beginning work in the Hebrides in 1947, told the *Glasgow Herald*: 'Time is vital. The really good storytellers are mostly over 70 years of age. Their stories must be recorded before it is too late.'[4] The Irish Commission, Maclean added, had 9 full-time collectors, 30–50 part-time collectors and 500 local correspondents working in Ireland.

With no government support, the Folklore Institute of Scotland could not hope to match that and even to begin work on a small scale it had to raise funds, but it was an uphill struggle. After three years John had to announce that the plan to publish a journal had been postponed and he called for more members to contribute to funds. At the annual meeting the following year he renewed his appeal with a note of desperation, declaring that the present small membership was not creditable to a nation professing to be keenly interested in the preservation of its traditions, but doing very little about it. He also revealed that the Arts Council and the Rockefeller Trust had both turned down applications for funds. A reply was awaited from the Carnegie Trust, but when it came that was also negative.

John explained the refusal by saying that charitable trusts like the Rockefeller and Carnegie were not used to the concept of oral tradition – and in Britain, in contrast to many other countries, there was still a prejudice against spoken as compared to written history. But this may not have been the whole story. John acknowledged privately that his own outspokenness was also a problem. In a letter to Delargy he explained:

> I am well aware I have made a good few enemies over *Gaelic in Scottish Education and Life* [a polemic pamphlet he had published in 1945] – and equally amongst the admirers of Mrs Kennedy-Fraser★ who seem to have no scruples about the suppression of the 'originals'. Also I sense a certain jealousy amongst professional scholars – perhaps because I have been able to finance some of my own publications myself. Macdonald Aberdeen's fight to the end against the McCaig Trust giving any grant to the Gaelic folksong booklet was a symptom – and I had never crossed

★ See Chapter 15

swords with him in any way. Sometimes I think that Murchison [the Rev. T.M. Murchison, a Church of Scotland minister, Gaelic scholar and writer who was chairman of the council of the Folklore Institute of Scotland] himself is under disapproval for his friendship with me.[5]

John had good grounds for this opinion. Under pressure from educationists the Secretary of State for Scotland commissioned a report on the possibility of state support for Gaelic, but the investigating committee ignored John and the Folklore Institute – and eventually the initiative came to nothing. John wrote an account of his own collecting and publishing for the English Folk-song Society, probably as a prelude to asking for financial support for future work, but got no response. He appears not to have realised that the society's president, Douglas Fraser, was the brother of Marjory Kennedy-Fraser, whom John had criticised in print.

In 1952, after five years in the post, John resigned as president and the Folklore Institute of Scotland faded away. It may have failed and John's hopes for a government-funded Scottish Folklore Commission had come to nothing, but in 1951 Scotland got a good alternative with the founding of the School of Scottish Studies at the University of Edinburgh, with Angus McIntosh as a prime mover. With the resources of the university and an energetic leader, the School became the focus for folklore studies in Scotland, especially after McIntosh launched the ambitious Linguistic Survey of Scotland.

Although he held the title Forbes Professor of English Language and General Linguistics and had a lifelong research interest in Old and Middle English, Angus McIntosh had learned Gaelic and had a deep affection for and knowledge of the language and culture of the Hebrides. He was to prove a powerful ally and warm friend to both John and Margaret and in 1951 arranged that John receive a grant from the Leverhulme Foundation. It was only £200 to last two years, but it was the first financial contribution he had received in 15 years of collecting and publishing. His actual spending was far greater. In 1951 he estimated that he had spent £640 on recording machines and blank disks and wire, and a further £200 on photocopies of documents, travel and accommodation costs in the Hebrides and Nova Scotia. 'All paid for out of capital,' he wrote,[6] but

John at this time had no capital. He was financing his Gaelic work from his overdrafts and combining it with a full-time job as a working farmer.

If it could not help with cash, the School was able to help in other ways. It procured wire for John's wire recorder – not a simple or cheap matter in the age of post-war shortages – and it started an archive where John was at last able to deposit copies of the recordings he had so painstakingly collected in an institution which was pleased to receive them, would look after them and make them available to scholars and other interested people. Scotland at last had an archive where an important part of its heritage was being preserved.

★

John's work was beginning to attract attention outside Scotland and towards the end of 1950 he received a letter posted from the Palais du Chaillot Hotel in Paris. The writer addressed him as 'Dr Campbell' – although it was more than a decade before John would receive his doctorate – and spent little time in introducing himself, beginning 'I believe you will know me from my various publications in the field of American folksong.' It was signed Alan Lomax.

If the world of folksong collecting could claim to have an international star, then it was Alan Lomax. Building on the work of his father, he had pioneered the field recording of songs across the United States, concentrating on the poor and the dispossessed. John Campbell would surely have sympathised with Lomax's motivation 'to give a voice to the voiceless'. He had brought many singers to public attention. A record of *Goodnight Irene* by the black singer Huddie Ledbetter, known as 'Lead Belly', whom Lomax had first recorded in prison, had been a popular hit and earned money for both men, with Lomax ploughing his share into financing a trip to Europe. His interests were wider than the US and his radio programmes on both sides of the Atlantic had brought world folk music to a general audience. As Assistant in Charge of the Archive of Folksong at the Library of Congress from 1937–42, he had academic credentials too.

The letter invited John's help in 'a project of interest to all folksong specialists . . . A world library of folk and primitive music'. Lomax went on to explain that he had been commissioned by the Columbia Record Company of New York to assemble material to be issued as one 12-inch long playing record for each nation or region. In contrast to the attitude of the BBC, which did not broadcast untrained singers, 'all the material [will be] authentic folksong, recorded wherever possible in the field from country singers and players'. Each album was to have an editor, or co-editor, who should be an authority and would be paid a modest honorarium in dollars. Royalties would be paid to the archives furnishing the songs so that at their discretion 'singers can receive recompense or the money can be used for further collecting'.

The note concluded 'actually the conditions of this publication are, for the scientist and folk-music enthusiast, practically ideal. Columbia does a fine technical job. They are leaving it up to me and to my colleagues . . . about what should be included. I think that in two or three years a musical library of the peoples of the world might be a reality – and out of that will come the use of long playing master records to preserve all our best things from decay. Well, I'm an optimist, but one must be when one sets out on a long job . . . Would you be so kind as to give me a hand and write me right away because I'm at the beginning of a long pull.'[7]

On the face of it Lomax's offer was a godsend to John. Here was an international collector with an established reputation offering him the chance to showcase his best material and to earn some money from it to use for further collecting. Unlike previous attempts to popularise folksong, this was to feature original authentic recordings – ordinary people were for the first time to be given a chance to be heard. John wrote back positively. The only archives of authentic Gaelic music in existence were his own and that of the School of Scottish Studies Linguistic Survey, he said. 'As I have made 365 folksong recordings in the Outer Hebrides on wire during the past 12 months there would be no difficulty at all in providing any material needed from my collection, so long as the singers consented.' He also suggested six types of song which ought to be included, but added two qualifications: since his own collecting came only from one district of Scotland he ought to consult

Professor Angus McIntosh about songs from other districts, and there ought to be a separate Scottish album, rather than including Scotland in a British record.[8]

Lomax replied by return of post. He wasn't against a separate Scottish album, but he was concerned that it should be a commercial success. 'Now, there is no reason that a Scots album couldn't do very well, provided only that there is in Scotland an hour of song and music, sung or played by authentic and pleasing performers and already recorded or easily available for recording now. If you think that between your own collection, that of Angus McIntosh, the BBC and elsewhere there is such an hour, why that's fine. We'll make a Scots album.

'Please consult with your friends and associates there and let me know. And please believe me when I tell you that my motive in this project is that of folklore generally – to bring light into dark places, to give voice to the voiceless. It seems to me that a Scots album ought to include the material you suggest in your letter + piping, fiddling, the ballads of the border, some of the lyric songs of the period of Burns (things that he imitated) and should be partly in English and partly in Gaelic. What is your opinion?'[9] He ended by offering John the job of editor and asking him to gather all the recorded material together in advance of a visit Lomax planned to make to Scotland after he had been to Ireland to talk to Delargy.

Far from encouraging him, this letter unsettled John. The venture was far more commercial than he had at first realised and if a Scottish album had to include piping, fiddle music, border ballads and Burns-era songs – sung presumably in English or Scots – would there be room for authentic Gaelic material? If he became editor, could he trust Lomax not to alter his selection of songs? John wrote to Frank Collinson, a musicologist with whom he had started collaborating, Angus McIntosh and to his fellow office bearers in the Folklore Institute of Scotland suggesting that Lomax's offer should be rejected and the Institute itself should bring out its own album of Scottish folksong.

This was a reasonable position to take, but the Institute had no money to produce an album of its own and over the ensuing months John hardened his attitude. During this period he was under the strain of the Major Michael affair and its financial fallout, and his letters to Collinson, Delargy, McIntosh and others started with a retelling of his woes. It may well have coloured his reaction. He refused Lomax's offer of the editorship and tried to stop the project altogether.

When Lomax, denied the co-operation of local collectors, arrived in Scotland to do the recording himself, John became alarmed. He had spent years pioneering folksong collection in the islands at considerable personal expense and with very little recognition. Now he feared an outsider would reap the benefit. He wrote to Collinson: 'Lomax appears to have been through Uist, Benbecula and Barra with a comb. I gather from a confidential letter from Delargy that he made himself thoroughly unpopular in Dublin. But I'm afraid it's the go-getters like him and not the pioneers who do work at their own expense who reap the rewards. That's always been the way of the world.'[10]

He wrote to Annie Johnston and the Coddy and other friends in the islands accusing Lomax of 'making a beeline to get a certain item from a certain singer of which he could only have heard through a recording of mine being talked of – a thing which is absolutely contrary to the ethics and etiquette of folksong collecting. That etiquette demands that one collector does not try to get songs etc. from a reciter who is already singing for another collector without at first at least attempting to reach an understanding with the collector who has discovered, and is working to record, the reciter in question. Feelings are very strong indeed on this point amongst the collectors of folk music.'[11]

Partly driving John's concern was a fear that Lomax might claim copyright of the songs he recorded and that, even though he himself had previously recorded the same songs from the same singers, he would lose out. Lomax's past association with the Library of Congress now appeared a threat rather than a recommendation. He wrote in alarm to Annie Johnston telling her that previous collectors and plagiarisers had been able to claim copyright of songs and stories from the islands. 'So you can see that my warning, which was about copyright and not about recording, was very necessary. It is probable that Lomax would not know of the present existence of folksongs in the Hebrides were it not for the copies of Ruairi Iain

Bhain's songs I presented to the Library of Congress when I visited them in 1947 *at my own expense.*'

This was a complete misunderstanding of the law of copyright and it wasn't until John was reassured by Angus McIntosh, by Frank Collinson who had consulted the BBC's lawyer, and by Lomax himself that he accepted that Lomax could not claim copyright over anything other than specific recordings he had made and certainly not over original folksongs, nor over other recordings, even of the same singer and the same song.

Other issues were also troubling John. The story was going round that Lomax was paying singers. 'I'm afraid the harm this incursion will do is incalculable. Once the payment of reciters had begun, there will be no ends to what will be expected,' John wrote to Sidney Newman, Reid Professor of Music at the University of Edinburgh. 'I am not in a position to make such payments and even if I were I would scorn to work on such a basis. As a consequence of this matter I have decided not to return to Barra to record songs until the misunderstanding is cleared up.'[12] This was another red herring and Lomax again denied that he was either paying singers or asking them to give up their copyright.

Angus McIntosh did his best to defuse the situation, telling John that Lomax could not be stopped from visiting the islands to record willing singers and storytellers and he was experienced enough not to need much outside help in getting what he wanted. 'He is an amiable character, who can be trusted to make his way in a rural area,' he wrote, 'and he is not entirely devoid of guile.'[13] Delargy also seems not to have taken the matter too seriously, although he was not happy with Lomax's activities in Ireland, where he had been collecting material for an Irish album. He wrote to John from Dublin: 'My real wish is that the claymores be brought out from under the thatch and that he be carved into small pieces and the pieces thrown into the sea. I told him that when he was here and [learned] that he intended to go to Scotland.'[14]

Since Alan Lomax was having to stay longer in Scotland than he had planned, he had arranged to base himself at the headquarters of BBC Scotland, where he was being paid to produce radio pro-grammes, including a 'ballad opera' featuring Gaelic folksongs. Who had commissioned him? John jumped to the conclusion that it was

Hugh MacPhee, head of Gaelic for BBC Scotland and a fellow council member of the Folklore Institute of Scotland. The two men had clashed before, probably over the BBC's policy of broadcasting only trained singers and excluding amateurs from the islands. He wrote a strong letter to MacPhee and got back an equally robust reply.

John wrote to Collinson: 'I consider his letter beneath contempt but the fact that he is involved in this will at least produce the effect of swinging the islanders to our support. There is of course a long background of disagreement between MacPhee and myself on this matter. One of us should at the next FIOS general meeting move a motion condemning the BBC for passing over native scholars in favour of Lomax for this work.'[15]

In a later letter John looked for a 'showdown' with MacPhee and said he would treat it as a matter of confidence in his presidency of the Folklore Institute and would resign if he lost. Collinson at first was prepared to go along with a protest to the Controller of BBC Scotland, but after inquiries with friends in the BBC in London he backed off. MacPhee was not the culprit, he had been ordered by London to accommodate Lomax. Collinson wrote again in September 1951 to tell John that the whole Scottish BBC was 'seething with anger at the foisting of Lomax upon them by London' and MacPhee, far from sheltering Lomax, was indignant and had made an internal protest. He had more news: he and Professor Newman had met Lomax in Edinburgh at the School of Scottish Studies and had decided to accept Lomax's offer to give them copies of everything he had recorded in Scotland.[16]

Lomax himself wrote to John on 15 September 1951 regretting any misunderstandings and adding that from the more than 70 reels of tape he had given to Edinburgh University he had taken 40 songs in Gaelic and English for his Scottish album for Columbia. He ended hoping that the letter would be accepted by John as a gesture of friendship. 'I only wish I had the Gaelic so that I might really share more fully the pleasure of you, Calum Maclean, and others who have it.'[17]

But John was not placated. He had been baffled how Lomax had discovered where to go and who the best singers were. He had at first suspected a leak from the records of the School of Scottish

Studies, but when he was assured this had not happened, turned to those who might have assisted the American. The mention by Lomax of the name of Calum Maclean, who had left the Irish Folklore Commission and was now employed by the School of Scottish Studies, inflamed him. The two men were old friends. Maclean had visited Canna several times to work on transcriptions of recordings made by John and Margaret. They shared more than their love of Gaelic tradition; both were converts to Catholicism and had adopted a romantic allegiance to the Jacobite cause.

John could not confront Maclean, who was on a six-month research sabbatical in Uppsala, Sweden. So he wrote to him and his tendency to express himself vehemently on paper, when he might have been more circumspect face to face, led him into a bitter row. Maclean countered the accusations with a new charge of his own that John had kept manuscripts of transcriptions of songs recorded in Raasay which ought to have been returned to the Irish Folklore Commission in Dublin.

The two men continued to trade insults until January 1952 when John, realising the damage that was being done, not only to his friendship with Calum Maclean, but to the cause of folklore collecting in Scotland, wrote 'withdrawing and apologising for anything I have said about ingratitude or jealousy'.[18] Maclean responded by withdrawing his accusation – the manuscripts had been found in Dublin – and also apologising. 'As for Lomax, I helped him mainly because of his record. No one in Scotland will ever record 20,000 folksongs as John and Alan Lomax have done in America.'[19]

The exchange repaired the relationship between John and Maclean and in 1960 John wrote to his friends at St Francis Xavier University, Nova Scotia, asking them to consider awarding an honorary degree to Calum Maclean in recognition of his work in preserving Hebridean folklore. Maclean, who was suffering from cancer, heard that he was to receive a doctorate, but died before it could be conferred. John, however, did not forgive Delargy, whom he suspected of encouraging Lomax to come to Scotland.

Alan Lomax produced his World Library of Folk and Primitive Music, although it took him many years longer than he had expected, and he did include a separate Scottish record as his third volume. It featured a wide variety of music from the Glasgow Police Band, to pipe and fiddle music and Burns' *My Love is like a Red Red Rose*. Half the 44 songs were in Gaelic, most of them recorded in the islands by Lomax. Many were, however, heavily cut to fit so many tracks on one disk.

# CHAPTER FOURTEEN

# The End of Inverneill

John's father died on 19 August 1953 – by a strange coincidence, John noted, the same day of the year on which his great-great-grandfather, also Duncan Campbell, had died in 1840. John and his father had never been close and he had sought guidance from father-figures in other men – his professors at Oxford, Compton Mackenzie and the Coddy on Barra – but there was no animosity between them. 'We never quarrelled,' John wrote, 'we just had less and less to say to each other.'

Duncan had remarried in 1940 and took his new wife to live at Inverneill with his unmarried sisters, the formidable Olive and the younger Una. The arrangement did not work any better than it had when Duncan's first wife Ethel had met Olive and after a short while the two sisters moved to Alltnacraig, an imposing Victorian house on the estate, overlooking Loch Fyne. After the war, prompted by his wife, Duncan began to think of the future of the estate and made tentative inquiries of his sons as to whether any of them would be prepared to take it on. In August 1947 John returned to Inverneill, the first time he had slept in the house since 1928.

Seeing his father in his ancestral home, surrounded by so much of the history of the Campbells of Inverneill of which he might be the last laird, moved John and, despite his unease in the house and his dislike of the military and imperial tradition it embodied, he wanted to do all he could to enable him to end his days there. But the poor state of repair of the building and his father's lack of money were obvious.

For the first time John demanded a full statement of the financial position of the estate, its income from rents and its debts and obligations. There were no immediate answers and he had returned to Canna before the information he had requested began to arrive. When it did come John was far from convinced that he was being told the full story. What was revealed was that his father had inherited a substantial debt of £26,000.* John had long since suspected that the family owed money, but he had not realised how much. Where had it come from? The origin and cause of the debt were not explained; Duncan just implied that his own father, Old Inverneill, had inherited a bankrupt position, so obscuring the origins of the liability in the past.

What this made clear, however, was that Duncan's sale of land, the Scotnish estate for £5,000 and later Taynish, which John had expected to inherit and manage, for £17,000 were nothing to do with the family's lack of confidence in John. They were necessary to pay off the liabilities. How different his life might have been had this been explained to him when he came of age, or before Taynish was sold. But there was still a puzzle: on the figures John was given, the proceeds of the land sales together with £11,000 from a life assurance policy on his grandfather, should have been more than sufficient to clear the debt, leaving a substantial positive balance of £7,000.

It was hard to reconcile this healthy conclusion with his father's obviously impoverished situation and John also knew that there was a family marriage settlement – a legal obligation common in Highland landowning families – to provide for younger sons and daughters. He did not know the details of it because, against custom and practice, he had not been made a trustee of the settlement on the death of his grandfather. Instead Aunt Olive had become privy to information he was denied – an arrangement he resented since it kept him in the dark about the true state of the family finances. Besides, Olive was a beneficiary of the settlement and therefore ought not also to have been a trustee.

His questioning of his father on this point did not get him very much further. He was told that, were he to take on Inverneill, he would not have to take on the marriage settlement as well, because his aunts Olive, Una and widowed Ysobel were willing to waive their entitlements.

John's own situation at this time was not conducive to an attempt

---

* At the time John's father took on the debt it was the equivalent of £1,500,000 in 2010 prices.

to take over Inverneill. His health was poor, he had debts of his own without, as he then believed, any obvious way of repaying them and the only offer he had received to buy Canna would have left him with a loss. The strain of living with his own precarious financial position had helped to bring about a mental breakdown from which he was not yet fully recovered. The prospect of shouldering responsibility for further borrowing cannot have been easy to contemplate.

He was also reluctant to return to the claustrophobic society of the Argyll gentry. He knew his departure had caused disparaging comment and his lifestyle since then – learning Gaelic, choosing to live among people who were not of his own social class and turning his back on the Conservative and Unionist political philosophy so ingrained in his former neighbours, not to mention declining to fight in the war – were not likely to help him to fit back in. Even so, it was not an easy decision. The pull of family even after so long a period of estrangement, was strong and despite the emotional distance between him and his father filial loyalty still compelled him to try to find a way to secure the estate in the family and put Duncan's mind at rest.

None of this, however, counted for much beside the stark financial facts. He reluctantly concluded that he could not afford to take on Inverneill, and his brothers, George, now established in his career as an engineer, and Colin, living permanently in the United States, also lacked the capital to rehabilitate so big an estate. John did make an offer to buy the Inverneill library and leave it in the house, but it was rejected by his father.

John's decision must have been a severe blow to Duncan. Apart from doing nothing to alleviate his own financial situation, which was deteriorating as the estate sucked up cash, it threatened the end for the line of Campbells of Inverneill which had started with Sir Archibald's purchase 170 years previously. But again, he offered no rebuke to his son and bore his disappointment in silence. His desperate need for money soon became apparent. He sold the magnificent mature beech trees surrounding Inverneill House which had been planted by Sir James Campbell in the 1790s. He received £2,000 and within a short time they were all felled.

The telegram bringing the news of Duncan's death in 1953

arrived on Canna five hours after the ferry had left for the mainland. There was a strong north-easterly gale blowing, but a yachtsman with a powerful motor vessel offered to take John and Margaret to the mainland, leaving his own wife and family to stay in Canna House with Sheila Lockett, John's secretary. The sea was rough and the direction and strength of the wind prevented them from sailing into Mallaig harbour, but another yachtsman rowed out to take them off and bring them ashore.

From there the Campbells went by train to Fort William to stay the night before taking a MacBrayne's steamer down Loch Linnhe to Oban. A bus took them to Ardrishaig on Loch Fyne where they were met by John's Aunt Olive, who drove them the last few miles to Inverneill. They arrived late and Margaret slept in a small room in the baronial wing of the house added by John's grandfather, which John had always felt had a sinister atmosphere. The Gothic gloom cast by walls hung with swords, muskets, spears and pictures of men in red uniforms and battles from the imperial past of his family was now deepened by a smell of damp and mould. The house was in mourning, and not only for its dead laird. John made a bed for himself in the dining room.

Although it had taken John only a little over 24 hours to make the difficult journey, Olive had already taken charge, making most of the funeral arrangements and even writing an obituary of her brother for the press. John was relieved when the following day his brother George arrived with his wife Wendy and put up at a local pub. The two brothers conferred on all the issues of the next few days and acted together – a strong support for John over decisions which he expected might be difficult. The same day a copy of his father's will came from Murray Beith & Murray, the Edinburgh law firm which had been solicitors to the family for generations. It was simple: apart from a few small legacies to his sisters, nephew and nieces in lieu of the family marriage settlement and provision for his widow, Inverneill House, its contents and the estate were offered in turn to John, his brothers George and Colin and then their cousin Duncan Lorne Campbell.

The day of the funeral was fortunately fine in an otherwise poor August. The local Episcopal and Presbyterian clergymen said prayers at the door of the house before a piper led the mourners from the house to the family mausoleum a few hundred yards up the hill. A path had been mown through the long grass and undergrowth and Peter Graham, tenant of the home farm which now made up most of the estate, had lent his best horse and cart to carry the coffin. There Duncan was laid to rest beside his father and mother. Plaques commemorated his brothers, both killed in action in France during the 1914–18 war: Torquil Lorne, buried on the Somme, and Neill Diarmid, whose body was never identified. Another remembered his second son Tearlach (Charles), whose ashes had been taken to the Waterbury family cemetery in America at his mother's insistence.

The Episcopal priest conducted the graveside service and the party returned to the house for tea and drinks. John was delighted to meet again some of the old tenants of his father from Taynish and to speak to them in Gaelic, this time more fluently than he had been able to do when he had last seen them at his twenty-first birthday party. But he noted the coolness of the Argyll County set, few of whom spoke to him or offered any sympathy.[1]

After the guests had left, John, George and Duncan Lorne met the lawyer in the Inverneill library for the formal reading of the will and to decide the future of the estate. John and George declined to take it on and the refusal of Colin, who did not intend to return to Britain, was assumed. Duncan Lorne, who had an agricultural contracting business in Dorset, said that he wanted to do so and the lawyer thought this would be possible, provided the aunts waived their rights under the marriage settlement. Duncan had plans to develop the estate and exploit its potential for forestry and tourism, but over the next few days, as a succession of valuers arrived to assess the estate for death duties and probate, the plans began to unravel. The estate was in a poor condition and badly needed investment and the opportunities for increasing revenue by putting up rents and felling timber were small.

While Duncan was considering his prospects, John and George were going through their father's papers, trying to piece together the real financial state of Inverneill. What they found was not encouraging. Their father had a portfolio of stocks and shares, but when a large overdraft was deducted from its value and legacies paid there would be little left to provide for his widow. A bigger shock was to come. Their grandparents' marriage settlement, which they had been led to believe was an internal family affair, had long ago been converted into a substantial mortgage★ secured on the Inverneill estate. Any new owner had either to continue to pay interest – a considerable extra burden on an already loss-making enterprise – or to redeem it, demanding substantial extra capital. On top of this there were outstanding improvement loans which had been taken to provide electric light in Inverneill House and build a new cottage on the estate.

A few days later the family attended Olive's birthday party – described by John as 'a tense, sticky and insincere function' – in the course of which John was taken aside by his aunt, who as a trustee of the marriage settlement since 1922 knew the true state of the family finances better than anyone. He was told that she and her sister did not think Duncan Lorne should take on the considerable risk of inheriting Inverneill.

Nevertheless, over the next week John and George tried to find a way to respect their father's last wishes and to enable Duncan Lorne to inherit the estate and so keep it in the family. With their wives, they drove to Edinburgh to meet John's own lawyer to discuss the problem with him. He strongly advised the brothers not to take on the financial risk of accepting the bequest.

They then drove to Glasgow – where Margaret caught a dawn train to Mallaig, en route for Canna – before returning to Edinburgh to discuss possible solutions with Duncan Lorne and Murray Beith & Murray. At one stage the brothers considered paying off their father's overdraft so that his share portfolio could be used to provide an income for his widow and to redeem the mortgage on her death – although John's contribution to an arrangement like this could only have been made by increasing his own substantial borrowings still further. The lawyers suggested other schemes and they considered them all, but the figures were not convincing and they would not overcome the opposition of the aunts, whose consent was needed under the terms of the marriage settlement. It became clear that the matter could not be resolved quickly and John and George both returned home, John taking with him a large chest and several suitcases full of Inverneill papers.

★ £4,800, equivalent to £275,000 in 2010 prices

A few weeks later John wrote to his aunts setting out the options for Inverneill, which included leaving it to Duncan Lorne, it being acquired by the trustees of the marriage settlement and an outright sale. He travelled to Alltnacraig to find out their answer. They were strongly in favour of a sale. The family would lose its link with the land and so much of its history, but the proceeds would be used to pay off the debt and free the family of a financial burden which it had carried for generations. A few weeks afterwards John, George, their lawyers and the aunts met in Edinburgh to complete the details. John and George still had to clear the outstanding land loans and taxes from their own pockets and top up an income for their stepmother, but Inverneill was to be offered to Peter Graham, the farm tenant, with the hope that he would take it at a price which would enable the mortgage to be paid off. Duncan Lorne was informed and, although disappointed, accepted that the financial situation made any other course impossible.

In October 1953 John, George and their wives motored to Inverneill to begin clearing the house and dividing up its contents. John went to Graham to put the proposal to him and the following day was relieved to receive a positive answer, with no quibbling over the price. The sale was to include the house and all the land except the mausoleum, which was to be owned by a new family trust, and Inverneill island in Loch Fyne, which was to pass to Colin, who wanted some small part of the estate to remain in the family.

Technically John was now 'Campbell of Inverneill', a title he did not use and which, since he had no son, would die with him. He resisted Colin's requests that he be named as heir to the title, a change which would have to be sanctioned by the Lord Lyon King of Arms, the heraldic arbiter in Scotland, but after two decades of disputes the two brothers agreed. Colin became 'Younger of Inverneill'.

The poor state of the house, with peeling wallpaper and wet crumbling plaster everywhere, particularly in the newer wing, were testimony to John of the secrecy and pride which had brought down the family. The melancholy task of going through centuries of accumulated possessions took the two couples days and was relieved by dinners in a nearby hotel and by the presence of Jolly, the overweight marmalade cat, who oversaw the proceedings with a proprietorial air.

As the house began to be emptied the brothers and their wives noticed a steady clearing of the air. With the family secret breached and the building stripped of its military adornments and heavy furnishings, the haunted atmosphere which John had described as exuding hostility and 'the feeling one gets when someone of strong personality who dislikes you intensely comes into the room',[2] began to dissipate. Books, furniture, crockery and silverware were divided among the family. John inherited Sir Archibald Campbell's silver teapot, which was taken to the dining room of Canna House to stand on the mantelpiece opposite the teapot of Ethan Allen, his old foe during the American War of Independence, which had been inherited by Margaret from her family. John also took back to Canna as many of the Inverneill papers as he could find and later had delivered by puffer his grandfather's 12-foot dinghy and a supply of cut beech logs – the last remnants of the famous trees.

After the aunts had taken a last look, the keys were handed to Peter Graham, who refused to see Olive. He later demolished the older part of the house and sold the newer part, ploughed up the garden, felled the remaining timber and sold plots of land along the shore of Loch Fyne for bungalows. 'One could sense his animus against certain members of the family for their attitude to him as tenant,' John concluded,[3] but his own relationships and those of other members of his family with the Grahams remained cordial.

★

Back in his attic study on the second floor of Canna House, John began to go through the trunk, the suitcases and the boxes of papers he had brought back from Inverneill. A year before his father's death he had tried to piece together a financial history and to work out the sequence of events which had brought about the end not only of his own inheritance but of the whole family's estates. He did not get very far. The story was not complete. He did not yet have enough information to resolve the mystery and ended only with a list of questions to which he did not have the answers. Now he tried again.[4]

Some of what he found surprised him when he learned that the family had only been landowners – as opposed to tacksmen – for a much shorter period than he had been led to believe and he learned the source of Sir Archibald's fortune – the man had been 'in trade'! As he worked his way down the years, John also came across the 'entails', legally binding trusts established to keep the landholdings together and prevent them being sold by the family's black sheep, or pledged against personal debts. There were also marriage settlements designed to do the same thing. He discovered an illegitimate son, again not mentioned in the family, who had brought to the family the Kilpatrick estate on Mull.

Debts were not uncommon and more or less once every generation land or other assets had had to be sold to keep the family solvent. By the time John's grandfather, Old Inverneill, had inherited the estate it was heavily indebted, as John had been told by his father. However, he now discovered that his great-grandfather had had a substantial insurance policy on his life and the payout on his death had cleared most of the borrowings. Old Inverneill had started his stewardship of the family estates in reasonable financial shape. He had a healthy income and had married into money. The mystery was, where did the money go?

Then John noticed the name Joseph Yardley Johnston.

Yardley Johnston was an American who described himself as an engineer in the printing trade. Who first introduced him to Old Inverneill John could not say for certain, but it might have been Lieutenant-General Sir James Bevan Edwards who, like John's grandfather, was an old soldier and a former India hand. He had served with the Royal Engineers in the Indian Mutiny, the Crimean War and the Mahdist War, when a British Expeditionary Force had arrived at Khartoum too late to save General Gordon. After retiring from the army he had started a second career as a politician, but he resigned his seat four years later. Edwards was a respected figure, but Old Inverneill's brother-in-law Frank described him as 'a plausible optimist'.

Johnston told the two men that he had come to Britain to further exploit patents he held for a new press which would revolutionise the printing of high-quality images. With the growth of literacy in the late nineteenth century there had been an explosion in demand for printed matter – newspapers, magazines, books, pamphlets, posters and advertising materials. Now there was a new demand for printed illustrations, in black and white and colour, photographs as well as drawings. The problem besetting printers was how to produce these with acceptable quality at a speed high enough to produce the large number of copies needed to satisfy a mass market. Johnston claimed he had the answer.

He formed the Johnston Die Press Company Ltd and Colonel Duncan Campbell – Old Inverneill – became a director, followed by Sir James Bevan Edwards. In order to qualify, each man had to own a hundred £1 shares, but Johnston made these a gift to Campbell and Edwards. They offered to pay, but Johnston would not hear of it. It must have looked like a promising opportunity: the profit margin forecast by Johnston was substantial and sales were assured and Johnston was taking all the risk by taking payment for his patents largely in shares.

The company took 'comfortable' offices at 22 Bride Lane in the City of London and Johnston, who appears to have been a man of taste, had them furnished in 'artistic and extravagant style'. Lunches of several courses with wine were served in the offices each day.[5] Johnston ran the company almost entirely himself, 'doing the work of eight men', working long days and delegating very little to his company secretary and accountant. Some of the other directors attended the office but there was little for them to do.

He hosted lunches and invited 500 members of the press to visit to see the demonstration machines he had installed. He boasted that he had a scrapbook of 700 pages filled with newspaper clippings. The Johnston Die Press Company was merely the start, and in quick succession he formed a string of companies to exploit his inventions across Europe. Old Inverneill joined the boards of all of them. The world appeared to be at their feet, the company's shares rocketed and the directors, afraid of missing out, started to invest.

But all was not well. Of the first 27 presses sold, 17 had been returned by customers dissatisfied with their performance. Writs flew across London and rumours of fraud reached Old Inverneill's stockbroker brother-in-law, who advised him to resign, sell his shares and get out. The advice was rejected on the grounds that to resign would be to show disloyalty and would risk losing his director's fees – which had never been paid. It was too late, one by one the companies collapsed. The case had become a scandal in the City – it was a fraud. The shares had been ramped up by accomplices of Johnston and investors had lost fortunes. The Official Receiver, a senior official of the Board of Trade, began a public inquiry before a judge at which all the directors were summoned to appear. Old Inverneill got off lightly, being called to give evidence only at the end of a long day.

He avoided public humiliation, but he had committed the enormous sum of £26,000, using up all his savings and investments and borrowing heavily. He was overstretched and could not repay his overdrafts, at any moment one of his creditors might precipitate his bankruptcy, adding social disgrace to his financial collapse. He had already prejudiced his oldest son's future by pulling him out of Oxford in a vain attempt to turn the situation around. Now he called on him again to save the family. Duncan – John's father – agreed to the 'disentail' of the family's estates in Argyll – freeing them from the legal strictures which prevented them being used as security for personal debts.

A loan of £26,000 was raised from the Church of Scotland Ministers' Widows Pension Fund to pay off Old Inverneill's liabilities and a further mortgage of £4,860 was obtained to provide for Duncan's brothers and sisters under the terms of their parents' marriage settlement, since any rental income from the estates would now be eaten up in interest payments.

Sitting alone in his study in Canna House, John now realised that the sale of Taynish and the unbridgeable emotional gulf between himself and his father were not caused by his failings, but by those of his grandfather.

He also understood the profound tragedy of his father's life. At the age of 21 everything was before him. He was handsome, intelligent and successful, yet he had been summoned home from Oxford to hear news which was to shock him and stunt all his ambitions. Out of loyalty to his own father, Duncan had taken on debts which were so large they were to overshadow everything he did – even beyond his death, since they prevented his wishes that Inverneill remain in the family from being realised. He had worked his whole adult life to keep his family's reputation and estates intact. The debt and the vow of silence had contributed to the break-up of his marriage and made strangers of his sons. He had ended his days in poverty amid the decay of a once great house.

John wrote in his notebook:

I think with profound sorrow of my father caught up in a chain of conflicting loyalties, tied I strongly suspect, by an early promise never to reveal the secret of his father's financial disaster, weighed down throughout his life by the disastrous terms of the Inverneill 'disentail' of 1902 and the Taynish transfer of 1908; taken out of Oxford at the start of 1901 to be faced with the . . . complete responsibility for his father's debts and the Inverneill marriage settlement, consenting to the secret terms of the Taynish transfer out of affection and sympathy for his father who he obviously idolised . . . the secrecy in which he was entangled eventually ruined his family life. All this from immature actions motivated by filial loyalty and devotion.

Of my mother I can only say that a person of very strong character and practical experience might have guessed what lay behind all the secrecy, driven my father to disclose it and kept the in-laws at bay. But she was not that kind of person. No more was I; a combination in fact of Hamlet and Esau, born to set right a situation it was beyond my power to do more than wind up at the bitter end.

# CHAPTER FIFTEEN

# Illuminating the Celtic Twilight

*What are these isles, but a song sung by island voices?*[1]

By the early 1950s John had begun to get control of his life again. His decision to rely on Canna people rather than bringing in outsiders meant that the island became a happier and more settled place. The farm was beginning to pay its way and with Sheila Lockett keeping the accounts up to date he knew exactly where he was from day to day. He was still heavily in debt, but at least now he knew that one day he would inherit enough money from his American grandparents to be able to pay off his borrowings. The nervous breakdown had taken a big toll on his health, but steadily his strength and his confidence were returning. After the hardship and depression of the war years, the new decade was a period of optimism and it was with this spirit that John returned to his work collecting and preserving Gaelic language and culture.

He had been a pioneer in his early work in Barra and Nova Scotia, but although he had the encouragement and enthusiasm of his wife Margaret and a few close friends, he received scant support or recognition from elsewhere. He paid all his own travelling and recording expenses and often the cost of publication too – with a few exceptions commercial and academic publishers were not interested in the material he was collecting. He thought of himself as a scholar and was painstaking in his research, verification and attribution, but was mostly shunned by university departments.

He had briefly considered a conventional academic career when his Oxford Gaelic teacher Professor John Fraser had suggested he spend a year studying in Germany and a year in Ireland before looking for a post in Britain. He was glad he had rejected the idea, saying later: 'Had I become a wholetime professional academic I might well in Scotland have become involved in some unpleasant feuds and politics later on. As it was, being an amateur and non-competitor I was able to maintain friendly relations with scholars who had little in common.'[2]

Only rare researchers, such as Fraser and Angus McIntosh at Edinburgh University, accepted oral tradition and field recording as valid academic exercises. Most academics were still contemptuous of the idea that anything of value could be learned from poorly educated or even illiterate people. As a historian in an age when history was still dominated by studies of 'Great Men' and battles, John was ahead of his time in believing that the lives of ordinary people recounted in their own words could add a new dimension. He understood the incomprehension with which his work was viewed, but he could not sympathise with it and never considered compromise.

'Communities where an oral tradition predominates are so much out of the experience of the modern Western world that it is extremely difficult for anyone without first-hand knowledge to imagine how a language can be cultivated without being written to any extent, or what an oral literature is like, or how it is propagated and added to from generation to generation,' he wrote.[3] To John the Gaelic mind existed in a vertical plane – it had 'historical continuity and a religious sense', whereas the consciousness of the modern West existed in a horizontal plane – it had breadth, it knew a little about a lot, but it was concerned with purely contemporary happenings which were forgotten soon after they happened. 'There is a profound difference between the two attitudes, which represent the different spirits of different ages, and are very much in conflict.'

Working in this 'vertical plane' could yield amazing results – storytellers in the Hebrides could go back 1,000 years to the Vikings for material for their stories, which they made vivid with a strong sense of reality. But these sources were not easy for the outsider to access. Recitals of oral tradition did not often take place in public, but were much more informal, belonging to the fireside or integrated into everyday repetitive tasks such as rocking the cradle, milking the cows, waulking the home-made cloth, or rowing boats. To be present at these events required the collector to be trusted by the performers and invited into their homes or their working lives, and that took time, patience and empathy.

John thought of himself as a historian and his youthful first book, *Highland Songs of the Forty-Five*, had shown that a knowledge of Gaelic language and songs, albeit from written rather than oral sources, could bring to light new information which challenged accepted orthodoxies. The more he read the primary sources, particularly in Gaelic, the more he became sceptical of what he scornfully called 'the Whig view of Scottish history' which sought to justify everything that had happened since the 1707 Act of Union joining Scotland and England. His problem was that those who espoused and propagated the 'Whig view' were in most of the positions of academic power.

He was also a linguist, and here again he took a radically different approach from many of his academic contemporaries. In Gaelic scholarship there was a 'Received Gaelic', just as broadcasting at the time was dominated by 'Received English'. The language was simplified into a standard form to make translations easier and an 'artificial literary dialect'[4] had been developed at the time of the translation of the Bible.

But the language that John Campbell encountered did not conform to an ossified standard, it was a living entity, capable of change and variation. In particular, the standard 'official' form ignored vernacular speech, dialect words and regional differences. To John, these variations not only added to the richness of the language, they were important pointers to the origins and history of the speakers, as he had found in Nova Scotia, where several generations after their families had left Scotland he had heard Gaelic spoken in accents and using distinctive words or phrases easily recognisable as originating from a particular island or area of the Highlands.

There were no standard texts to enable him to look up unusual words, so he used dictionaries of old Irish words or started to create his own, or to seek out the original manuscripts of others who had done so before him.

The work was absorbing, but he had to find time for it alongside the demands of being a full-time farmer. The notion that his collecting and writing might be supported by the Scottish, let alone the British government, was remote. He believed strongly that the reverse was the case: officialdom was working to discourage the use and survival of Gaelic. He had seen recent examples of this when, at the outbreak of the war, Gaelic broadcasts and telegrams had been banned. He contrasted the enlightened attitude of the British Empire, where the right of minorities to speak their mother tongue, to have it taught in schools, to be able to listen to broadcasts in the language was enshrined in local legislation, to that of Scots Gaelic, where the state was indifferent and the bureaucracy hostile.[5] John looked with envy to the official support given by Scandinavia, the US and Ireland to similar work.

There was a lot of public interest in 'Celtic' songs; recordings and sheet music had been hugely popular in Britain and across the world. These had superficial resemblances to the songs of the islands, but they were not authentic and the people who sang them and made money from them hardly acknowledged their origins. The islands, it seemed to John, had been consistently exploited and misrepresented. It was an injustice he wanted to correct.

In 1936 he had been asked by the magazine *Outlook* to review the second edition of *Father Allan's Island* by an American folk-song collector and writer, Amy Murray. She had been one of four women who had visited the tiny island of Eriskay at different times around the turn of the twentieth century to seek out the parish priest, Fr Allan McDonald. John was very drawn to Fr Allan, even though the priest had died of pneumonia, aged only 46, the year before John was born. His character was still vivid in the memories of the people of Eriskay, South Uist and Barra in the 1930s and John heard many stories about him. He had been a kindly, intelligent and studious man who was not only loved by the islanders for the conscientious and compassionate way he carried out his pastoral as well as his spiritual duties, but also respected as a poet, writer and collector of Gaelic folksong, folklore and stories.

Much of Fr Allan's poetry concerned religious themes, but he also had a very quick wit. John might especially have liked the Gaelic toast he proposed at the wedding of his housekeeper, a Campbell, who was marrying another Campbell. The priest used the historic animosity following the massacre at Glencoe as the basis for a comic verse:

> I have never before performed such a service –
> A toast to the venomous Clan Campbell
> Proposed by a man of my kin, of Clan Donald

After admonishing the bridegroom for stealing his housekeeper, he used the Gaelic meaning of the name Campbell to conclude:

> If I happened to be a man of action
> Campbell would feel the force of my fist,
> I'd leave some defects on his chops
> And land him a dozen or so on the nose
> Until he'd have two affiliations
> Campbell (Bent-mouth) and Cameron (Bent-nosed)![6]

Over 20 years John was to devote a considerable amount of time and money to tracing the work of Fr Allan, publishing much of it for the first time, righting wrongs he believed had been done to the priest and writing a short biography. The more he learned of him and read his work, the more he identified with him.

In an article in 1958 he gave a detailed picture of the priest's character, describing the 'sensitivity and scientific detachment' with which he approached the study of Hebridean oral culture, but also going further: 'Fr Allan [himself], although possessed of a sense of humour, was a man of austere temperament and disciplined intellect. He was well acquainted with the concreteness of Gaelic oral literature as with the earthier side of human nature. He hated anything savouring of sentimentalism, affectation or pretence . . .'[7] There were a number of contemporary accounts of Fr Allan and John, an assiduous researcher, would have read them all. He also interviewed people who had known him. But it is possible that the description he gave was as much his own assessment of his own character as that of his hero: a man with an instinctive understanding and love of Hebridean culture, working more or less alone and having to battle against poor health and poverty.

Priests in the islands were often remarkable men. They were usually Gaelic speaking – Fr Allan was not a native speaker, but became fluent – and were given a broad general education by the Church. With the suppression of Catholicism in Scotland during the Reformation, the education of priests was forced to move abroad and even in the late nineteenth century there were still Scots colleges in Rome and several European countries. Fr Allan had studied at Valladolid in northern Spain. Once in their parishes, the priests saw themselves as representatives of their community as well as of the Catholic Church.

Until the Crofters' Act the people of the islands still had no security of tenure and were terrified of taking an independent line. They were often afraid to support their own representatives in public in case it led their landlords to evict them from their homes and livelihoods. Priests like Fr John Mackintosh, one of Fr Allan's colleagues on South Uist, made statements on their behalf to the Crofters' Commission, which had been taking evidence of oppression of working people by their absentee landlords. Fr Allan himself had stood up for the Catholic crofters, who, despite being in the overwhelming majority, had no representation on school boards until 1888.

Life in the islands before the age of motorised transport could be hard. Walking or voyages in small open sailing boats were the most common forms of travel and Fr Allan, whose first parish included a large part of South Uist and the small island of Eriskay, often had to walk for hours in bad weather to preach, make sick calls or visit the nine schools under his care as chairman of the school board.

Frederick Rea, an English teacher who arrived in South Uist in 1890 to become headmaster of Garrynamonie school, was met at Lochboisdale by Fr Allan.

A few men were grouped on the little pier, among whom stood a tall figure clad in clerical black. As I reached the end of the gangway onto the pier, this figure left the group and advanced towards me with an extended hand. 'You are the new schoolmaster I believe,' he said in a deep, strong voice, and with a stronger grasp of the hand. He was a well-proportioned figure, over six feet in height with strongly marked weatherbeaten features, about thirty years of age, and his grey eyes under bushy sandy-coloured eyebrows bent upon me kindly but penetrating looks. Seizing my bag with a short 'Come along' to me, and a wave of the hand to the group he had left, he started off through driving misty rain along a rough stony road.[8]

After ten years in South Uist caring for a parish of 2,300 souls spread over 40 square miles of some of the most difficult terrain in Britain and at the mercy of the Atlantic gales, Fr Allan's health broke down.

A sympathetic bishop transferred him to Eriskay, where he spent the last 12 years of his life. His new parish was smaller, but no more comfortable and he threw himself into local causes to improve the lot of his parishioners and to raise enough money to build a new church for the island. In this cause he sold his Gaelic manuscripts, the fruit of more than 20 years of collecting, and gave the proceeds to the building fund.

The four women who travelled to Eriskay came to exploit Fr Allan in one way or another and he, a celibate, guileless and generous man living in relative isolation, was probably flattered by their attention and easily persuaded to help them. He willingly shared with them all his years of research and collecting. On a scale of exploitation, Amy Murray was one of those who offended least. Written in an odd – some would say irritating – folksy style her book was nevertheless an affectionate and not inaccurate portrait of Fr Allan and life on Eriskay at the beginning of the twentieth century. It enjoyed considerable success in the United States, where Margaret had read it as a young woman.

John already knew that the priest had been a meticulous documenter of his work collecting songs, stories, folk remedies and Gaelic words, but while reading *Father Allan's Island* he discovered that there had been ten notebooks, many more than he had thought. He set himself the task of trying to recover them and met with early success in 1937, when one of the books, entitled *Strange Things*, turned up in Compton Mackenzie's library in the house he had built on Barra. John immediately borrowed it to begin to type it out, but the task and the search for the remaining nine notebooks was interrupted by the war, the purchase of Canna and his nervous breakdown.

The quest did not resume until 1949, when a second notebook was discovered in the library of Glasgow University. Later the same year Angus McIntosh, who had now become a professor at the University of Edinburgh, unearthed two more volumes in a bequest of material left to the university library. The following year McIntosh found three more – a book of lexicographical material and proverbs including a glossary of 2,500 'hard words' from Eriskay and Barra, a collection of waulking songs and a collection of Gaelic hymns.

Shortly afterwards John obtained one of Fr Allan's diaries from a priest in Fort William and himself discovered a further notebook in the library of Glasgow University. He now had eight of the ten notebooks, plus a diary and several small collections of notes. Word spread, prompting others to give him letters to and from Fr Allan. Together they revealed a life's work by a diligent and sensitive man who not only faithfully recorded the stories and songs of others, but himself wrote poetry in Gaelic and English and translated hymns and a mass into Gaelic. But why had none of this been published under Fr Allan's own name at the time? And what had attracted those women to seek him out?

A second visitor to Fr Allan in 1905 had been Marjory Kennedy-Fraser, a singer and musician who had heard that an American folk-song collector, Evelyn Benedict, was already on the island and that Amy Murray was expected to come in the autumn. Benedict published nothing from her trip, but like Murray, Mrs Kennedy-Fraser was to profit hugely from her visit to Eriskay and later other islands. She was already a singer of Hebridean songs and writer about the music and folklore of the islands, but after her visit her fame increased. She became a pop star of her age, touring and performing in Europe, the US and Canada and her songs, which she published in three volumes of *Songs of the Hebrides,* were immensely popular. She also produced several other books and numerous recordings of performances by herself and her daughter Patuffa. Some of the songs, such as the *Eriskay Love Lilt* and *Kismuel's Galley* continue to be sung and recorded up until the present day and are widely accepted as the authentic sound of the Western Isles.

Mrs Kennedy-Fraser had died in 1930, but her reputation lived on and she was credited − by Prime Minister Ramsay Macdonald, among others − not only with recording Gaelic song, but of being the principal preserver of a culture which had now vanished. To John, however, she was not much more than an exploiter. What annoyed him most was the impression among her many supporters that she had collected and translated the songs herself, whereas in fact she had used songs collected and published by others, including Fr Allan, who got little credit. There was also a misconception that because of the large number of songs she had published and recorded, there was nothing left − the entire musical culture of the Hebrides had been recorded and was now extinct.

By her own admission Mrs Kennedy-Fraser was unable to speak or understand more than a few words of conversational Gaelic, so she turned the tunes she heard into 'art songs' – using approximate English translations made for her by others or sometimes writing all the words herself – 'faithfully . . . within our Scoto-Celtic melodic heritage',[9] as she called it. Having done this she found that the new words would not fit the original melodies, so she also had to modify the tunes to fit the English words and often to change the key to suit her own voice. To make them 'acceptable to the refined ear', she also abandoned the modal form which is so distinctive of Gaelic song. Western music commonly uses only two modes, the major and the minor, whereas Gaelic song uses as many as eight. With changed words and music they could hardly be described as original or authentic.

Part of the appeal of her songs was the romantic 'Celtic Twilight' context in which she presented them, a vision of pastel shades and misty landscapes which appealed to her audience. She described Eriskay – 'an enchanted island'– in the words of Keats:

> Magic casements, opening on the foam
> Of perilous seas in faery lands forlorn.[10]

Kennedy-Fraser had first been recommended to go to Eriskay by the artist John Duncan, who specialised in ethereal portraits with a Celtic theme (he painted the rather portly frame of Mrs Kennedy-Fraser in middle-age against the rocks and sea of Eriskay). Fr Allan she called a 'Celtic dreamer', a description which would have infuriated John. The whole movement, it seemed to him, wanted to see the culture of the islands in 'muted colours of gloomy mysticism', whereas they were the reverse, 'brightly coloured, concrete and epigrammatic'.[11] It treated the islands as a sort of idealised Avalon, rather than real places where real people went about their everyday lives, often involving hard manual work, disease and poverty. John's attempts to put the record straight, which he started to do in the 1930s, did not win him many friends. As two of Mrs Kennedy-Fraser's supporters wrote: 'To deride work of this kind as a tampering with the genuine product of the folk-spirit is inept and ungracious.'[12]

Being described as 'inept and ungracious' was never going to put him off and in 1969 he and his musical collaborator Frank Collinson returned to the theme, publishing the original versions of the songs

Mrs Kennedy-Fraser had used and showing how she had changed them.[13] But Campbell and Collinson were out of step with the age. Later scholars and performers of traditional song would look askance at highly arranged folksong, sung by classically trained professional singers to orchestral accompaniment. But in *Country Magazine*, a radio programme he presented, Collinson had been obliged to work to BBC practice, which was against 'untrained' singers marring the airwaves, thus excluding the singers John was anxious to record. When native Scottish singers were eventually broadcast in the late 1950s, popular reaction was remarkably hostile, even including fervent Scottish Nationalists such as the poet Hugh MacDiarmid.[14]

John was fiercely critical of Mrs Kennedy-Fraser in several books and articles, but when he came to write her entry in the Oxford Dictionary of National Biography, he softened his disapproval. She had never concealed what she had done and she had inspired many people – his own wife Margaret among them – to seek out the originals of the Gaelic songs she had popularised.

He was much less inclined to give any credit at all to the fourth woman to visit Fr Allan. Ada Goodrich-Freer first made her way to the island in 1895 while she was researching the phenomenon of 'second sight' in the Highlands and Islands on behalf of the Society for Psychical Research. At that time in her late 30s, she was an attractive and engaging woman who always looked younger than her age and she easily won Fr Allan's confidence. He allowed her to read and make use of the material he had collected for her research, but now that John had found the notebooks and could read them for himself, he discovered that she had gone much further than merely drawing on them as source material.

In the last years of the nineteenth and the first few of the twentieth centuries Miss Goodrich-Freer built a reputation for herself as an authority on Hebridean folklore, giving lectures to learned societies in London and Scotland, writing papers and in 1902 publishing a book, *Outer Isles*. This reputation persisted until her death in 1931, marked by an obituary in the magazine *Folklore* eulogising her achievements. Yet, as with Mrs Kennedy-Fraser, by her own admission, she could not speak or understand Gaelic and had only visited the islands on a few short summer visits, so how was she able to amass the volume and quality of the material she presented?

John found that she had occasionally acknowledged the help given to her by Fr Allan, but in a way that implied that he had made introductions for her, accompanied her on visits to storytellers or singers, but that she, herself, had collected the songs and stories used in her papers and lectures. Reading through the diaries, John found several references to work Fr Allan was doing to provide material for Miss Freer's lectures, sometimes working late to meet her deadlines at the expense of his own failing health.

With painstaking thoroughness, John and Sheila Lockett went through Ada Goodrich-Freer's lectures, papers and book and compared them with Fr Allan's notebooks. They discovered at least two dozen instances of blatant plagiarism, sometimes of extensive passages with only small changes of words. Sometimes she flagrantly misrepresented his findings. To support her argument that 'second sight' existed in the islands, she reproduced his retelling of folk memories as if they had happened recently. Where he added qualifications, she substituted certainties.

John published a short book about the life and work of Fr Allan in 1954,[15] followed by printing several of Fr Allan's own writings for the first time. In 1958 he returned to the subject, writing an article detailing the extent to which Miss Freer owed her renown as a folklorist to Fr Allan's work. The piece was not universally well-received. Despite the evidence, some academics and folklorists believed that John had overstepped the bounds of decency in attacking the reputation of a dead woman. He countered by arguing that only by destroying Miss Freer's reputation could he rescue that of Fr Allan, whose notes had been plundered to such an extent that publication of his own work had been stifled. To add insult to injury, Miss Freer had claimed copyright of the material in her book and papers.

Several journals, including *Folklore*, which had published Miss Freer's papers and lectures, refused to take John's article, despite the fact that it dealt with people long dead, and it remained unpublished until the University of Edinburgh's department of Scottish Studies, headed by Angus McIntosh, printed it.[16] His willingness to engage in controversy and make fierce accusations against established figures like Mrs Kennedy-Fraser and Miss Freer came back to haunt John when he was turned down for grants or other support. He had the feeling that a strong lobby was working against him, but he was unrepentant and drew strength from the opposition and the feeling that he was putting the record straight.

He never forgot Ada Goodrich-Freer and how she had betrayed Fr Allan. In 1968 he collaborated with Dr Trevor Hall, who had previously written about the Society of Psychical Research which had employed Miss Freer, and together they published *Strange Things*, which reproduced John's article and reprinted Fr Allan's original notebook of that title and contained a thorough demolition of Miss Freer's character, exposing her as a fantasist, charlatan and habitual liar.

# CHAPTER SIXTEEN

# Recognition and Contentment

The collaboration John had started with Frank Collinson was to prove a successful and harmonious one, lasting over 30 years. He was eight years older than John and when they first met was working in London for the BBC as editor of the radio programme *Country Magazine*. Although a trained classical musician, his tastes and experience were incredibly varied. He was proud not only of having conducted for both Cole Porter and Richard Tauber, but also of having restored William Walton's *Ballet* from a single piano score when the original music was destroyed in the London blitz.[1]

In 1949 he visited John and Margaret on Canna and began transcribing the tunes of the songs collected by them and by Calum Maclean. Few people owned machines on which the recordings could be played and by publishing them in printed form John and Collinson hoped to bring them to a wider audience.

With John's discovery of the way in which Fr Allan's work had been misappropriated, they were concerned about copyright and agreed that they should share any rights in the songs John had recorded and Collinson had transcribed. 'Mrs Kennedy-Fraser made a fortune out of phony versions of Gaelic songs, perhaps there is a little money to be made out of arrangements of authentic versions as well,' Collinson wrote.[2] Later he joined the School of Scottish Studies as its first musical research fellow. It gave him a secure income and he and his wife moved to Scotland, enabling him to spend more time on his work with John, which was to include joint field trips as well as desk work on material already collected. The partnership did not earn either of them anything – in fact it may have cost them money – but it did yield three volumes of *Hebridean Folksongs* (1969, 1977 and 1981), numerous articles and papers, and secured their reputations in the field of Gaelic folksong.

This was a productive time for John. He recovered and published for the first time much of the work of Fr Allan, including his collection of Gaelic words and some of his Gaelic poetry. At his own expense he published the Coddy's stories from Barra, other books of stories from South Uist and narratives of first-hand history of the Highlands and Islands. One of these was *The Furrow Behind Me*, the life story of farm worker Angus MacLellan, originally from South Uist, which John recorded in Gaelic and transcribed, edited and published in both English and Gaelic. He also edited and published *A School in South Uist*, the charming memoirs of an English schoolmaster, catapulted from the Midlands to the very different world of the Hebrides in the late nineteenth and early twentieth centuries.

All his work was well received in the Gaelic-speaking areas, but had limited popular appeal elsewhere. Although he was still working outside the universities and was viewed by some academics as an irritating eccentric, John's methods and his results were gradually winning acceptance. Recognition came first from Canada, when St Francis Xavier University, which John had first visited more than 20 years before, awarded him an honorary degree in 1953. In 1962 he submitted a thesis to Oxford University on his work in recovering, analysing and publishing the works of Edward Lhuyd, a seventeenth-century Welsh polymath, who had travelled in Scotland and studied Gaelic, and was awarded a doctorate as a result. In 1965 the first acknowledgment in his own country of his achievements came when he received an honorary degree from the University of Glasgow, where Derick Thomson, his former colleague in the Scottish Folklore Institute, was now Professor of Celtic.

John's scholarly work was to be regularly accepted by leading journals, such as *Scottish Gaelic Studies*, published by the Aberdeen University Celtic Department, and *Ériu*, the leading Irish language publication, but he was also keen to bring Gaelic culture and history to a wider public. Over several decades he persuaded the editors of the *Scots Magazine* to take pieces by him on Mrs Kennedy-Fraser and *Songs of the Hebrides*, the work of Fr Allan McDonald, Highland links with Nova Scotia, obituaries of Hebridean bards or storytellers and a two-part account of the founding of the Sea League on Barra by Compton Mackenzie and himself. The subject matter sometimes looked a little out of place among the more folksy articles which were the magazine's usual fare, but John was convinced that there was a curiosity among general readers both at home and abroad.

Oral history and the past as told through the lives of ordinary people were increasingly being acknowledged as valid historical evidence but John was still unusual in concentrating on this form of scholarship. His research and fidelity to his sources and subjects were of a high standard, but he had little use for over-arching historical theories, preferring to let his subjects speak for themselves. This kept him out of the academic mainstream and thus denied him research grants. His work, rather than earning him money, was a financial burden.

Commercial or academic publishers took up his major projects, such as the three volumes of *Hebridean Folksongs*, but even this was hard going. In 1980 he wrote complaining bitterly to Oxford University Press about their decision to limit the print run of the third volume to 1,000 copies, fewer than either of the previous two volumes – even after £1,750 had been raised from donations towards the publication costs and John and Frank Collinson had waived their royalties.[3] No Scottish university was interested in John's translation of the autobiography of the Uist farmworker Angus Maclellan and it was first published in Gaelic in Norway. Many of the shorter or less academic works he either had to publish himself or subsidise a printer to produce. He never questioned this use of money – it was what had to be done to help preserve a culture under threat.

It was also a labour of love. He and Margaret did not see themselves as detached professional collectors or anthropologists, but as part of the culture they were recording. They had made many friends in the islands, including the Coddy and Annie Johnston from Barra and the Macrae sisters from South Uist, all of whom were frequent visitors to Canna. Songs and stories were often recorded at ceilidhs which, although they were arranged for them specifically for this purpose, were as much social as working occasions. They also held regular ceilidhs for local people. Canna in the 1950s was still a predominantly Gaelic-speaking island, as it had been 20 years earlier, and many of the old people had rich memories of songs and stories.

At the same time as concentrating on his own work, John was encouraging his wife to publish the songs of South Uist she had collected during her five years living there. Margaret would never regard herself as a scholar, but she did want to do something with the

songs and folklore she had in her notebooks. Her work was less well-
known than John's but it had been recognised in 1949 when she
presented at an international folk music conference in Venice. The
International Folk Music Council asked her to play her recordings to
Zoltan Kodály in London, which led in turn to her being invited to
contribute to a festival in memory of the Hungarian composer and
ethnomusicologist Béla Bartók in 1956.

★

For most of the late 1940s and early 1950s Margaret had been
preoccupied with Canna, nursing John through his breakdown and
running the farm in his absence. As he got back to full strength she
had time to get her own book together and in 1955 produced
*Folksongs and Folklore of South Uist*[4], a selection of the songs she had
taken down, including songs in praise of South Uist, love-songs,
lullabies, laments, songs of exile, songs as accompaniment to dancing
or working, such as milking songs, spinning songs and waulking
songs. She also included stories and anecdotes, prayers, proverbs,
herbal medicines, charms and recipes.

As a foreword to all of this she wrote an account of her own daily
life which demonstrated a natural fluency and, in colourful descrip-
tive images, conveyed her affection for the island and its people. The
book was an immediate critical success and attracted international
attention, but the reaction it received on South Uist pleased
Margaret more than anything. When she, John and Sheila Lockett
took copies to Peigi and Mairi Macrae and their neighbours they
accepted it as a warm and authentic tribute to their culture and way
of life. Her friend Fred Gillies, poet and shopkeeper in Lochboisdale,
wrote movingly:

> *an eibhleag anns an gann bha 'n deo*
> *Sheid i oirre, 's thug i beo a rithist*
> ['an ember was dying; she blew on it and brought it to life again']

In 1977 John persuaded Oxford University Press to republish
*Folksongs and Folklore of South Uist*, but they would not accept
any risk. He had to do it on a 'commission basis,' meaning that he

paid the costs of printing and binding and recouped his expenditure from the royalties which, despite Oxford's misgivings, he did easily. It has been reprinted twice more and Margaret was awarded four honorary degrees on the strength of it. The easy, accessible style in which it is written and the charm with which Margaret evokes a past age, gave the book more general appeal than John's more scholarly works. Although she received the sort of instant recognition he had struggled to attain, John never resented it and took pride in her achievement. Margaret did not publish any further Gaelic or folksong work, but the book's success established the husband and wife partnership as authoritative, and brought Canna a reputation as an intellectual and cultural centre.

Canna House, which had never lacked visitors from among John and Margaret's wide circle of friends and relatives from both sides of the Atlantic, was now attracting a stream of writers, artists, musicians, naturalists, academics and politicians keen to learn their opinions on anything from transport policy to Celtic languages. The visitors' book resembled that of a British embassy, rather than that of a house on a remote island. Some signatures occurred again and again, like that of the poet Kathleen Raine, who valued the healing properties of the island on the many emotional scars she carried, and found inspiration in its landscape. Others included the artists Helen Binyon and Gilbert Spencer, brother of Stanley, the cellist Vivien Mackie, the engraver Reynolds Stone and the Scottish poet Helen Cruickshank.

Compton Mackenzie had introduced the Swedish painter and writer Roland Svensson, who specialised in islands, to the Campbells. He became a regular house guest, painted the island many times and wrote about it in his book: *Övärld, Ett urval ur hundra dagböcker 1946–1960* (Insularity, A selection from a hundred diaries). The opposite of the dark, brooding Scandinavian of Ibsen and Bergman, being round and jolly with a full beard, he was an eager participant in John's games and entertainments. He produced a poster of cats and billiard balls for a 'Welcome home Canna House snooker championship' for Margaret in 1955 when it was asked: 'John Campbell will risk his title – and who will venture?' Another, two years later, advertised:

A Great Event, A John Lorne Campbell Public Lecture!!
(Colour and Film),
New York's Waterfront,
Mr and Mrs Campbell World Cruise,
Mr Campbell's Exploration of the Faroese Islands.
Tickets will only be available by personal invitation to the booking
office at Canna House. Gaelic murmur may be heard.

As a counterweight to what John described as the intolerable lone-
liness of winter, when bad weather could sometimes cut the island off
from the mainland or other islands for days or even weeks at a time,
house parties would be arranged on any excuse – visits from friends,
chance meetings at cattle sales, foreign yachtsmen in the harbour,
particularly Americans. Any hospitality offered to the couple when
they were travelling would be repaid with an invitation to Canna.

Among friends John lost his reserve and became the life of the
party. Usually scruffily dressed during the day, he would always put
on a jacket and tie for dinner. Guests would be summoned to the
table with a fanfare on the bugle. He delighted in being the perfect
host, showing off his knowledge of fine wines and ordering good
food from Young & Saunders, Edinburgh, or Fortnum & Mason in
London. Boxes of delicacies lined the corridor to the kitchen. There
was always music in the house, from Margaret at the piano and John
on flute or other wind instrument. Any musically proficient guest
was pressed into performance.

The photo albums in Canna House document the change in
John's demeanour far more graphically than words. In pictures taken
during the 1940s and early 1950s he is often serious or frowning. In
those taken later he is often seen smiling, laughing, clowning,
wearing one of his eccentric collection of hats or entertaining his
guests on the flute or a whistle.

For the most part the couple thrived on the conversations which
resulted over the dinner table and the house would ring with laughter.
But occasionally the attention was uninvited, an unwelcome inter-
ruption to their daily work. Strangers would arrive at the door with a
bewildering variety of requests. One wanted advice on tartan, another
assumed it was a hotel and demanded accommodation. A professor
from an obscure US university claimed he could decipher musical

notes from the patterns on Canna's carved Celtic stones and insisted on playing the resulting discordant tune. Margaret would mostly bear these with wry good humour, often turning them into amusing stories in her letters to friends, which were the equal of the comic novels written by Compton Mackenzie. She was invariably the last to go to her room and, with a packet of cigarettes on one side of her table and a glass of whisky on the other, would be heard pounding her upright manual typewriter deep into the night, keeping up a constant correspondence with friends and relatives in Britain and abroad.

John's patience was thinner; he had no facility for small talk and acute shyness stayed with him all his life. Faced with an unwanted visitor asking apparently silly questions, he would lapse into silence, or turn his back and mutely walk away. Margaret had a habit of inviting congenial strangers she met on her travels to spend a few days on Canna. John did not always approve of her choices and would sometimes go to lengths to avoid them. Fred Pattison, the former schoolboy farmworker who had brought his wife Anne back to holiday on the island, remembers John inviting them for a picnic so as to be out of the house when Margaret's visitor arrived. It was raining hard, but he was undeterred, driving them to a sheltered spot where they ate lunch under a large umbrella, John grinning like a schoolboy playing truant.

On Sundays John took control of the kitchen to give Margaret a break from cooking. His repertoire did not extend very far – sardines-on-toast was a favourite – but it was served with affection. Sunday was also the day of his favourite television programme, the legal drama *Perry Mason*. Margaret refused to have a set in the house and John tried to get around the ban by buying a small one to keep in his study, but the reception was terrible. So each Sunday evening in a twentieth-century version of *droit de seigneur* he would walk down to the Square to watch the programme in the home of Jessie MacKinnon, who owned the only functioning TV on the island. A cake would be baked, the best china would be brought out for tea and her grandchildren would be warned to be on their best behaviour. Whenever Jessie or her sister Mary-Ann MacLean felt the programme had reached an unsuitable point she would try to distract the children by pointing out a fishing boat at the pier or humming loudly. John, engrossed, never noticed.

Margaret regretted that she had never been able to give John 'the curly-haired child' he would have loved, but he had the next best thing. He had never lost touch with his Basque friend Saturnino, who had worked for his mother in St Jean de Luz. Ethel Campbell did not return to the house and Saturnino, by this time married with two young daughters, Maria Carmen and Magdalena (Magda), earned a living the best he could in depressed post-war Spain, often having to leave his family to work away from home. In 1958 his wife died and John and Margaret travelled to Spain to be with the family. They invited him to bring the girls to Canna for a summer break and in 1961 he did, beginning a series of annual trips which were to lead to an important and lasting relationship.

The girls grew up speaking Basque, Spanish and French. During their extended holidays on Canna Margaret – dubbed 'Marguerite' by them – spoke French and taught them English by reading out Peter Rabbit and other Beatrix Potter stories. John, called by them 'Juan', spoke fluent French, but had also picked up some Spanish and Basque. He read them P.G. Wodehouse. They came every summer and, with the permission of the nuns at their convent school, stayed for three or four months at a time, living at Tighard. Saturnino did odd jobs, farm work or fishing with John and the girls grew up with the Canna children. Maria Carmen fell in love with Michael, handsome, fair-haired son of the widowed Mary-Ann MacLean, a relationship frowned upon by her father, but the boy tragically died of a kidney infection in 1964.

John found Saturnino's company strengthening and calming. Returning from a long day's fishing together, Margaret would ask what they had talked about. 'Nothing,' he would reply, 'we never said a word to each other. A perfect day.'

He looked forward to the annual summer visits and usually met them in London off the boat-train from the Continent to give them a treat. There would be a meal and a trip to a cartoon cinema to see *Tom and Jerry* or *Mickey Mouse*. The humour transcended language and appealed to John as much as to the girls. When they arrived in Canna he would prepare treats and surprises for them, modifying board games to use Spanish pesetas or 'El Banco de Canna' notes in denominations of 'Francos', which he illustrated with pictures of cattle, ducks or the Canna stamp he had had printed featuring a shearwater in flight.

As they entered womanhood and stopped coming as frequently,

Saturnino would come alone, but John would arrange secretly for Magda to come to Canna, surprising her father. The visits continued until Saturnino died in 1974. After his death, John assumed the role of surrogate father, giving Maria Carmen away at her wedding and taking on a grandfather's duty with her daughter – even managing to write to the child in her first language, Basque.

Compton Mackenzie, who had been one of John and Margaret's first visitors when they moved in, had spent most of the 1940s and early 1950s living in the south of England, but in 1953 he bought a flat at 31 Drummond Place in Edinburgh's New Town and retired to Scotland. The Campbells renewed their friendship with him and his home became their base whenever they were in the Scottish capital. Margaret had not liked Mackenzie when she had first met him on Barra, feeling he excluded her from the all-male evenings of billiards, whisky and conversation at his house. But now, in an early-hours conversation round the fire in Drummond Place, they put their differences behind them and she told him she was grateful for giving John confidence and making him work.

Compton and his wife Faith had been living apart for several decades, but they remained close. As well as being an author herself, sometime actress and sculptor, she was an accomplished pianist who had studied with a pupil of Clara Schumann. She became a regular visitor to Canna House, writing her novel *The Crooked Wall* there and playing duets with Margaret on the Steinway grand, with John occasionally adding a bass line on the French horn.

The Mackenzies were Catholic converts, did not believe in divorce and publicly celebrated their Golden Wedding in 1955 – despite the fact that they had been apart for half of the 50 years. After Faith died in 1960 Mackenzie, now Sir Compton, married Chrissie McSween, his secretary with whom he had been living since his time on Barra. She died a year after their marriage and two years later, in 1965, Mackenzie married her younger sister Lilly. John and Margaret were witnesses at the wedding and to foil the press, booked the wedding car and the dinner in their names. Margaret was one of the last to visit Mackenzie before he died in 1972, and long afterwards they continued to stay with Lilly when they visited Edinburgh.

★

Alongside the folksong work, there was the Canna farm to run and work on wildlife conservation, which received much less public attention than the couple's efforts with Gaelic culture, but was considered by them to be equally important. John's interest in nature and wildlife had been kindled by his solitary walks on his father's Taynish estate as a child and the skills and concerns learned then had never left him. Canna had never been a sporting estate, but the Thom family were keen shots. John did not regard killing birds or animals as sport. Immediately on taking possession of the island, he had banned shooting or the killing of birds and animals. He made an exception for rabbits, which were out of control and a threat to pastures and the habitat of other species, and the occasional shooting of predatory gulls and hooded crows. At the same time he continued traditional farming practices, rejecting extensive use of chemical fertilizers, insecticides or pesticides and went out of his way to create special protected areas for butterflies, moths, birds and mammals.

Canna was home to a rich variety of birdlife. Its cliffs supported breeding colonies of puffins, razorbills, brown and black guillemots, fulmars, kittiwakes and Manx Shearwaters. Its waters boasted many species of duck, divers, cormorants and shags. Geese grazed on its fields, corncrakes and waders inhabited its shoreline and raptors, including golden eagles, buzzards and the rare peregrine falcon, soared above its hills and crags.

The island had been visited by bird watchers and professional ornithologists for decades and John was keen to encourage their surveys and sightings, allowing them to camp without charge, but he discouraged mass tourism, which he feared would ruin habitats and discourage the breeding of birds. After neighbouring Rum was bought by the Nature Conservancy Council, John integrated his conservation programme with theirs. To encourage and shelter wildlife on the island he planted 16 acres of woodlands as windbreaks and small plantations. Canna has no natural lochs, so he dammed a stream to make a pond on Sanday in which planted bulrushes and lilies and established small stands of willow on its margins.

He took a keen interest in birds, but his first love from childhood had been entomology. The scientific skills in trapping, identifying and recording moths and butterflies he began to learn as an 11-year-old boy were developed and perfected over the years. He began his

Hebridean collection on Barra in 1936 and continued on Canna from 1938. In 1951 he was able to buy an advanced mercury vapour moth trap which increased his take and he eventually built up to 30 cabinet drawers containing 283 species of macrolepidoptera, including the first recorded specimen of the noctuid moth *Dianthoecia Caesia* taken in Scotland, which he found in 1952.

When he bought Canna he was advised by a visiting cattle valuer not to speak Gaelic to his employees and tenants and not to let them see him chasing butterflies. He ignored both pieces of advice and before long the islanders and their children were bringing him moths, butterflies and insects they could not identify themselves. He was the official migrant recorder for Canna, a task he persuaded the lighthouse keepers on the tiny islet of Heisker to share. From the early 1950s he pioneered the marking of moths and butterflies to track their migrations and published numerous articles in learned journals and pamphlets, including *The Macrolepidoptera of the Parish of Barra* in 1938 and in 1970 *Macrolepidoptera Cannae*, which was the definitive work on moths and butterflies on Canna, describing 267 species, until John himself rendered it incomplete by recording 16 more.

His reputation as a conservationist and naturalist led him to expose another academic fraud, although this time involving butterflies rather than Gaelic songs and stories. In 1948 John had been contacted by John Raven, a Cambridge classics don who was also a keen and knowledgeable botanist. Raven was investigating a suspicious series of remarkable findings of rare plants on the Isle of Rum by John Heslop Harrison, a professor at Newcastle University.[5] The problem was how to get to Rum with his two companions, since the island, then owned by Lady Monica Bullough, widow of Sir George, was closed to uninvited visitors. John Campbell had a solution. He wrote to Raven: 'If you wish to enter by the back door, this has been done, by campers who landed on the isle of Canna and then hired the boat of Mr Allan MacIsaac, crofter, to ferry them to Rum, where they remained unbeknown for several days and were ferried back again, getting the mailboat the next morning.'[6]

The party arrived on Canna some time later and were perplexed by their brief stay. Raven's friend Tom Creighton recalled that they were camping near the pier when 'a boat came by and a completely unknown Canna resident threw two lobsters, ready boiled, on to the turf beside us and went off. I've never understood the reason for this generosity, and the lobsters were extremely good to eat.' Later they presented themselves at Canna House, to be greeted by John. 'Without even mentioning our names or acknowledging our visit, he said, "Oh, how nice that you could come. Now we can play a flute quartet."' The musical evening did not happen, since only Creighton could play the flute and he could not master the spare instrument that John Campbell produced. But, he recorded, 'the meeting was enjoyable, amusing and, like the laird himself, highly eccentric.'[7]

The three men did get to Rum, but Raven's eventual paper, throwing considerable doubt on the professor's discoveries was suppressed. John Campbell's interest was not primarily with the plants Heslop Harrison claimed to have found on Rum, but the three specimens of *Maculinea arion*, the Large Blue butterfly, which Heslop Harrison alleged he had caught there. John was immediately sceptical; there had been no other reported sightings of such a rare butterfly in the Hebrides. He did not follow it up immediately, but never forgot it and 25 years later, when, prompted by an article in a learned journal, he tried to track down the three specimens Heslop Harrison claimed to have caught and given to friends or to Oxford University. His findings – or lack of them – convinced him it was a fraud or a hoax and he recounted the tale in an article in the *Entomologist's Record* in 1975.[8]

★

Most of Canna was farmed by John as an owner-occupying farmer – a description he preferred to laird or proprietor – but several of the islanders held crofts on Sanday, which they cultivated or used to graze cattle. Although they also worked for the estate, their crofts gave them a measure of independence and legal security of tenure which John valued as adding to the sustainability of the community. He was rare among Highland landowners in actually creating new crofts rather than trying to extinguish those which already existed. John viewed the Crofters' Act of 1886, which gave small farmers protection from summary eviction by landlords, not only as a measure of social justice, but the basis for the political and economic regeneration of the north of Scotland by creating a 'peasantry' – a class of independent and entrepreneurial smallholders capable of countering the dead hand of absenteeism.

His attitude to land ownership in the Hebrides had been spelled out in a joint letter with Compton Mackenzie to the magazine *Outlook* in 1936. The two public school-educated Oxford graduates set out a programme which was almost Marxist in its radicalism, calling for legal limits on the amount of land any one person or body could hold and the establishment of a strong development board with powers to compulsorily purchase land to establish new small-holdings.[9]

He returned to the subject in 1944, when he compared Scandinavia with Scotland. In the former 'political theory favours peasant proprietorship, where everything is done to preserve and enrich rural life on a distributionist basis where education and communications and the protection of fisheries are conceived in the crofters' interests, where absenteeism is an impossibility.' In the latter the prevailing political theory was still *laissez faire*, 'where conditions favour the big farmer and landowner, where absenteeism is permitted and where rural education, communications and the general protection of the small man's rights is far inferior'. The demand for land was there, he added, but it was not being met. There were 8,870 applications outstanding for smallholdings in the Outer Hebrides alone at the end of the war, many of these claims ten years old.[10]

When he bought Canna John had reasonable grounds for hoping that the Government would buy part of the island to create new crofts. Land raids by returning servicemen after the First World War had prompted the Land Settlement (Scotland) Act of 1919, which gave the Government powers to force large landowners to create smallholdings and also to buy land and lease it back to crofters. The powers had been used in Skye, Raasay, South Uist and other parts of the Highlands, but since then subtle changes in official attitudes had been taking place. Crofting was increasingly being seen as part of the problem rather than the solution to the economic development of the Highlands. Lord Leverhulme, the industrial magnate whose own estates on the island of Lewis had been subject to land raids, condemned crofting as inefficient and inhibiting investment. By 1945 when it came into Government, the Labour Party thought the same way.

The change of policy was starkly illustrated in 1948 when seven men, most returning servicemen, staked claims to land on the Knoydart estate on the mainland close to Canna, which was owned by the absentee millionaire Lord Brockett. The case became a *cause célèbre* and Nationalists and Liberals, including John's former class-mate John Bannerman, rallied to their side. Hamish Henderson wrote a protest ballad about it. But the 'Seven Men of Knoydart' did not get their land – they were persuaded to leave and take legal action, but they lost a court battle and the Government refused to use its powers to give them their holdings.

John was bitter. 'The break-up of great estates and the settlement of smallholders on them in other countries is hailed as a great act of progress by the British left-wing press and leftish public opinion; but this approval does not extend to land settlement in Great Britain itself, where it is felt in such circles that smallholders, crofters and peasant proprietors are a tiresomely independently class of person more likely than not to vote Liberal or Conservative at elections and providing very poor material for a servile State.'[11]

He went on to attack the Labour Government for failing to control speculation in agricultural land, absenteeism or the amount of land which could be owned by one individual. In fact with Super-tax (the highest rate of tax on income) at £19s 6d (97.5p) in the £ there was an inducement to wealthy men to buy Highland estates and run them at a deficit in order to offset the losses against their private income tax.

'All this means that we have arrived at a fantastic state of paradox. Under a Labour Government which was expected to give the crofter and small farmer a square deal and which might reasonably have been expected to encourage the breaking up of great estates, land settlement has come to a dead stop; speculation in agricultural land and multiple ownership are unchecked; large landowners have every inducement to take farms and crofts into their own hands and appoint managers instead of looking for tenants; and public money is given to men who don't need it to raise their estates to a condition of over-capitalised perfection, whereas the men who need capital but can't afford to spend it on such a scale get nothing.'

Unable to alter the ownership of his own estate, John continued to farm it as best he could. This was long before 'self-sufficiency' and organic farming became fashionable, but Canna had to get as near as it could to both for economic reasons rather than considerations of taste. Everything imported was more expensive than it would be on the mainland, so there was an incentive to produce as much as possible on the island, whether it was fertiliser or food. Canna produced its own meat and diary products, Margaret and most of the crofters kept hens for eggs and the occasional fowl for the pot. The fertile soil was good for potatoes and, in gardens, vegetables and fruit. The plants Margaret had bought from nurseries when they first took possession of Canna House had paid off and she had established an attractive and productive south-facing garden with fruit trees, soft fruit and vegetables as well as flowers.

Although some fields were cultivated, Canna was largely a live-stock enterprise, with two flocks of Cheviot and Blackface sheep and two herds of grazing cattle, half of which were Margaret's pedigree Highland cattle, which John had come to accept as a permanent feature of the farm. After the recovery in agricultural prices in the 1950s John was able to run the farm on the basis that it broke even or made a small operating profit – it earned enough from livestock and sales of other produce to cover wages and supplies which had to be bought in. But as soon as his financial state improved he embarked on a sustained programme of investment. This included bringing water, sanitation and electricity supplied by diesel generators to every house on the island, renewing land drains and fences and, after 1971 extending the pier and building a new house for a shepherd. The farm was not earning enough to repay this spending, but John justified it to himself because he was benefiting his tenants, increas-ing efficiency and improving the capital value of the estate.

Justifying it to the tax inspector, however, was another matter. During the 1950s and 1960s John kept up a spirited exchange of letters with Inland Revenue officials who were suspicious of the fact that the farm seldom made a taxable profit. John responded to one inquiry: 'I cannot help wondering why an individual who is prepared to spend capital improving land should be regarded by the Inspector of Taxes as an object of suspicion? There is no prospect of this state of affairs altering as long as I am in occupation of Canna: i.e. supposing the capital is available I intend to continue spending it on the estate.'[12]

# CHAPTER SEVENTEEN

# Fighting for a Lifeline

The ferry service was the lifeblood of Canna and since 1930 the island had enjoyed a golden age. That year saw the introduction of the *Lochmor* and the *Lochearn,* large, comfortable ships operated by the company of David MacBrayne, which provided a regular and reliable link with the mainland railheads at Mallaig and Oban, and the Hebridean islands.

At first not everyone was impressed by the staid lines of the two ferries – squat funnels, high superstructure and almost vertical masts – but all agreed they were a great improvement on previous vessels on the routes. They were bigger, at 452 tons, and thus able to ride out the Minch storms more easily, and offered a higher standard of comfort in their wood-panelled saloons, restaurants and cabins for overnight sailings. The *Lochmor,* operating from Mallaig, sailed by way of Skye, Eigg, Rum, Muck and Canna, to Harris and South Uist, where she linked up with the *Lochearn,* which served South Uist, Barra, Tiree, Coll and Tobermory, reaching the mainland at Oban. Canna may look remote on the map, but these interlocking services enabled the islanders to reach the neighbouring Hebridean communities on the Inner and Outer Isles and two mainland ports, both served by the railway. The ferry network was an essential part of their lives.

MacBrayne's had operated ships in the Minch since the mid-nineteenth century, and its captains, such as Duncan 'Squeaky' Robertson of the *Lochearn* and Donald Joseph MacKinnon of the *Lochmor* were known and respected throughout the isles. Mac-Kinnon had the double advantage from John's point of view of being a very capable ship's master and a Gaelic speaker with a fine singing voice, which could often be heard booming from the bridge, particularly in rough seas, when he would sing at full volume. John persuaded him to record in Canna House.

Canna was the mid-point on the *Lochmor's* run. Its deep-water harbour provided shelter from storms and the pier, constructed by the Thoms, enabled the ship to tie up, so that passengers and cargo could be easily loaded aboard. It was the only one of the Small Isles with this facility. The sea at the piers on the other islands was too shallow to allow ships in close to land and people and freight had to be taken out to the ferry in 'flit boats' – an inconvenience in good weather, uncomfortable, dangerous or impossible in bad weather. The island benefited socially from the ferry link, with residents able to visit their friends and relatives easily, and Canna was part of the parish of Bornish, on South Uist, whose priest visited to preach in the chapel.

The gain was also economic. The *Lochmor* could take 120 sheep or 35 cattle in addition to passengers and other freight, and the farm often sent livestock to the weekly sales at Corpach, near Fort William, transporting them in pens on the deck or in the hold of the ferry and then transferring them to the railway at Mallaig. Livestock and other produce were bought and sold in the marts of the outer islands. Canna also had a long-standing arrangement to supply potatoes to shops and hotels.

But times were changing. The ferry companies had been acquired by railway operators before the war and consolidated into one line, Caledonian MacBrayne (CalMac), and when those companies were nationalised in 1947 CalMac, too, passed into public ownership. In the early 1960s it began consultations on replacing the *Lochmor*, but it was clear from its proposals that a fundamental reassessment of the role of the ferry was coming. Post-war prosperity had opened the Highlands and Islands to a much larger population of visitors than had made the journeys to the islands in the pre-war period. The new tourists wanted to bring their families and their cars and were not prepared to wait hours at ferry ports for bus or train connections or to have their vehicles hoisted aboard by derricks. They represented a new market and CalMac was keen to exploit it. The company wanted to serve the larger islands with much bigger ships than the *Lochmor* – roll-on, roll-off car ferries which would all operate from Oban, leaving Mallaig as home port for the inshore services to Skye and the Small Isles.

This spelt disaster for Canna; not only did the island not have a slip, where cars and other vehicles could drive ashore, but its pier was not long enough to allow the new big ships to tie up alongside, even if that had been allowed. But that is not what MacBrayne's had in mind. It proposed instead to serve the Small Isles with a much smaller vessel, a 70-foot motor boat. This would have much less room for passengers, freight or livestock and be more susceptible to bad weather and thus less reliable. The smaller boat would be unable to cross the more exposed waters of the Minch between Canna and the outer islands, cutting off social and economic links which had existed for generations. To John and Margaret this was a particular blow. Many of their friends and contacts were on the Outer Islands. Under the proposed new arrangements, to reach them they would have to catch the mailboat to Mallaig, travel by train to Oban, changing at Fort William, and there take another ferry to Castlebay or Lochboisdale. A journey which previously had taken hours, now might mean an overnight stay and two days' travelling.

John's dream of reviving crofting on Canna and Sanday as a means of growing the population ended with this news. The island now boasted ten crofts, but as the older people died, their holdings were either amalgamated or left uncultivated. Canna had a primary school, but children had to leave at the age of 11 for secondary school on the mainland and higher or further education after that. Some never came back. John had hoped to attract new crofters from the Outer Islands, but the end of direct transport links back to their families and friends reduced the attraction of starting afresh in a new place.

British Railways, led by Dr Richard Beeching, who was intent on reducing its operating losses, ended the practice of carrying livestock at normal freight rates. Access to markets in the Outer Isles was to be cut off and now, if Canna's sheep and cattle were to be transported from Mallaig to Corpach by rail, special arrangements had to be made at a much higher price. It struck at the viability of the farm and the community.

To John these changes were symptomatic of the attitude towards the Highlands and Islands in the south of England, where he was convinced the decisions had been made. The north of Scotland was now regarded as a tourist destination and the interests of car-driving holiday-makers were being preferred to those of the inhabitants. He was as convinced of the vital importance of transport to the islands as he had been of fishing 30 years earlier when he and Compton Mackenzie had founded the Sea League, and he tried to rekindle the campaigning spirit of those times.

In a pamphlet published in 1963 he proposed the slogan 'No taxation without transportation' and called for a massive protest[1]. No one living on the islands could believe that the new ferry arrangement would be suitable, he asserted, although 'to someone sitting in an office looking at a map it might appear so'. One of the remedies, he suggested, would be for the local authority to take over Canna pier and lengthen it, so that bigger ships could tie up alongside. If the pier were publicly owned it would qualify for a 75 per cent grant, whereas this was not available to a private landlord. He offered not only to give the pier free of charge, but to make an *ex gratia* payment to the council to cover the remaining 25 per cent of the work.

In the same pamphlet John took the opportunity to air other grievances. He railed against another nationalised industry, the telephone service, pointing out that Canna's local calling area extended only to the other Small Isles and the island of Soay, where there were relatively few telephones. Mallaig was counted as a national call at four times the cost, although this was where the exchange was and where Canna residents made most of their calls to trades-people, suppliers and transport offices.

He hit out again at British Railways for not allowing refunds on sleeper reservations unless 24 hours' notice was given. This might be fair to mainland travellers, but island residents could find themselves 'storm-stayed' at any time and would lose their money. He criticised the Farm Improvement Act for not allowing modifications to piers, slips or jetties in their list of improvements which could be grant-aided and he drew attention to the discrepancies in the level of proof required and the penalties for deer poaching compared to sheep stealing. The law went a long way to protect the rights of sporting landlords, but sheep farms like Canna – which had lost animals to theft by fishing boat crews – was disregarded.

Despite his campaigning, there was no 'massive protest', even on the scale of the Barra car tax revolt of 20 years earlier. MacBrayne's proposals were not universally liked, but this time the motorists and their powerful lobby groups were on the other side, they wanted the freedom to be able to drive to the Outer Islands. The government saw tourism as a means to countering economic decline and depopulation in the islands. The livelihood of crofters and farmers was secondary.

John did not give up and returned to the fray the following year: 'It is felt here,' he told the Highland Panel, which advised the government on economic matters, 'that the needs of the inhabitants of the Highlands and Islands should take precedence in the organisation of transport over the needs of summer visitors. The tourist industry is no doubt of importance to some districts, but the fundamental industry of the country as a whole is agriculture. If transport is not adequate to meet the needs of the inhabitants all the year round, then there may very well eventually be no inhabitants to entertain the summer visitors'.[2] Three years later he was making his case to the Department of Agriculture in Edinburgh. The proposed downgrading of the ferry service represented a backward step and would severely threaten life on the islands.[3]

John's ancestors may have defended their communities with swords; his weapons were a typewriter, his copious address book, an endless supply of Canna headed notepaper and the Canna Post Office. He backed up his pamphlets and official statements with a daily stream of letters to anyone he felt could advance or support Canna's cause. He won the backing of local politicians and neighbours on the other islands and made himself a constant nuisance to bureaucrats who were either advancing the opposing case or would have influence over the final decision.

Despite his campaign, the *Lochmor* was taken out of service in 1964, but his worst fears, that Canna would be served by a passenger launch unable to take livestock or freight, were not realised. Perhaps because of his protests, Caledonian MacBrayne bought a 20-year-old wooden-hulled former minesweeper and renamed her *Loch Arkaig*. She was a quarter of the tonnage of the *Lochmor*, but at 117 feet long was nearly 50 feet longer than the launch MacBrayne's had originally proposed – and she could carry 160 passengers, albeit that most of them would have to sit on deck, rather than in the cramped saloon. She was modified to be able to transport 120 lambs in pens on deck and provided with a derrick which could lift 1 ½ tons of cargo. The situation was not as bad as it could have been, but Canna had lost its link to the Gaelic speakers of the Outer Isles and with it a big part of the social and cultural life of the island.

To transport greater numbers of cattle or sheep to market from now on meant hiring a bigger vessel to make a special journey and John worried that as Caledonian MacBrayne replaced its fleet with larger ships, they would eventually have nothing which could tie up at Canna pier. His offer to the local authority to take over the pier was ignored and in 1971, fearing that the island would someday find itself cut off, he borrowed the considerable sum of £35,000 and had the pier lengthened. He removed one more excuse for the ferry company to downgrade the service, but for his pains received a bill from the Crown Estates Commissioners for rent on the extra area of seabed the pier would now occupy.

The whole episode reinforced John in his view that government and bureaucracy in all its forms were indifferent to the depopulation of the islands, or even wanted to encourage it. For the time being the lifeline to Canna was safe, but the battle over shipping was not yet over.

★

In 1966, after owning Eigg for 40 years, the Runciman family had put the island up for sale. Although they had been absentees and used Eigg as a holiday home, they were regarded by the population as model landlords who had invested in the estate and treated their tenants and employees with respect. They wanted to sell to someone who would follow their tradition and chose a Welsh sheep farmer, Captain Robert Evans, but his enthusiasm lasted only five years and in 1971 the island changed hands again. The new buyer, Bernard Farnham-Smith, introduced himself as 'Commander Farnham-Smith', a title which owed as much to its owner's Service career as that of 'Major' Michael, Canna's erstwhile factor. The Commander announced a plan to use the island as an adventure school for handicapped boys, but this proved as insubstantial as his sea-going experience and three years later, having been unmasked by the press as a former commander in the fire brigade rather than the Royal Navy, he put the island up for sale again.

One of John's demands in *Act Now for the Highlands and Islands*, the booklet he had co-written in 1939, was for an economic agency for the north of Scotland and in 1965 the demand had been met with the establishment of the Highlands and Islands Development Board. It now tried to counter the negative impact of absentee landlordism on the Highlands by buying Eigg, offering just above the £200,000 asking price set by Farnham-Smith, but its bid was easily beaten by another absentee, the businessman Keith Schellenberg.

Schellenberg, a former Olympic bobsleigh competitor, power-boat racer and driver of vintage sports cars, objected to being called a 'playboy' and unsuccessfully tried to sue two newspapers which called him that and criticised his ownership of the island, but play formed an important part of his activities on Eigg. The annual 'Eigg Games' attracted his friends from across Europe, including the German millionaire Gunter Sachs and the current Captain of Clanranald, whose ancestor had sold the island to help pay off debts. Not for Schellenberg were tossing the caber and throwing the hammer traditional to Highland Games. His guests dressed in costume and refought old battles using tennis balls rather than firearms. One year it was Hanoverians versus Jacobites, another British versus Germans. His tenure on Eigg evoked comparisions with that of the Bulloughs on Rum, particularly when he shipped in his yellow-painted vintage Rolls Royce to convey himself from one side of the tiny island to the other.

However, Schellenberg did invest in the farm and tried to stimulate the tourist industry on the island. A passionate advocate of free enterprise, he resented the state subsidy paid to keep the ferry running and in 1975 when CalMac again began consultations on the type of service the islands wanted, put forward a radical plan of his own. The ferry company, perhaps in response to local pressure from John and others, was proposing to replace the now ageing *Loch Arkaig* with a purpose-built vessel capable of carrying six cars, freight or 100 sheep. It would still not be up to the standards of the old *Lochmor*, but it would be bigger and better equipped and would be able to convey passengers in more comfort than the Spartan vessel it was to supersede. The plan was unveiled to representatives from the four Small Isles at a meeting in Inverness, to general approval from John.

Schellenberg was unimpressed and proposed instead that the subsidy be taken away from the state-owned company and given to a new venture, based on Eigg, which would provide a passenger and freight service to the Small Isles using 'a small fast motorboat, a landing craft and an 80-foot mailboat'.[4] He argued that his proposal would be better for the three islands without deep-water piers – Eigg, Rum and Muck – because the small boats would be able to tie up at their jetties and the landing craft could be loaded from the beach. Also, since it would be based on Eigg, it would create jobs on the island and contribute to its economic sustainability.

John was horrified. Seas around the two westernmost islands – Canna and Rum – were significantly more exposed than those around the inner and more sheltered islands, Eigg and Muck. Already the service provided by the *Loch Arkaig* was less reliable than previously because it was unable to sail in rough weather, now the prospect of the route being taken over by even smaller boats threatened the economic viability of the island. Landing craft, being flat-bottomed, can only operate effectively in calm seas and if Schellenberg's boat was unable to reach Canna in time to get its sheep and cattle to market the profitability of the farm and the livelihoods of those who depended on it were at risk. John became even more concerned when he learned that the Highlands and Islands Development Board – the body he had himself helped to call into being – was backing Schellenberg and prepared to put money into the Small Boat Scheme. For a while it appeared that officialdom was ranged against him. The Scottish Office appeared to favour Schellenberg's scheme as offering a substantial financial saving over the MacBrayne's subsidy.

He immediately resumed his letter-writing campaign, this time adding a new weapon to his armoury, one of the first fax machines to appear in the Hebrides. Although now nearing 70 years old, he was at the height of his powers and the fight galvanised him. He felt he was literally fighting for the life of his island.

The beauty of Canna and the intellectual stimulation of Canna House had attracted a host of admirers and supporters over the three decades that John and Margaret had owned the island; now he summoned them to the cause. He wrote and sent copies of articles and official documents to the scholar priests of St Francis Xavier

University, Nova Scotia, academics in Canada, the US and Norway, the vice-premier of Canada (who had relatives in Mallaig), to New Zealand, to Chile – to anywhere he thought there might be a sympathetic ear. He called for help from the Nature Conservancy Council, the Royal Society for the Protection of Birds, the National Trust for Scotland, the Crofters' Commission, the Commodore of the Scottish Motor Yacht Club, to the poet Kathleen Raine and the artist Roland Svensson and anyone else who might write in support. The name John Lorne Campbell appeared frequently in the letters columns of Scottish newspapers, and journalists from publications as geographically dispersed as the *West Highland Free Press* and the *Financial Times* made the ferry trip from Mallaig to Canna to hear the argument first-hand.

The fight did not all go one way. Proponents of the Small Boat Scheme also had their allies in remote places and letters began to appear in the *Oban Times* and the *Stornoway Gazette* from across the UK and beyond. Neither of these newspapers was a particular friend to either John or Canna and the *Oban Times* ran a cartoon depicting the Canna demand for a larger ferry as an ocean-going liner subsidised to the cost of £10,000,000 a year. Russell Johnston, Liberal MP for Inverness, whose vast constituency took in the Small Isles, joined the battle. Schellenberg may have had support in government, but he had failed to convince the population of his own island. In 1977 the Small Isles Community Council was formed and its chairman, Fergus Gowans of Eigg, organised a referendum; the result was a rejection of the Small Boat Scheme by 80 votes to 11.

Matters came to a head at an official meeting in Fort William in May 1977. The Scottish Office had by this time worked through the financial figures and realised that the Small Boat Scheme would cost very little – if anything – less than the MacBrayne's subsidy, for a much less reliable service. Muck turned against the small boat service, Lawrence MacEwan, one of the two brothers who farmed the island, declaring: 'Mr Schellenberg is temporal, MacBrayne's is eternal.'[5]

The proposal was killed, but the two-year delay it had caused had forced up the cost of the new ferry and as a result the specification had to be reduced; it would carry fewer passengers in more cramped conditions. In a final twist to the sorry tale, the ageing *Loch Arkaig* was holed during a fierce storm in the Sound of Sleat off Skye, and sank at her mooring in Mallaig harbour. Substitute ships had to take over the service until the new ferry was ready. In a resumed stand, John again wrote to Russell Johnston MP, who interceded with the Scottish minister. The new ship, by this time on the slipway, was cut in two and a new section inserted to lengthen her and provide more passenger and freight space.

The lifeline to Canna was preserved, but there was one last skirmish for John to fight. MacBrayne's proposed to name the new ship *Loch Mhor*. He was disgusted, not only that they would invite comparison with the illustrious former bearer of that name, but that they would commit a grammatical crime in Gaelic by pairing a masculine noun with a feminine adjective. This time his protest produced an immediate change of policy.

# CHAPTER EIGHTEEN

# A Succession Problem

For the time being John had won the struggle to avoid 'economic strangulation', but the battle over ferries had unnerved him. By the late 1970s he was over 70 and still farming the island after more than 40 years. No longer fit for hard physical work in the fields, he delegated a lot of the day-to-day running to Ian MacKinnon as farm manager, but he still kept the accounts and made the major decisions. Crucially, also, he provided the capital to invest in the island. The question he asked himself repeatedly was, who would take on those roles if he were no longer able to it?

From the early 1950s he had been concerned about how to perpetuate the work he had started on Canna. He and Margaret had no children and his attempts to get some sort of community ownership going had come to nothing. He had no intention of ever selling the island (despite what he told the tax inspector) and was in reasonable health, but he feared that after their deaths it could fall into the hands of an absentee landlord and become another rich man's plaything. With the examples of the Bulloughs' tenure on Rum and Lord Brockett's Knoydart estate on the mainland, he had good reason to fear that all he had done to try to preserve a Hebridean way of life might be undone.

In 1954 he discussed with lawyer Robin McEwen the practicality of leaving the island to the National Trust for Scotland (NTS) in his will.[1] The Trust had been founded in 1931 and had initially concentrated on acquiring and preserving stately homes and other historic buildings, but in 1954 it accepted Fair Isle, off the north coast of Scotland – an island with an existing community which was even more remote than Canna. John wanted to attach conditions to any bequest: that if Margaret survived him, she be allowed to rent grazing on Compass Hill for her pedigree Highland herd and that the rest of the island be split into small farms, with priority for the tenancies given to local people. What he had failed to achieve in life – repopulating the island with crofters – he hoped he still might achieve after his death.

There did not seem to be much urgency and it was two years before John returned to the plan and asked McEwen to approach Jamie Stormonth Darling, director of the NTS. Over several meetings they explored how the Trust might take over the island to fit in with John's wishes that the farm continue to be run on traditional lines and that Margaret, should she outlive him, be allowed to continue living in Canna House rent-free.

Stormonth Darling, who knew Canna and had holidayed there in the 1930s, indicated that the Trust would be sympathetic, but he could not make commitments which might not come into effect for years or even decades in the future. He added that it was unlikely that the Trust would agree to accept the island if there were conditions which would tie its hands in the way it was to be managed. There also might be problems with death duties, and the Trust would need an endowment to cover the running costs of Canna.[2] The talks continued on and off for a few years. John dropped his conditions and did name the Trust in his will as his preferred choice as the eventual inheritor of the island.

In the 1970s, with ferry problems starting to worry him, he began to reconsider. Leaving the island to the Trust after his death might solve the succession problem, but it meant he would be in charge for the whole of the rest of his life with no opportunity to step back from his responsibilities, which he took extremely seriously. He began to think that it might be better for the Trust to take over the island while he was still alive, alleviating him of some of the burdens and allowing him to retire from farming and managing the estate and concentrate on his Gaelic library and writing.

The American trust fund set up for him by his mother's parents, might provide an endowment to persuade the NTS to accept Canna. Its clout as a large, well-connected and well-respected organisation was sure to count for more than his own name if it came to fighting Canna's corner again. The council of the Trust, led by its president, the 12th Earl of Wemyss, and chairman, the 6th Marquess of Bute, was stuffed with the great and good of Scotland. They had political and establishment connections which John, through temperament and geographic isolation, had never acquired. In 1973 he wrote to Stormonth Darling suggesting that the NTS might take over the island, and a Trust manager was despatched to Canna to report on the practical details.

The matter still did not seem to be urgent on either side and two years later, in 1975, the director was speculating that the Trust could lead a consortium of public bodies, to include the Highlands and Islands Development Board and the Nature Conservancy Council which had bought Rum, Canna's nearest neighbour, in 1957.[3] The NTS would still need an endowment and John was still considering using some of the money in his American trust, but complications over the tax implications of moving money across the Atlantic delayed the plan and it made little headway until the end of the decade.

By 1979 Stormonth Darling was hooked: he had visited Canna and seen around Canna House and the library and, perhaps even more persuasive, he had been entertained and charmed by John and Margaret. John's initial objective of continuing to run the farm along traditional lines and encourage resettlement by providing new smallholdings now seemed to have been relegated in the director's mind. He wrote enthusiastically to Lord Wemyss, the council and senior Trust officials, describing Canna House as 'the most out-standing storehouse of knowledge on our western seaboard'. He added: 'So much knowledge is still in the heads of the two of them [John and Margaret] and, therefore, so much can be learned by the intelligentsia being in their company.'[4]

Ideas started to be flung around which had nothing to do with farming or conservation: Canna could become an educational establishment, with partners including a Scottish university and St Francis Xavier University, Nova Scotia. Tighard could be made available for scholars and John and Margaret paid honoraria as 'honorary professors'.

Detailed negotiations now commenced and by November 1980, when John attended a meeting of the Trust's executive committee in Edinburgh, the outline of a deal had been established. By this time practical considerations had outweighed fanciful schemes. Forgotten were the ideas of Canna as an educational establishment, or of the Trust leading a consortium of public bodies. It would acquire the island alone.

John's own valuation of the farm, the crofts, the houses, woodland and pier came to £1,345,000 – perhaps a little optimistic, since he included a sizeable sum for 'amenity value' – plus his Gaelic library which he priced at £56,000. He was prepared to pass the island and his books to the NTS as a gift, but needed to sell Canna House to the Trust for £50,000 in order to pay off the estate overdraft.

Under the plan finally agreed, John was not to be an 'honorary professor', but curator of the library, which now became the property of the Trust.[5] The thought that he could do all this and give up farming, however, proved to be illusory. Canna, like every other hill sheep farm in Scotland, had been receiving subsidies, and if John now stopped farming he would have to repay them. Ironically, he had never paid pension contributions for himself from the farm income and thought that by doing so he was helping the sustainability of the island. Had he been a pensioner he would have been exempt from repayment of the subsidies, but as it was he would have to continue as a farming tenant of the Trust for five years, paying an annual rent of £2,000.

The deal was not yet finalised, with legal work still to be done and finance to be sorted out. The Trust needed an endowment before it could take on the island and Stormonth Darling also had to win over some members of his management team, who – perceptively – felt that the NTS had already been taking on too much and that the difficulties and costs of running a remote island had not been fully appreciated. On his side, John had not explained to the island community what he was intending to do, but before the agreement could be signed the news unexpectedly leaked out. The *Sunday Telegraph* found out about the proposal and published a brief story.

John was outraged – not so much that his plans to hand the island to the Trust had been prematurely made public, but that the article named his wife as 'Ethel', his mother's name, carelessly copied by the reporter from John's entry in *Who's Who*. A 'furious lawyer's letter' was despatched: '[The story] caused some of our more distant friends to wonder if there had been a divorce and remarriage, quite a frequent thing these days.'[6] But he was pleased that negotiations with the Trust had gone well. 'This plan would bring more life into the place and ensure continuation of a sympathetic administration, and relieve me of the worries and responsibilities of landownership.'[7]

With his intention now public, John hurried to explain the arrangements to Ian MacKinnon and to reassure him that there would be no change in their relationship, at least for five years. John would continue as farm tenant and Ian as manager.

Despite the publicity, the transfer of Canna was still far from certain. The National Trust for Scotland's surveys of the island identified a lot of work to be done in modernising properties and improving infrastructure, such as the replacement of the electricity system, which still relied on the generators that John had bought as wartime surplus. In spite of his assertion to the Trust's factor that the farm 'if strictly accounted would show a handsome profit',[8] there were doubts about whether the island could be run on a break-even basis.

Stormonth Darling had the support of his president, but in order to overcome opposition from some of his own professional team and members of the Trust's council, he knew he would have to raise a substantial endowment for the island. John had pledged four fifths of his American trust fund towards the endowment and Trust officials estimated this could be worth £75,000–£80,000, but it would not come until after the death of the last survivor of John and Margaret. In any case it was far less than the £500,000 Trust staff calculated would be the absolute minimum needed to provide sufficient regular income to offset continuing losses and meet the £50,000 purchase price John needed to repay his overdrafts.

In 1981 the Trust launched an appeal to mark its Golden Jubilee, hoping to raise enough to be able to devote £150,000 towards the Canna endowment. To cover the rest, it drafted an application to the National Heritage Memorial Fund, whose chairman was Lord Charteris of Amisfield, Provost of Eton, former private secretary to the Queen and brother of Lord Wemyss. The application was to stress the unique history and attributes of Canna and the value of John's Gaelic library. It would outline the Trust's plan to encourage tourism by modernising two of the cottages and suggest that it might be an idea place to trial renewable energy schemes such as windmills or a tidal generator sited between Canna and Sanday.

John also wrote personally to Lord Charteris emphasising the value of his library and giving the names of academics from around the world who would testify to its worth.

The draft application worked up by NTS staff envisaged a total fund of £500,000 – with £150,000 coming from the Jubilee appeal and £350,000 from the Heritage Fund; however, by the time the claim was submitted the sum required had risen considerably. Trust staff now employed the so-called 'Chorley Formula' developed by the National Trust in England to calculate how much would be needed to provide an adequate regular income. The English body took a much more cautious view of the likely costs and risks involved in taking on a property and had been successful in using the formula to obtain substantial endowments. Under the Chorley methodology the sum demanded for Canna doubled to £1 million. Deducting what the Trust thought it could raise, the Heritage Fund was asked for £850,000.

If any Trust official believed the Wemyss-Charteris family connection would make the application a formality, he was mistaken. Stormonth Darling had no such illusions, knowing that the two brothers did not get on. The Heritage Fund decided to do its own assessment of the island and its financial needs. It was said jokingly that Lord Charteris only knew one accountant, and that was the Queen's accountant – Michael Gerrard ('Gerry') Peat, son of the founder of the blue-blooded firm of Peat, Marwick, Mitchell & Co. He was duly summoned and headed the investigating team himself. His report, hard-headed and thorough, questioned the Trust's ability to correctly estimate the costs of running Canna. It was true that it had taken on other islands – Fair Isle in 1954 and more recently Iona and St Kilda – but the first two had much larger populations and better transport links and the third was uninhabited, so none of them was strictly comparable. It also cast doubt on one of the Trust's central assumptions, that after John stopped farming, the NTS would be able to find a tenant who would take over the farm at his own risk and pay rent.

The Peat report revealed that the farm, far from making a 'handsome profit' as John asserted, had aggregate losses of £37,000 in the five years up until 1980. Tellingly, it added: 'It would therefore seem open to doubt whether such a [farming] partner would be found, in which case it is also open to doubt whether the existing population who depend on the farm for their livelihood could be supported without the Trust incurring the burden of the farm losses.'

The conclusions were not hopeful. The application, Peat added, was not supported by any detailed calculation or extensive research, and the sum required for 'contingencies' at £200,000 was excessive. 'Viewed against the existing endowment funds of the Trust, the amount requested for Canna appears disproportionately large.'[9] Their recommendation was that any grant be scaled back to £350,000–£400,000 – the amount originally estimated by National Trust for Scotland's own managers.

When Stormonth Darling saw a copy of the report he was downcast. 'Where I am naturally getting worried is over the pruning of the various estimates to such an extent that the diffidents (almost dissidents) around the Executive table may have further grounds to say that the whole Canna proposition should be dismissed,' he wrote to Brian Lang, the Heritage Fund's secretary. 'In our discussions here so far, in order to maintain unanimity, we have been careful to use the saving clause "if fully funded".'[10]

If a rebellion against the plan did materialise, it was overcome by Stormonth Darling using his considerable charm and the respect with which he was held within the Trust. His executive committee and the council approved the acquisition of Canna in April 1981 and a legal agreement was signed the following month. John feared an onslaught by the press when the news was officially announced in June and thought he and Margaret ought to decamp from Canna House to a vacant shepherd's cottage to avoid telephone calls. He was persuaded to stay put and although the news did attract considerable press interest, the coverage was moderate and approving.

Many journalists saw the story as a modern fairytale – the husband and wife who had turned their backs on their monied families to nurture and preserve a remote island. Julie Davidson, filling a whole page in the *Scotsman*, wrote of John: 'His story is a romantic one, the story of an individualist whose island isolation has made him something of a visionary but never a fantasist. His strikes against those mainland institutions "who would like to be able to forget the islands" have been conducted by a pen which, at its most astringent, has never been venomous; and by taking the kind of action which cuts the feet from the opposition – usually the Scottish Transport Group, the Scottish Office and the Highlands and Islands Development Board.'[11]

She concluded: 'The Trust may have bought Canna House, their home, with its extensive Celtic and Scottish library, recordings of traditional Gaelic songs and collection of Lepidoptera; but the Campbells will remain, running the library, breeding more Highland cattle and entertaining a stream of friends to good food and music and conversation in the summer dusk.'

It was fair comment. John had given up ownership of the island he had struggled to buy 43 years before, but if he felt the loss in his heart, little else had changed. He was still running the estate, albeit as a tenant farmer rather than owner. He was still living in Canna House surrounded by his unrivalled Gaelic library, extensive collection of original recordings of songs and stories and the eccentric accumulation inherited from his and Margaret's families, or picked up during decades of travel and living in the Western Isles. The farm workers – all members of the MacKinnon family – still took their ultimate orders from him and members of the Trust staff were careful to consult him on anything which concerned the island. To all outward appearances he was still the laird of Canna, although he preferred the Gaelic term 'Fear Chanaidh', which does not carry the same connotation of superiority.

The National Trust for Scotland had become the new owner of Canna, but with a much smaller endowment than several of its managers had thought essential. Stormonth Darling wrote to John in the autumn to tell him that £50,000 had been allocated from the Golden Jubilee Appeal to the Canna endowment[12] – not mentioning that the Trust had promised the National Heritage Fund that its contribution would be three times that amount – but even this was stretching the truth because two years later an internal memo revealed that the £50,000 had still not been passed across and cautioned 'this year with its financial difficulties may not be the year to do so'.[13]

As the old owner to the new, John wrote to Jamie Stormonth Darling with some guidance, learned through his own often painful experience. 'Major' Michael and his own failed plans to repopulate the island were not forgotten.

In due course I'll write you a memorandum on the difficult subject of crofting introduction here, but there is no hurry about that. The main thing is that anybody who comes should be approved beforehand by the people who live here already, should row in the same boat as far as possible and not be competitors with the people who gain their livelihoods here by working on the land, or at lobster fishing – or possible rival centres of power with the farm tenant or the NTS administration.

It is a difficult thing to make the right choice. Here I could talk more freely than I could write. I hope the NTS might be able to take on the farming here after my time with Ian MacKinnon and after him his son Donald as manager; I'm sure that would be better than introducing a new farm tenant.[14]

It was good advice and needed sooner than either man realised.

# CHAPTER NINETEEN

# The Old Order Changes

For a while all went well. Grandees from the Trust council came, were entertained in Canna House and went away impressed by the Gaelic library and seduced by the beauty of the island. John tolerated these occasions more often than he enjoyed them. He knew they were a duty, but his shyness made them painful. On one occasion he complained to Ann Berthoff, who with her husband Warner had been visiting regularly since 1950, that a lunch he had to attend would be 'ridiculous'. 'If you think it will be a "Mickey Mouse" affair wear your Mickey Mouse badge,' she suggested. So he sat through the lunch with a Disney button sent to him by a friend in the US on his lapel, much to the puzzlement of the guests. No one dared to ask him why he was wearing it.

On a lower stratum, work parties of volunteers came to do labour-intensive jobs which the islanders lacked time to do: repointing stonework on the pier, rehabilitating Kate's Cottage, the most remote and isolated of the abandoned dwellings, as a bunk-house for future work parties. There was always rubbish to remove from the beaches, a problem renewed with every incoming tide and becoming more obtrusive as plastic replaced wooden fish boxes, hemp ropes gave way to day-glo blue, green or orange nylon and glass bottles and tin cans were superseded by PVC containers. The detritus of modern life disfigured the beaches and rocks and refused to rot away.

John carried on much as before, although as tenant rather than owner he realised there was no incentive for him to invest in the long-term productivity of the farm. He found new causes to fight. A proposed ban on part-time lobster fishing, which would have hit the income of the MacKinnon family, who had taken over lobster fishing now that he was unable to do it himself; the closure of the Oban telephone exchange; and he continued to supply Jamie

Stormonth Darling with ideas. Some were practical, like looking for new inhabitants who could make things from wool, 'a raw material which we produce in quality and quantity'. Others were a little more speculative: the dream of a small malt whisky distillery producing 'Canna Cream', was, John conceded, a distant prospect – he did not mention that Canna was unlikely to have been able to produce enough barley, nor that its water supply was hardly adequate for the existing population, let alone industrial production. 'The introduction of Gentoo Penguins at Garrisdale might be achievable sooner,' he thought.[1]

However, change had come and in subtle ways began to be felt. Important decisions were no longer made on the island, but in the regional office of the National Trust for Scotland more than 100 miles away in Inverness, or even more remotely, in the Edinburgh headquarters. Donald John MacKinnon, Ian and Norah's oldest son, who was still living with his parents, wrote to the Trust requesting a house of his own. All five MacKinnon children were living with their parents or their aunt and the Trust began to realise the scale of the task it had taken on. As they reached adulthood it was important that they had places of their own, so that they could marry and – it was hoped – bring their partners to the island.

For this to happen the Trust, which owned most of the properties and all the land, either had to make houses available for them, or provide sites where they could build their own houses – as John had done with Angus MacKinnon, Ian's younger brother who had built a new bungalow on Sanday. Trust officials were sympathetic and began to think about how homes could be provided, but their discussions were internal and not communicated to Canna. Donald John wrote: 'The islanders always seem to be kept in the dark about things which affect them more than anyone. Surely they could be consulted about matters which concern them?'[2]

More personal changes were coming too. John's health was not good. He was in his mid-70s, the stamina he had enjoyed even a few years before was deserting him and he was starting to suffer pains in his chest. His doctor told him he had a heart condition – he had to give up farming and would soon need major surgery. To add to his discomfort, the winter of 1982–83 was extremely cold, the worst John had experienced since Barra in 1936 – 'Damart seems right out of winter underwear,' he complained, 'are they selling it all to the Russians?'[3] At the beginning of 1983 he wrote to the NTS telling them he wanted to give up tenancy of the Canna farm on Whit Sunday (23 May). He also wrote to the Department of Agriculture for Scotland enclosing his doctor's letter and asking that, since he was being forced to give up farming because of ill-health, he be excused repayment of the outstanding sheep subsidies.

This transition was coming very much sooner than John had hoped or planned and he was very concerned about who would take over the farm. The Trust still favoured a tenancy arrangement, with the farming tenant not only paying rent, but also taking on the risk of the farm losing money. Ian MacKinnon was offered the tenancy, either alone or in partnership with his brother Angus, but he turned it down. As a farm worker, paid at the statutory level all his working life, he had no financial resources to fall back on if the farm could not be made to pay.

John, with his education in estate management and long years in farming, knew very well how Canna could be turned into a commercial success. An absentee tenant farmer could get rid of all the cattle, turn the whole island over to sheep either left to fend for themselves or under the care of one shepherd, with contractors brought in for lambing, shearing and rounding-up animals for sale. The Trust might make a profit from such an arrangement, but the community and the conservation value of the island would be damaged, perhaps fatally.

He tried as much as he could to influence the decision: 'I can't see the Trust would want a commercial farmer here, who would bring in his own men, disperse the Highland herd and throw weed killers and insecticides around on the arable land, but if I were to be succeeded by such a person in the tenancy, I would expect to be paid full value for my farm live and dead stock and I doubt very much if Margaret and I would want to go on living here if such a person took over.'[4]

Stormonth Darling was in two minds, perhaps remembering the warning from the Peat, Marwick report that the Trust could be left shouldering the losses of the farm. In an internal memo he weighed two alternatives – that the Trust might find an outsider to take on the farm and continue with the present workforce, or that it would take over the farm itself and look for a benefactor who might donate £10,000 a year for four or five years to cover any shortfall.[5] A major problem was that the farm provided the only full-time employment on the island and was currently paying the wages of five people, Ian MacKinnon and his brother Angus, Ian's sons Donald and Patrick and daughter Geraldine.

Everyone realised that the farm was overstaffed by modern standards and that an outsider was unlikely to guarantee employment. That would force the younger MacKinnons to leave and would put the population of Canna on a downward path. Faced with this stark decision, the Trust director opted to keep the community intact. NTS itself would take over the farm, employing Ian as manager, three of his children and his brother. Stormonth Darling visited the island, but clearly had some apprehensions about the financial consequences of what he had decided. 'I was impressed (or depressed!) by the amount to be done everywhere – especially on Sanday, where everything is so run down,' he wrote to a colleague. At a meeting of all the islanders in Canna House he explained the heavy financial burden the Trust had taken on and stressed the need for everyone to work with the Trust to make the estate viable.

John was very pleased. The formal arrangements were quickly decided. He and Margaret would donate the herd of pedigree Highland cattle to the Trust, which would buy all other 'live and dead stock' – cattle, sheep, machinery and implements – at valuation. Shortly afterwards Jamie Stormonth Darling was knighted and retired from the NTS. Margaret was in no doubt about the debt she and John owed him. She wrote congratulating him on his knighthood. 'It is [owing] to you that Canna belongs to the Trust today and makes us secure in its future. You also know what love we have for this precious island and for the cherished friends here who are part of its very earth.'[6]

The employment situation on the island eased a few months later when Angus MacKinnon told the Trust he was emigrating. Like his brother, Wee Hector, Angus had married a New Zealand girl who had worked as an au pair in Canna House, now he was following his brother to make a new life on the other side of the world. He hastened to assure the Trust that his departure had nothing to do with the transfer of ownership of Canna and Stormonth Darling gave him a glowing reference, but his departure was a blow to the island. Angus was popular and a hard worker, but he also had two young children, who were attending the island's primary school. It was largely their future which had persuaded him to go, they lacked friends of their own age on the island and when they reached secondary school would have to board on the mainland.

The family's departure reduced the population by a quarter. His jobs – he combined farm work with being the mechanic and electrician – were given to his nephew Patrick, known as Packie. Later Geraldine left the island to go to agricultural college and get farming experience on the mainland.

John was now free of responsibility for the farm, but had found another project to keep him busy. Stormonth Darling had suggested that he write the definitive history of Canna and, with some secretarial help partly paid for by the Trust, he had thrown himself into the work. He had already amassed a wealth of source material and with his knowledge of Highland history and expertise in scholarship he was ideally placed to write the book.

The Trust was not going to produce the work itself, but had promised to help find a publisher. If they expected a straightforward uncontroversial volume, they were mistaken. In telling the story of the island from its days as a Norse and early Christian settlement, John was determined to write the book 'from the point of view of a Gaelic-speaking Jacobite islander, turning a good deal of official Hebridean history upside-down'.[7] He began with the startling assertion that Canna had been visited by St Columba, founder of the Celtic Christian Church in Scotland, and was in fact the island described in an early biography of the saint as 'Hinba'. He produced a lot of circumstantial evidence to back his claim, but few scholars were convinced.

He thought the Trust would be excited by his claim – they already owned Iona, where Columba had founded his monastery, now he was offering them the chance to claim custodianship of a second important religious site, but the Trust were unconcerned about a 1,400-year-old controversy. What did alarm them when they saw the manuscript of John's chapter on Canna in modern times was his retelling of the political battle to stop the Small Boat Scheme.

He had a few old scores to settle, particularly against the Highlands and Islands Development Board, which he felt had betrayed him by backing Keith Schellenberg, the owner of Eigg, who had wanted the subsidy withdrawn from the state-owned ferry company Caledonian MacBrayne. With the same fearlessness he had shown in his first book* published 50 years before, he laid into the establishment with relish, alleging that the Board had acted 'with a noticeable degree of hostility towards its opponents'.

The Trust was trying hard to develop friendly relations with the HIDB and particularly to persuade it to co-finance projects on Canna. The Trust's factor called for the toning-down of 'somewhat intemperate language' but the president, Lord Wemyss, went further, demanding the suppression of the chapter on transport on the grounds that it was 'the most boring subject conceivable for those not involved' and that John's account was 'not quite complete, slightly inaccurate and misleading in places'.[8] John defended himself: 'Authors can be difficult about the futures of their brainchildren. In the case of this book, it hasn't just been researched – it has also been lived, which makes for an even stronger involvement.'[9] But he agreed in the end to take out some material and moderate his language.

This was not the only embarrassment. Around the same time NTS senior managers and its new director, Lester Borley, had been wooing Ranald Alexander Macdonald, 24th Captain of Clanranald. They intended to ask him to finance the restoration of the stone bothy on the shore below Canna House and adopt it as a Clan Macdonald project. Their argument was that it was popularly called 'the Clanranald House' and there was a story that Dòmhnall Dubh of Clanranald – a notorious chief of the clan – had died there in 1686.

Macdonald seemed quite interested, visited Canna and was entertained in Tighard. He sent the Trust director copies of pages from *The Young Chevalier, Or a Genuine Narrative of all that befell that Unfortunate Adventurer*, a nineteenth-century history which claimed that Bonnie Prince Charlie had visited Canna during his escape after his defeat at Culloden. But John torpedoed the Trust's funding case by showing that the house in question had not been built until nearly 100 years after Dòmhnall Dubh's demise. It should not be called

---

* *Highland Songs of the Forty-Five*

Clanranald's house, but more accurately MacNeill's house, he insisted. 'Bang goes my chance of getting any money out of Clanranald,' wrote one exasperated Trust executive.

In August 1984 John went into hospital in Edinburgh to have a mitral valve in his heart replaced and was in intensive care for several weeks, with only close relatives allowed to visit. Morton Boyd, director of the Nature Conservancy Council, put on his white lab coat to bluff his way past the ward sister. John, still coming round from the effects of the operation and the anaesthetic, recognised his close friend, but was convinced that he was in hospital in the north of Sweden and that the nurses were speaking Swedish. John later told the story against himself with amusement. The operation was a success, but he needed a long recuperation and he and Margaret went for six weeks to the Villa San Giralomo in Fiesole near Florence, a guest house surrounded by gardens and run by the Blue Nuns, an Irish order who spoke Gaelic. The Campbells had visited several times already and it had become one of their favourite places to rest and recover.

The National Trust for Scotland was also changing. The benevolent patricianism of Sir James Stormonth Darling, with his myriad connections among the Great and Good of Scotland, was replaced by a much more direct – some would say abrasive – managerial style. The new director, Lester Borley, was a grammar school boy from Dover and although he was at pains to tell John that his university degree had been in geography and anthropology, it was his background in tourism which most attracted the NTS. He had been chief executive of both the Scottish and English tourist boards and he believed that increasing visitors to Trust properties was a way of bringing much-needed income into the organisation.

His focus on building up visits and membership certainly produced results. By 1989 membership had topped 200,000, double the number of a decade before, and visitor numbers exceeded 1,725,000, but that success brought criticism that the Trust had abandoned conservation for the entertainment industry. Borley defended himself against his accusers in robust style. He told the journalist Anne Johnstone: 'We are a conservation body which has become more and more involved with tourism.' When she tried to put more detailed criticisms to him he waved her aside with responses such as 'stupid' and 'nonsense'. 'These questions are asked by people who aren't in the business of conserving and opening to the public. They don't understand.'[10]

The problem Borley faced, however, was stark. From caring for 38 properties in 1944, by 1989 the Trust had 104 and in only a handful of cases did the individual endowments which came with them provide enough income to cover running costs and essential maintenance. Canna was no exception. While John was the farming tenant, bearing the risk on the estate and paying rent to the Trust, the island managed to break even or show a small profit, but as soon as the Trust took over the farm itself the losses started to mount, from a deficit of £17,000 in 1983–84 to over £100,000 by 1991–92.[11]

There was heavy expenditure on modernising cottages – to a standard John felt was far in excess of what Hebridean farm workers would expect – and on rebuilding The Square, the main farmhouse, which had burnt down. The Trust again infuriated John by deciding to pull down the ruin and build the new house at right-angles to the original, giving it a view over the harbour, but destroying the concept of a 'square'. He went to the length of employing his own surveyor to show that the house could be rebuilt on its old foundations, but to no avail. How much of this was the former owner showing characteristic inconsistency? John hated the new house, describing it as 'hideous', but it was a white-harled cottage which looked very similar from the outside to the building it had replaced. While he had been the proprietor, he had built Caslum, a pre-fabricated, pebble-dashed bungalow for a shepherd, but seemed not to care about the incongruous blot it made on the landscape.

There were other more justifiable criticisms. The Trust was spending much more on the farm than John had done. With no farming experience of its own, it brought in a farming adviser. 'The island is now in a very irritated mood following the Trust's appointment of a Berwickshire farmer, unexperienced [*sic*] in island conditions, as "Budget Controller", (i.e. boss) of the farm here,' he wrote to Angus McIntosh.

He came in June with the other administration, was not introduced to the staff, who thought he was a visiting farmer come to look on at the fank,* and who were astounded and furious when he started to issue brusque orders. One of the things he said, on the basis of this minimal acquaintance with local conditions, was that the herd of Cheviot sheep should be got rid of – this without bothering to consult my records – the Cheviot sheep always produce more money than the blackfaces, even if they usually produce fewer lambs.[12]

That was not the only point on which John disagreed with the new appointment. On the adviser's recommendation the Trust bought a new, large muck spreader, only to find that it was too heavy to be pulled by the old, small tractors which had been taken over from John. New, heavier tractors were bought which shattered the tile field drains, making the fields boggy.

The Canna endowment had grown with good investment returns, but it was still inadequate to meet the costs. The Trust obtained grants to cover some of its improvements, but it was still having to dip into its general funds to meet the deficits. Borley did not see why Canna could not be made to pay more of its own way by attracting more visitors and therefore income – a proposal which met with stout opposition from John. Canna, which lacked a shop, a café – even public lavatories – did not have the facilities for more than a few visitors at a time and the available accommodation was needed for the local population.

The Trust director accepted that Canna House could not be opened to the public while John and Margaret were living there, but he wondered whether visitors might be allowed to visit the unique Gaelic library the Trust had acquired with the island. The idea was dismissed outright by John and at a confrontation in the dining room at Canna House he got up and walked out when it was suggested. He was happy to show his books to *bona fide* scholars, but argued that the library was too small for parties to look around and in any case there was a risk that some of the rarer, more valuable books might be pilfered.

The exchange set the tone for the steadily deteriorating relationship between Lester Borley and Canna's former proprietor. John and Margaret began to see him as the root of all the slights, real and

---

* Sheep fold

imagined, they felt were being dealt to their island legacy and they were prepared to express themselves publicly. John spoke openly to reporters voicing his misgivings and telling *Country Living* magazine that he bitterly regretted giving the island to the National Trust for Scotland. 'There were no strings to the gift because I felt I was making it to friends. Instead of conditions there was a gentleman's agreement which was never codified. The understanding was that the Trust would leave things as they were. It would conserve, not develop. But there are new men in charge now at the National Trust for Scotland and I suspect they have plans that would completely ruin the place. Most likely they are just waiting for me to die, then they will be able to do as they like.'[13]

Strong words, but perhaps the conflict brought some personal benefits. More than one old friend thought the battle with the Trust helped to keep John sharp and alive in his declining years.

# CHAPTER TWENTY

# Despair and Recovery

At the end of 1985, Angus McIntosh had written to tell John and Margaret that a group of influential supporters had met to discuss forming a 'Friends of Canna Society.' Prominent amongst them were the Trust 'Old Guard', including Lord Wemyss, Jamie Stormonth Darling and Kate Hardie, who had been the director's secretary at the NTS and had become a special friend to the Campbells. The aims were said to be to support the Trust in carrying out projects on Canna and to help by raising funds from foundations, corporations and individuals, but John saw the 'Friends of Canna' as a way of bringing more pressure to bear on the Trust management.

Although he said that he wanted to stay in the background, he took a lead by inviting the distinguished diplomat and author Sir Fitzroy MacLean to become the Society's first president. 'Admittedly the Trust is well-intentioned, but not always imaginative or well-experienced,' John told him. 'there is the general matter of priorities, e.g. while the idea of making a causeway between Canna and Sanday is on their scheme of projects, that is much less important than the repair and improvement of the present roads on Canna, which are now in a deplorable condition, indeed dangerous in some places.'[1] He complained about the heavy-handed administration of the farm, then added: 'The Trust agreed at the time of donation to maintain Canna as a traditional Hebridean community which, to our minds meant seeking Gaelic-speaking incomers from Barra or South Uist – I don't know to what extent any real effort was made to do this. Promises made then don't seem to have been codified or passed down through the administration.'

The Trust may not have done much to find new immigrants from the outer isles, but Lester Borley was keen to keep the Gaelic heritage of Canna intact. When a new teacher for the primary school had been appointed by the council, he asked why a native speaker could not be chosen. The response he received was not encouraging. 'No Gaelic speaker applied,' the Trust's Highland factor told him. 'I find that islanders and West Highlanders do not on the whole want to go to more isolated places than those where they are at present. The people who want to go to isolated islands are those who come from England and the main cities and want to get away from it all.'[2]

This was to prove to be the Trust's own experience when it started advertising for families to move to the island. Overwhelmingly the response came from people living in towns and cities, not from the Gaelic islands. To replace Angus and Geraldine MacKinnon, the Trust brought in a farmhand, his wife and three children from mainland Scotland and an English building contractor, with his wife and their young children. With the newly appointed schoolteacher and her husband, this increased the size of the community by more than half. For a few years things seemed to go reasonably well and incomers and indigenous residents appeared to get along. The new families were invited to the weekly billiards evenings in Canna House and often stopped in for tea on their way to or from the pier, traditional meeting place for the island whenever the ferry called.

But in small communities minor personal differences, which might be absorbed by larger populations, can be magnified out of all proportion. John had found this himself when he tried to introduce new blood in 1938. Now the Trust was facing the same problems. The first sign that something was wrong was an investigation by the Inverness regional headquarters of the Post Office of issues raised by an unidentified complainant. Mail was reportedly being delivered late or not at all to individual houses on Canna and Sanday; and the Post Office, a shed on the shore staffed by Winnie MacKinnon, was not open all the hours that it should have been.

The identity of the protagonist did not stay a secret very long as the story was leaked to local newspapers. Leading the attack was the schoolteacher's husband, who demanded a postal delivery service to individual houses on Sanday, rather than residents having to pick up their mail from the Post Office, or have it dropped off by their neighbours, which had been the practice on the island for decades. The Post Office revealed that in addition to his other jobs as farm manager, piermaster and coastguard, Ian MacKinnon was the island's postman.

Some newspapers treated the story as a 'Monarch of the Glen' type farce – a chance to make fun at the expense of the islanders. John did not take it lightly and he reacted with fury at what he saw as an unprovoked attack on his friend and on the whole indigenous population. His attitude to his ownership of Canna had been gradually changing since the radical reformer and redistributionist of the 1930s. He still wanted to fight for the rights of crofters and farm workers, but now he identified much more with the traditions of his family and was content to be called (in fact to call himself) a laird, even though he did not own the island.

'It was from my Campbell grandfather that I learned that it was the duty of a Highland laird to defend his tenants and employees – as Highlanders we did not consider a cash nexus the sole basis of our personal relationships with them,' he wrote. 'That was the basis of my own relationship with the Canna people. I can see that nowadays it is considered to be an old fashioned one, but I am prepared to stand by it at all times. If the laird wants loyalty from his tenants and employees, he must be loyal to them.'[3]

He wrote in uncharacteristically restrained terms to the *Oban Times* protesting at the mountains which were being made out of molehills, but in private he railed against the 'White Settler mentality of the incomers.' John's letter only provoked a prolonged exchange, with former residents and visitors writing to give their experiences and opinions on one side or the other.

It may have been a storm in a teacup, which was resolved in the end by a compromise, but the emotions stirred up did not die down so quickly. The issue split the community, with the contractor and his family lining up behind the complainant while the Campbells and the MacKinnons defended Ian. The Trust was at a loss to know what to do to restore calm and one manager wrote to a councillor on the education committee: 'Apart from inciting the *West Highland Free Press* to publish a long and critical article last summer he [the schoolteacher's husband] has reported not just the Trust but more seriously other individual islanders to the Health and Safety at Work authorities, the Nature Conservancy Council, CalMac, the Trust headquarters and the GPO.' Talks had failed to resolve the issue so the Trust manager asked for drastic action. 'I appreciate you cannot sack a teacher because of her husband – and she is actually an extremely good teacher – but if there is anything that could be done, perhaps to transfer them elsewhere, then the folk on Canna would, I think, be forever grateful and it would certainly be greeted with relief in this office.'[4]

The transfer was not forthcoming, but a new crisis brought matters to a head. The farm worker whom the Trust had brought to the island was convicted of assaulting the schoolteacher and the contractor's wife. The court case, with its story of the women forced to flee into the hills barefoot in their nightclothes to hide while the police were called, made lurid headlines and again focused attention on the small, by now unhappy island and reopened old divisions. In a sad note to Lester Borley, John reported that the Saturday evening billiard sessions had ceased after New Year's Eve 1989, 'ending a continuous run since 1947, owing to the increasing hostility of the Sanday settlers towards the Canna people'.

This time the Trust felt it had to take decisive action, sacked the farmhand and banned him from the island, despite appeals from the MacKinnons and the Campbells to allow him to stay. This did not resolve the problem. The schoolteacher resigned and moved elsewhere, but her husband stayed. The Trust had to go to court to evict him and decided also that the contractor and his family must go too. There were more newspaper headlines and accusations of racial and religious bigotry because those being evicted were neither Gaelic-speaking nor Catholic.

The publicity distressed John and Margaret, and he made a formal complaint about a news report on BBC television, but it was rejected. They were particularly bitter at the Trust for not defending the people of Canna in public, but the Trust did not know what line to take, everything it said seemed to make matters worse. Its attempts to increase the island's population had been no more successful than John's had been four decades before. All those it had brought to the island had been forced to leave and the school was closed, since there were no longer any school-age children on Canna or Sanday.

In 1992 Ian MacKinnon died at the age of 52. This was a tragic loss for his family and a severe blow to the Campbells. Ian had worked on the farm since leaving school at the age of 14. They counted him as a friend and supporter as well as an able farm manager, but his death also marked the passing of an era. He was the last person born on the island who had grown up speaking Gaelic and had assumed the mantle of the island tradition-bearer from the previous generation. He knew the history and folklore of the island and was an authority on its Gaelic place names. His death drove a new wedge between the Trust and the island.

The NTS regional head wrote to the director:

> The fact is that the family believe that Ian died of stress brought on by the Trust because we dismissed [the farmworker]. It was fundamentally my decision and responsibility, which they know. I still believe that decision was made carefully and in all the circumstances correctly, but this is a case where being right is not enough. I was told 'I hope you're satisfied now' and worse 'You b— killed him', all backed up by a determination that the Trust was not to be at the funeral. Knowing them well I am sure this was no unintended emotional outburst, and that they will neither forget nor forgive. I heard real venom in their voices.[5]

In an attempt to defuse the issue the Trust appointed a 'high level working party' to consider the future of Canna, but a more direct and personal intervention helped to mend damaged relations. Although the current Trust executives were *personae non gratae* when Ian MacKinnon was laid to rest in the small island burial ground, the Trust Old Guard in the form of Sir James Stormonth Darling and Lord Wemyss braved spring storms to make the crossing to Canna. Margaret wrote: 'To have David Wemyss and Jamie, brought to the MacKinnons as well as ourselves the Trust that we knew and loved. It was all God given and such a tribute to Ian.'[6]

★

The relationship between the NTS management and the Campbells improved when Lester Borley retired. Fairly or unfairly, he had come to symbolise everything they disliked about the Trust and his leaving gave them a reason to change their attitude. The new director, Rear Admiral Douglas Dow, brought his wife to Canna, met all the inhabitants and listened patiently to all John and Margaret's complaints. Nothing dramatic changed for the better, but the bad times were seen to have passed. 'John is in fine form, busy writing as usual,' Margaret wrote. 'Canna is looking her best, glorious weather and we are now so very happy with the new director. We had years of misery and worry before his miraculous appointment.'[7]

In fact, even before Dow's appointment, senior people in the Trust had become concerned that John, a distinguished scholar, was living out his late eighties unhappy and regretting having given Canna to the NTS. Lord Bute, who had taken over as president from Lord Wemyss, convened a meeting at Mount Stuart, his stately home on the Isle of Bute, which led to a decision to produce a comprehensive five-year plan for the island, encompassing the farm, Canna House and the Gaelic library. At the same time he used another of his positions, as chairman of the National Museums of Scotland, to approach Dr Hugh Cheape of the museums' curatorial staff to ask him to visit Canna.

Cheape, a historian and musicologist, had already met John Campbell once, but also felt he was in his debt. As a young student nearly 20 years before, he had written to ask for help and had been amazed to receive not only a long and carefully considered letter, but a parcel of books and articles: 'To someone he had never met this seemed to me to be a remarkable act of generosity.' He accepted an invitation to visit the island on board Lord Bute's yacht, the *King Duck*, in a party which also included Sir James and Lady Stormonth Darling and the editor of the *Scotsman*, Magnus Linklater, and his wife Veronica.

'We made our way up to Canna House,' Cheape remembered, 'and my first and lasting impression was of the warmth and hospitality we received from the Campbells in their home, typical of the old Highland tacksman's house – learning, civilisation and conviviality in the middle of the seas. Margaret's grand piano stood in the living room. There were butterflies and insects in glass cases and books occupying every available space.

'I was absolutely overwhelmed by the amount of material in the house. There was a very substantial library and cultural archive for Celtic and Norse Studies, Gaelic language, philology, literature and Scottish history and a collection of 1,500 Gaelic folksongs and 350 folk tales. It was one of the most comprehensive private collections of the Celtic languages and literature that I had ever seen. In fact nothing stands in comparison with the Canna House archive as a single historical resource for Celtic Studies amassed by a single scholar. It was an absolute treasure trove.'

In the following years Cheape became not only the champion of Canna within the National Trust, but a close confidant of John, helping him with the archive and preparing some of his shorter pieces for publication. During their work together John expressed his sadness that since he had donated the library, no one from the Trust had ever asked him about his work. To them the culture to which he had devoted his life was not a living thing, but another relic to be preserved. At the same time he expressed sympathy for the Trust: 'I must have been a hard act to follow.'

In 1994 Cheape and John Morton Boyd, chief executive of the Nature Conservancy Council, wrote a Citation of Heritage defining the island's natural and cultural assets and its resources. It was endorsed by 12 academic authorities in the sciences and 12 authorities in the humanities, who agreed that the library and archive must be preserved on Canna to become a focus for scholarship. It formed the basis for a £1.75 million application to the National Heritage Lottery Millennium Fund to secure the future of the island, its community and heritage. The intention was that Canna House become a centre for Gaelic scholarship and research, Corroghon, a listed stone barn overlooking the black sand beach, be converted as a centre for terrestrial and marine sciences and Tarbet, an abandoned farmhouse, become a field station for a nature reserve on the west of the island. After a huge amount of work, the bid was rejected, along with many other small or remote projects, as lottery cash was diverted to the 'folly' of the Millennium Dome in London.

Nevertheless, a Canna Advisory Group was established, including Cheape, Boyd, Professor William Gillies of the University of Edinburgh, Neil Fraser, the BBC's Head of Gaelic Broadcasting, and Neill Campbell, John's nephew. After a long period of neglect, efforts began to protect the library and fulfil its potential. The School of Scottish Studies at the University of Edinburgh was given a contract to construct an index of the Canna sound archive, the thousands of recordings made by the Campbells in the Western Isles and Nova Scotia. Digitisation began of nearly 9,000 negatives and prints taken by Margaret over 80 years of photography. The British

Library sound archive worked on the conservation of the wax cylinder recordings. Cheape wrote to university Celtic departments, alerting them to the value of the Canna archive and cooperation began to be established with the University of Aberdeen, the newly founded University of the Highlands and Islands and Sabhal Mòr Ostaig, the Gaelic college on Skye.

Having not sought wider recognition, John was becoming a minor celebrity. The BBC made radio programmes about him in English and Gaelic. In 1989 he was elected to a fellowship of the Royal Society of Edinburgh. He had always been wary of mixing with the 'Edinburgh Establishment', but he accepted the honour on the understanding that he did not have to attend meetings very often. The following year he was awarded the OBE. He claimed he was too infirm to attend an investiture at the Palace of Holyrood House, Edinburgh, although he made longer and more arduous journeys before and afterwards. The thought of bowing before a Hanoverian monarch may have been too much for him. The Lord Lieutenant of the county travelled to Canna to present the award, but the ceremony nearly did not take place. John was overcome by shyness and had to be coaxed into the meeting.

In 1992 he received a Papal Knighthood. This accolade pleased him most, since it was granted on the recommendation of the Catholic priests of the islands and West Highlands – men he respected and had worked with over decades. A traditionalist in religious matters who always favoured the Latin Mass, he nevertheless petitioned the Church authorities to have the service of investiture in Gaelic.

He was also keeping up his writing output, working on articles and essays. *Songs Remembered in Exile*, a book of the traditional Gaelic songs he had recorded in Nova Scotia in 1937 and 1953 appeared in 1990, although not without drama when the publisher, Aberdeen University Press, which had been bought by Robert Maxwell, fell victim to the collapse of the old fraudster's empire after his suicide. Margaret, too, had been busy. Her autobiography, *From the Alleghenies to the Hebrides*, on which she had been working for several years, was published in 1993.

Although in his late 80s, John scanned the news daily and maintained a lively curiosity. He took a deep interest in a case of alleged Satanism and ritualistic child abuse on the Orkney island of South Ronaldsay. Parents and the local minister were said to have been involved in sexual rites and police and social workers took the children into care. While others searched for contemporary answers, John saw parallels with allegations of witchcraft and sabbats in the Basque region reported to the Spanish Inquisition in 1614. In a rare instance of rationality, the Inquisition found that the stories were baseless and the product of mass hysteria.

John was convinced that the Orkney case was the same and he bombarded his friends with letters and articles. He and Hugh Cheape were preparing a collection of essays on the history and culture of the Highlands and Islands, provisionally titled *Echoes of the Hebrides.*[8] John insisted that his Orkney article be included. When the publisher demurred, he dug in his heels and withdrew the manuscript. 'John can be so cussed and no use boiling over', Margaret told Ann Berthoff.[9] However, a public inquiry proved him right, there had been no Satanism in Orkney.

The distraction from Gaelic did not last for long. In 1994–95 John was working on a major reappraisal of the life and work of Alasdair MacMhaighstir Alasdair, known in English as Alexander Mac-Donald. He was a renowned Gaelic poet and especially interested John because for a period he had been Baillie of Canna. He had written about him in his first book, *Highland Songs of the Forty-Five*, at more length in his history of Canna and in numerous articles, but was still intrigued by the gaps in his story and the apparent contra-dictions in his life. He was the son of an Episcopalian minister and for a while worked for the Society for the Propagation of Christian Knowledge (SPCK), a fiercely anti-Catholic and anti-Gaelic orga-nisation. But he became Bonnie Prince Charlie's Gaelic tutor and fought as a Jacobite officer throughout the '45 campaign.

MacDonald's book of 32 poems was the first volume of Gaelic poetry printed in Scotland and John was intrigued by its rich variety which, 'like his own personality is an unusual mixture of contra-dictions and opposites'.[10] There was a poem in praise of the Gaelic language, love poems, nature poems and one urging Highlanders to rise again against the Hanoverians, but also satires (John noted: 'some obscene') and a poem on the coming of venereal disease to Ardnamurchan. John commented: 'it is of great interest for the medical history of the Highlands, but has been suppressed as immoral since 1802'.[11]

He continued to pick and choose to whom he would talk. When the curator of Aberdeen Art Gallery arrived to discuss history, John sat (in Margaret's words) 'like a stone Buddha'. Two Highlanders arrived during lunch and asked to see the carved Celtic stones. 'John never moved from his plate.' But he was animated and articulate when in early 1995 a BBC film crew spent several weeks on the island filming *Fear Chanaidh,* an hour-long profile. The process was tiring, but John performed well for the camera and both he and Margaret enjoyed the experience and warmed to the Gaelic-speaking interviewer and crew. 'Cathy MacDonald is lovely to look at, smart and knew how to bring the best from John,'[12] she wrote to Ann Berthoff.

The stream of guests continued. In July Margaret was reporting that in little over a month 40 people had signed the visitors' book. She delighted in the weather: 'No one remembers such a summer on Canna, sunlight, blinding sun.' September brought a bumper crop of apples in the orchard and a 'surfeit of Red Admirals' which enchanted John. But the end of the year turned cold and on 16 December both Campbells retired to bed with bad coughs, although Margaret rose at 6 a.m. to stuff and roast a chicken for the captain and crew of the *Lochmor,* the Christmas lunch which she always cooked for them.

Both the bad weather and their poor health continued until the end of the year: 'Cables coated with ice have fallen from Shetland down through the Outer Isles, never was there such a Christmas for misery,' she wrote. 'I am taking time to pull myself together, John still in bed and I am trying to inspire him to put on his clothes. He will need a little energy in his wobbly shanks.'[13]

# Who Can Tell His Place of Dying?[1]

*S coma uair no àit' ar n-eug dhuinn*
*'S greadhnachas gun fheum ar tòrraidh*★

In April 1996 John and Margaret again visited Fiesole to stay in Villa San Giralomo. It had become an annual habit, a chance to recover from the Canna winter and refresh themselves in readiness for summer visitors. Several of the Blue Nuns, who ran the 50-room guesthouse, had become personal friends and John, recovered from his winter illnesses, relished the chance to speak Irish Gaelic with them. The villa's terrace gave an incomparable view across gardens, orchards and private villas to the roofs of Florence, dominated by the distinctive terracotta dome of Brunelleschi's cathedral. In the distance beyond was the Arno valley and its surrounding mountains.

On the morning of the 25th he had been netting moths in the garden. The day was warm enough to have lunch outside, but at the start of the meal John interrupted Margaret to point out a butterfly. As he did so he slumped to the table, dying instantly from a heart attack. He was five months short of his ninetieth birthday.

John's death brought to an end a remarkable 60-year marriage. It had been a partnership of equals. Margaret had established her independence and reputation as a folksong collector before she met John and she never gave up either. She was happy to be called Mrs Campbell, but she loved the fact that in South Uist she was still known by her maiden name and would be asked: 'Miss Shaw, how is Mr Campbell?' Husband and wife brought unique qualities to the relationship. She acknowledged his scholarship, farming expertise and capacity for prolonged hard work. He valued her grit and ability to speak her mind at times when he was too tongue-tied to do so.

★ The time or place of our death doesn't matter, Since happiness doesn't need a funeral. *From Bàrdachd Mhgr. Ailein*. The Gaelic Poems of Fr Allan MacDonald. Transcribed, translated and published by John Lorne Campbell, 1965.

It was also a long love story, against the most romantic of backgrounds – islands and boats, a life suffused with humour, music, poetry, a language and a culture which, although foreign to both of them, became their shared passion. When they first met, his tall, slim build, dark good looks, education and sharp intellect might have been intimidating had she not quickly discerned the vulnerability caused by his shyness and lack of confidence. She did her best to help him overcome both. Neither partner was very demonstrative in public, Margaret referring to John as 'you Old Goat', when correcting him on the date or place in which a photograph had been taken. She soon gave up trying to change him, but loved him for what he was. One birthday she gave him an embroidery sampler of designs for a waistcoat and a poem to go with it:

> Behold on the pier stands the bold laird of Canna,
> His eye to the sky as he wolfs a banana,
> The tatters and tears of his old coat aflutter
> Which his poor wife would gladly consign to the gutter.
>
> The hat and the shoes, the trews and the shirt,
> Along with his coat are covered in dirt.
> How can she take pride in her new suit from Jaeger
> If her man will insist on going clad as a beggar?
>
> Now here are some remnants of waistcoats so fine
> (They are framed to preserve them from passage of time)
> Such fine silks and satins the Campbells once wore
> Embroidered by Chinamen especially for
> The elegant gentry who took pride to see
> Their dress more suited their lofty degree.
>
> Birds, butterflies, flowers in stitches so small
> You must put on glasses to see them at all.
> What a contrast in coverage, alas we can say,
> But we love nonetheless – and so Happy Birthday!

She recognised that the young radical she had fallen in love with was also intensely proud of his family history – even if he had turned his back on its religion and politics. She cashed some shares to buy him Romney's portrait of Sir Archibald Campbell and allowed him to hang it in the dining room. That was a concession on her part considering 'Archie's' behaviour during the American War of Independence.

He liked to give her surprises: a white dinghy with *Mairead*, her name in Gaelic, on the transom; a wooden summer-house on the edge of a wood on the slopes of Compass Hill, which he had ordered from Sweden and assembled in secret. He recognised her need sometimes to be on her own. She could retire there to write, paint or, sitting on its verandah, contemplate the matchless view to Sanday and Rum.

Now Margaret was without John for the first time since 1935. Magda, at home in Spain, was shocked to receive a call from the National Trust for Scotland Inverness office telling her of John's death. He had telephoned her the evening before and had seemed fine. She called Margaret, who told her there was no need for her to come – the nuns would handle the arrangements. John had asked to be 'buried where he fell', and so would be interred in Fiesole. It was Maria Carmen who insisted that they should go and the two sisters arrived just as the requiem mass for John was about to begin.

After the burial Maria Carmen returned to her family and Magda accompanied Margaret back to Canna. They were met by Sheila Lockett at Mallaig. It did not take Margaret long to decide that she wanted to stay in Canna House, she did not want to move to the mainland and, at the age of 93 was not ready for an old people's home. Shortly afterwards Magda moved to Canna to be Margaret's companion and later the same year was given the post of archivist by the National Trust for Scotland, working to catalogue and conserve John's life work.

One of his last pieces of writing was published after his death, an essay on the Gaelic words from Eigg and Skye collected by the Rev. Kenneth MacLeod, which appeared in a Festschrift – a collection of learned articles – for Professor Derick Thomson. The three men, John, MacLeod and Thomson, had worked together in the short-lived Folklore Institute of Scotland half a century before. Among scholarly papers on 'The Irregular Verb' and 'Time and Aspect in the Scottish Gaelic Verbal System: a working paper on definitions and presentation', John's contribution stood out. It summed up his interest in the living Gaelic language, being the sayings of ordinary people, proverbs, metaphors and expletives. Among the more mundane phrases were a few which would have given John a wry smile as he typed them: *Buinneach air!* (May he get diarrhoea!) and *Tòn air eigh dha!* (Arse on ice to him!) Where are your pastel shades of Celtic Twilight now?

Hugh Cheape was called by Charles Fraser, John's lawyer, with the unexpected news that he was to be co-executor of John's will. The position gave him some authority with the National Trust and the opportunity to draw together some writings which were ready, or could be made ready, for publication. A further piece of news, however, was not so welcome. He was contacted by the *Ufficio di Stato Civile* of the commune of Fiesole to say that since John had been buried in the *campo commune* (municipal cemetery), his body must be exhumed and reburied after ten years. Cheape had some time to get all the necessary paperwork in order and to find an international undertaker. Margaret agreed that in 2006, rather than having John re-interred in Italy, he should be brought back to Canna.

John's will left most of his American estate – left to him by his Waterbury grandparents – to the Canna Discretionary Trust for the upkeep of the island. There were legacies to the Catholic Diocese of Argyll and the Isles (with the request that a Tridentine – Latin – mass be said for him), St Francis Xavier University, the National Scottish Gaelic Dictionary, the Scottish Gaelic Texts Society and the nuns of San Girolamo, Fiesole. There were also bequests to his relatives, the MacKinnon family, Sheila Lockett, his former secretary, Magda and Maria Carmen Sagarzazu and Maria's children. He left the tiny islets of Hyskeir and Humla, which he had excluded from the gift to the National Trust, to his cousin Duncan Lorne Campbell. To Patrick MacKinnon he left his two boats and fishing gear.

John's passing prompted obituaries in most British and Scottish national newspapers and several overseas publications. Roger Hutchinson, writing in the *Scotsman*, called him: 'A scholar and historian of incomparable originality and that rarest of human beings in the twentieth century, a working landowner who cared deeply for the failing traditions and stolen rights of the people of his area.'[2]

Neil Fraser, who had produced the profile programme *Fear Chanaidh* for the BBC, described him as 'one of the finest intellects that the Gaelic world has produced this century'.[3] Even *Folklore*, the learned journal which had ignored his books and refused to publish his articles, carried an article *in memoriam*, albeit a year late. By David Ellis Evans, who held the Jesus Chair of Celtic at Oxford, in succession to John's mentor John Fraser, it was a warm tribute, even if it did wrongly say he had bought the island of Barra.[4]

The publicity reawakened interest in his work, the Canna archive and in Margaret. Her books were reprinted and two of her four honorary degrees were awarded in the years following John's death. For eight years she led an active life, travelling as far afield as Nova Scotia and Pittsburgh. Her hundredth birthday attracted celebratory articles, a television interview and a visit from her friends in South Uist who brought her a special gift – potatoes from the *machair*.

She died a few weeks after her hundred and first birthday and was buried in the Hallan cemetery, South Uist, alongside her friends Peigi and Mairi MacRae. If that seems strange to people who did not know her, it was only logical to Margaret to return to the place where she had first learned to love the Hebrides. The graveyard is nearly full, but when inquiries were made there was a vacant plot next to the sisters. Did she know it would be waiting for her?

In June 2006 John's remains were exhumed from his grave in Fiesole and flown to Heathrow Airport. John's nephew, Neill Campbell, collected them and travelled to Edinburgh where he met up with Hugh Cheape and they journeyed on to Mallaig. The casket was placed in St Patrick's Catholic Church overnight and in the morning the parish priest, Fr Joe Calleja, said mass.

It was Midsummer's Day, a Wednesday, chosen because on that day the ferry *Loch Nevis* was scheduled to remain at Canna pier for two hours at lunchtime before going back to Mallaig. As a mark of respect Caledonian MacBrayne had donated tickets to those accompanying John and the plan was to complete the burial and return on the ferry. But the day started with a fierce storm and the ship could not leave the harbour. Cheape and Campbell spent several hours in the Mallaig Seaman's Mission drinking tea.

On Canna, Gordon Galloway and Julie Mitchell were also anxiously scanning the sky. They had been on the island for several days preparing for their wedding, which was to be on that day in the Presbyterian church, near the pier. But the humanist minister who was to conduct the ceremony and 30 of the wedding guests were also stuck in Mallaig.

By 3 p.m. the weather had improved and Captain Tony McQuade decided that they could sail. As they reached Canna the sun broke through the cloud, the wind lessened and the evening was fine and warm. While the minister and the wedding party filed into the church, a Land Rover met the *Loch Nevis* and took John's remains to a small birch wood behind the Catholic chapel which he and Saturnino had planted. In spring it is filled with bluebells. Now, on the longest day of the year, the late sun was casting dappled evening shadows. Magda had dug a grave in a small clearing and all the islanders gathered there while Fr Calleja said a blessing and Hugh Cheape and Neill Campbell lowered the box into the earth.

Two years later, the present owner of Taynish House, where John had been brought up, gave permission for a piece of stone to be taken from the garden for John's headstone. It was set in a small cairn, with the inscription:

*Iain Latharna Caimbeul*
*1.10.1906 – 25.4.1996*
*Fear Chanaidh*

CHAPTER TWENTY-TWO

# Essay: Return to Canna

The changes to Canna a decade after John's death were apparent even before we boarded the ferry. Fay and I waited in Mallaig harbour at the spot where we used to board the *Lochmor* and before her the *Loch Arkaig*. We put our bags down where a gangway waited to be hoisted onto the deck and a sign still said 'Small Isles Ferry'. It was a kindly American tourist bound for Rum who came to our rescue and directed us down the slipway on the other side of the quay to the car deck of the *Loch Nevis*. I was taken aback. At 941 tonnes, the vessel is four times the displacement of her predecessor and approaching twice the length. Surely a ship this size could not unload at the Canna pier or get anywhere near land on the other islands?

This question was answered at Rum, again at Canna and on the return journey at the other two islands. Nearly £20 million has been invested by the Scottish government, Highlands and Islands Council and the European Union in new piers and slipways for the four isles. As the ship docks at Canna the expanse of concrete looks vast, bounded by black steel piles and rubber fenders. The old pier, lengthened by John at his own expense in 1971 appeared big, but it has been smothered by the new one.

Scale seems much less of a problem when you land and from the other side of the harbour the new structure hardly stands out at all from the cliff behind. The benefits the pier and the ferry have brought to the island are considerable and they represent the first time since 1964, when the old *Lochmor* was taken out of service, that a change has meant a better service rather than a worse one. *Loch Nevis* can carry 14 vehicles and 190 passengers in reasonable comfort. This does not mean that car-based tourism has come to Canna, since only residents' and utility vehicles are allowed to land, but it does mean much easier handling of freight and livestock.

I noticed other good things even before landing. The fields were producing lush grass, fences and gates were in good repair and beasts looked healthy. The farm is now being run by Geraldine Mac-Kinnon, daughter of Ian, and her partner Murdo Jack. She returned to the island in 1997, a qualified and experienced farmer. Despite having been rejected for the vacant position of farm manager, she started a pony trekking enterprise. That meant she was on hand when the job came up again and this time the National Trust for Scotland was sensible enough to give it to her.

Anyone who stays more than a day or two on the island cannot fail to notice that Gerry and Murdo put more time and passion into the farm than is strictly demanded by any contract of employment. That is vital in a small island community. It cannot just be a job, it has to be a way of life. 'I just think I am part of it and it is part of me,' she told BBC interviewer Alan Dein.[1]

It was Gerry who while driving us to Sanday showed us another improvement. The latest in a century-old succession of footbridges linking Canna and Sanday having been swept away in a gale like its predecessors, the islanders and the National Trust persuaded the council to rebuild it as a road bridge, giving vehicle access to Sanday at all states of the tide. The new structure, bigger and stronger than the old one, has nevertheless been sympathetically designed, its deck and handrails made of timber rather than steel. It too does not look out of place in the landscape.

John Lorne Campbell would have approved of all these things, for which he had campaigned for over 50 years. Canna people pay national and local taxes like everyone else, but until now its pier – as essential to an island as a metalled road is to a mainland town – had had to be financed privately. He fought to force the council to concede that it owned and was therefore responsible for the old footbridge, digging back decades in council minutes to find the proof. He would have stood in wonder at the handsome construction now paid for by the local authority without a struggle.

He tried to pass on to the NTS his own hard-learned lesson that it pays to trust islanders with their own affairs, but it took the new guardians of the island as long to learn as it had taken him. He would have taken great pleasure from another MacKinnon in charge of the farm and been doubly pleased that the farm is still being managed on the same principles he established, conserving wildlife habitats alongside modern agricultural methods.

A lot has been done to protect Canna's wildlife in the past decade. The island is a Site of Special Scientific Interest and is specially protected because of its importance for nesting seabirds, supporting 13 species. But, alarmingly, research showed that numbers were declining rapidly, from 21,000 breeding birds in 1995 to 14,000 in 2004. The Manx shearwater, the graceful black and white bird whose image John chose for his Canna postage stamp, had almost disappeared. The eating of eggs and chicks by brown rats was found to be the reason. The solution was a sustained campaign to eradicate the predators from the island, taking several years and involving the placing of over 7,500 poison traps.

So as not to endanger Canna's distinctive population of wood-mice at the same time, families of the species had to be trapped and taken off the island while the poisoning was underway. They were successfully reintroduced afterwards. At the time of writing (2010) it is still only a few years since the project was completed, so it is too early for conclusive results, but initial indications are that it has been successful and the breeding seabird population is again rising.

John would also have been pleased to see golden eagles nesting on Canna. He was nervous that they might have been displaced by the reintroduction of sea eagles to Rum, but now both birds appear to co-exist. He would have delighted in the reappearance of the corncrake, a direct consequence of sympathetic management of the farm.

Not everything has gone well in the years since his death. Over £1 million was poured into a scheme to convert the abandoned St Edward's Church into a study centre – money which, so far at least, looks wasted. The site of the building had been chosen in 1886 for its prominence rather than convenience – a landmark and a status symbol as much as a place of worship. It is in the middle of a boggy moor with no road, no water supply and no power, away from the main settlement on Sanday and an hour's walk from Canna House. It has always suffered from damp. When I first visited it in the late 1970s it had already been deserted. Paint and plaster were mildewed and peeling and the building smelled of decay. Visitors later vandalised the church, so John sent the religious statues to the Catholic Diocese of Argyll and the Isles for safekeeping.

The idea that St Edward's could be rehabilitated appears to have started with Lord Bute, and must have owed more to his nostalgia for his great-grandmother, who built it as a memorial for her father, than for any practical consideration. Bute died in 1993, but the National Trust for Scotland persisted with the scheme. Most of the cost of refurbishment was put up by the Hebridean Trust, an Oxford-based charity which finances development in the islands, with other contributions from the local enterprise company, the lottery and an insurance company which paid out for a fortuitous lightning strike. Construction work started in 1999, but was by no means straightforward. Canna then had no roll-on roll-off ferry and there was no road bridge to Sanday.

Princess Anne was helicoptered in to open the building in 2001. Presumably she was not told that damp was already a major problem, nor that the Hebridean Trust, the architect and the builder were in dispute about who was to blame and who should bear the cost.* A financial settlement was eventually reached, but by then the Hebridean Trust had run out of money and patience and the NTS did not have funds to carry out remedial work. The building remains uninhabitable to this day.

The failure of the St Edward's project was a blow to the National Trust's plan to revitalise the economy of Canna. It was intended to provide paying accommodation for scholars working in the Gaelic archive and to employ a resident warden. It also meant that other plans, such as the rebuilding of Point House, the nearest derelict dwelling to the church, have had to be delayed.

The Trust produced a new five-year plan for the island in 2003. It envisaged an ambitious programme of infrastructure improvements, modest economic development to sustain a larger population and a commitment to involve the community more in decision-making. Seven years on, several of the major objectives have been achieved. The pier and the bridge, although built by others, came after extensive lobbying by the Trust, which has also improved the electricity supply by providing new diesel generators and refurbished several of the houses, either for permanent inhabitants or to provide

---

* The builder wrote and published his own account of the whole sorry story: A.R. McKerlich, *Restoring Canna's Chapel*, A, R. McKerlich, 2007.

more holiday accommodation. One new home has been built. Money has been raised for improving the water supply and rebuilding MacIsaac's, another of the derelict houses, but Point House, Corroghon Barn and Tarbet remain unfulfilled dreams.

Canna is still a drain on the resources of the NTS, at a time when recession has cut its income and it has had to make staff redundant and close some of its properties. But the island still exerts a strong pull and some of the Trust's wealthier patrons have provided funds for new developments.

The community has had its highs and lows since John's death. Island life seems attractive for those dissatisfied with urban living, but it imposes special strains. 'They come here to get away from everything, but what they need is to get away from themselves. This happens time after time,' I was told by Winnie MacKinnon. A number of people attracted to Canna by its quiet and open horizons could not settle and left. In order to keep the community together, the Trust also has had to ban others from the island, a landlord's responsibility it exercises with reluctance, but cannot escape.

Despite all this, there is new life and new hope on Canna. In 2006 the Trust advertised for two new families and received over 400 responses from all over the world. The whole community was involved in shortlisting and interviewing before choosing Sheila Gunn and John Clare to take over Tighard and run it as a guest-house. Sheila, from Skye, has some Gaelic and already knew the island from spells as a supply teacher. John, a former Royal Navy diver, is experienced in handling boats and engines. A second family, Neil and Deborah Baker, from South Wales, were chosen in 2008. Neil, a gardener, is on limited-term contract to restore the over-grown Canna House garden. Deb has become secretary of the newly constituted Canna Community Association and their two daughters have doubled the primary school population, the only other pupils being the children of Eilidh Soe-Paing, the schoolteacher. Her husband Geoff looks after their younger twins. In early 2010 another couple were recruited to run the tearoom.

The new families have integrated well and in a place where there are more jobs than people it is essential that everyone works together. Neil and John maintain the generators, except if they are away from the island at the same time, when Murdo takes over.

John is the piermaster and Murdo the deputy. Magda teaches French to the schoolchildren as well as managing the Canna House archive. Sheila speaks Gaelic with them, while also running the guesthouse. Winnie manages the Trust's rental properties, but is also the Postmistress. At lambing or shearing time, everyone helps on the farm.

The community is beginning to take more initiatives independently of the Trust and in 2009 commissioned a feasibility study for a renewable energy system to replace the expensive, noisy and polluting diesel generators.

With a population of less than 20, the future of Canna as an inhabited island is still not secure. Neil Baker's job is not permanent and unless the Trust finds a way to keep him employed on the island it will become difficult to stay. 'There are only two families that have children. If the other family left with their children, we would not stay and if we had to leave because the job came to an end I don't think the other family would be comfortable at all with just their own children in the school. Canna is a very fragile community, very vulnerable at the moment',[2] he told the BBC.

In recent memory the school has never had more than a handful of pupils and on occasion has been down to a single child, or has had to close. There is an urgent need to attract more young people to the island and to provide security of tenure. With the exception of Gerry and Winnie MacKinnon, who live in houses on their own crofts, everyone else lives in a tied house which goes with the job. It creates uncertainty for Sheila, John and Magda, all of whom would like to remain on the island when they retire from their current jobs. At present there would be nowhere for them to live. A healthy community has all age groups.

Canna House, the largest building on the island, has no one living in it and is the least used. The Trust has kept it weathertight, but seems at a loss to know what else to do with it. There are ambitious statements in the five-year plan about ensuring the long-term conservation of the listed building and its valuable archive, while giving more opportunity for access by serious scholars and general visitors. So far they have remained just words on a page. A previous proposal to build an annex to house the library and provide study rooms was, by the time the latest plan was prepared 'felt no longer to be appropriate', which sounds as though it means no longer thought to be affordable.

National Trust for Scotland members who knock on its door expecting to be able to look around, as they have done with countless other Trust properties, are disappointed – sometimes angry – to find it closed, but it is practically impossible to open the house to the public on a regular basis. Other Trust properties rely on volunteers, often from a local 'Friends' group, but Canna has no convenient pool of population to draw on. Volunteers are occasionally willing to come, but ferry schedules mean that they have to stay for at least two nights and the lack of accommodation on the island again becomes the block.

Visitors who do gain access are sometimes shocked by the state of the building. It is not typical of a National Trust house, freshly painted with furnishings appropriate to the period in which it was built. Its wallpaper is faded, its paint yellowing. There are damp stains on ceilings. It does not have a reception desk or a gift shop, no public lavatories or café. The dining room is no longer dominated by Sir Archibald Campbell, merely by an outline on the wallpaper where his portrait used to hang. The most valuable painting in the house, it was left by Margaret to the Scottish National Portrait Gallery with the hope that it would be on permanent loan in Canna, but for the last three years it has languished in the gallery's store in Edinburgh and is likely to remain there until the NTS can guarantee a more benign environment for its preservation.

In the years following John's death Hugh Cheape persuaded the Trust to buy from Margaret the furniture and books not in the library. It was an inspired proposal and a brave decision by the Trust to accept it. Some pieces are undoubtedly of value, but many are domestic and functional rather than elegant or historic. The books, which line the corridors and bedrooms, are unsorted and uncatalogued. Curtains are faded, carpets threadbare. Some pictures have artistic merit, many were hung only because they meant something to the former owners.* There are knick-knacks and ornaments, souvenirs, posters and postcards, the sort of things which end up at clearance sales.

But the effect is that the house remains much as John and Margaret left it, except for peeling wallpaper and brown stains

---

* Hugh Cheape and Neill Campbell, both of whom were left items in John or Margaret's wills, have left them in the house on long-term loan.

where rainwater has seeped in. It is possible to imagine it as it was in the days when there were frequent visits by poets and writers, schoolteachers and farmworkers, fishermen, artists, academics, priests and politicians and it resounded to music, argument and laughter. It remains a conundrum for the Trust: how to let more people see inside without destroying what they have come to see, how to preserve it without having to spend money it will never be able to repay?

A similar dilemma concerns the library. In 2006 a five-year project costing £3 million – Tobar an Dualchais (kist, or chest, of riches) – was launched to make available online the Gaelic sound recordings of the Canna archive, along with those in the BBC and the School of Scottish Studies at the University of Edinburgh. But there is as yet no comprehensive plan to make John's unique library of books and papers available to a wider audience without removing it from the island. The room in which it is currently housed is too small for even one person to work comfortably and the volumes within it too valuable to be allowed out on loan or left unsupervised.

When he gave Canna to the nation, John Lorne Campbell was aware that he was passing on a burden as well as a treasure. He had devoted his life to it and the cost, both in the money he ploughed into it and the proceeds forgone, meant nothing to him. Had he sold the island on the open market rather than given it to the Trust in 1981 he could have retired in comfort. His close friend Compton Mackenzie sold his library to an American university while he was still alive and retained the use of it until his death. John referred approvingly to this 'cake and eat it' arrangement many times, although he thought the price might have been higher. But there is no evidence that he ever considered a similar deal. In his mind land, literature and language were inseparable and he intended that they should always be so.

The vision which John outlined for the islands in 1938 with his manifesto *Act Now for the Highlands and Islands* has been fulfilled only partially. A Highlands and Islands Development Board was established in 1965 and, after a mixed record in its early years, has been reborn as Highlands and Islands Enterprise and is generally accepted as doing good work in trying to develop local economies.

Improved ferry and air transport has made it easier to get from individual islands to the mainland, but has also had the effect of breaking up the island community. It takes longer and costs more to go from Canna to South Uist than it does from Canna to Glasgow and there is very little interaction now between the Inner and Outer Isles. Road Equivalent Tariff is being trialled, over 60 years after John called for it, but there is no guarantee it will be implemented permanently and in the meantime high ferry fares are a disincentive to growth in population or prosperity. There are positives. There is now only one class on passenger services between Scotland and its islands and, partly thanks to money from Europe, all islands served by public ferries now have piers and waiting rooms.

There was a brief revival of the kelp industry and an attempt to establish co-operatives, both, alas, short-lived. Protection of the Minch fisheries came far too late to help the local industry which, except for a small number of boats, has died out in the islands. Crofting still exists, but it has never proved the engine of economic and social change which John hoped it might become. Absentee landlords are common and there is no limit to the amount of land one person can own, but legislation and social pressure have reduced the number of outrages against tenants and employees which were still common in 1938.

Community ownership has undergone a renaissance, although land raids have been replaced by public relations and fundraising campaigns. Close to Canna the estates of Knoydart and Eigg are now run by their inhabitants, with support and investment in renewable energy, refurbished housing, forestry and agriculture on a scale which Canna can only dream about.

Some of the measures John advocated to protect Gaelic have now been enacted. The Gaelic Language Act (Scotland) 2005, granted official status to the language for the first time and also established Bòrd na Gàidhlig, a Gaelic language board, with powers to undertake strategic planning for the language. It also became an officially recognised European language and able to be used on passports. There are now more schools teaching Gaelic, with several using it as the medium of instruction. The amount of broadcast Gaelic has increased, with the BBC operating an exclusively Gaelic radio service, Radio nan Gàidheal, and a television channel, BBC Alba. Bilingual road and railway signs are now more common.

John devoted an appendix in his book on Canna to correcting mistakes on maps, so he would have been especially pleased by the announcement from the Ordnance Survey in 2004 that it intended to make amends for a century of Gaelic ignorance and set up a committee to determine the correct forms of Gaelic place names for its maps.

Yet despite an unprecedented level of official support, the number of Gaelic speakers continues to fall and the last census in 2001 found only 58,000, half the number of 60 years earlier. The Outer Isles remain the stronghold of Gaelic, but sadly Canna has until recently been an exception. Now a group of the islanders, new and old, have begun to learn the language by distance learning. John, once a Gaelic learner himself, would surely have approved.

Ann Berthoff tells the story of a visitor to Canna who came across John sitting in the garden seemingly totally absorbed in mending a fishing net. 'Well you are certainly out of the world,' he said, to which John replied: 'On the contrary, I am at the centre of *my* world.' His legacies are memories of friends across the world, his books and articles, recordings, library, butterfly collection and the island which he bought and gave away.

> Many songs they knew who are now silent.
> Into their memories the dead are gone
> Who haunt the living in an ancient tongue
> Sung by old voices to the young,
> Telling of sea and isles, of boat and byre and glen;
> And from their music the living are reborn
> Into a remembered land,
> To call ancestral memories home
> And all that ancient grief and love our own.

From *Eileann Chanaidh, 2: Highland Graveyard,*
by Kathleen Raine

# Selected Bibliography

## By John Lorne Campbell

*A School in South Uist,* Frederic Rea (ed and introduction by John Lorne Campbell), 2nd edition, Birlinn 1997, reprinted 2001, 2003 (Routledge & Kegan Paul).

*A Very Civil People,* introduction by Hugh Cheape, Birlinn 2000, reprinted 2004.

*Act Now for the Highlands and Islands,* with Sir Alexander MacEwen, Saltire Society 1939.

*Bardachd Mhgr. Ailein: the Gaelic Poems of Fr Allan MacDonald,* transcribed by John Lorne Campbell from his MS, and ed with some translations, Campbell 1965.

*Canna, The Story of a Hebridean Island,* Oxford University Press for the National Trust for Scotland 1984. Revised reprint 1986, 1994, 2002.

*Edward Lhuyd in the Scottish Highlands,* with Derick Thomson, Oxford University Press 1963.

*Fr Allan MacDonald of Eriskay,* John Lorne Campbell 1954, 2nd edition (revised), Campbell 1956.

*Gaelic in Scottish Education and Life,* Saltire Society 1945, 2nd edition (revised) 1950.

*Gaelic Words and Expressions from South Uist and Eriskay,* collected by Fr. Allan MacDonald, ed. John Lorne Campbell, Dublin Institute for Advanced Studies 1958, 2nd edition with supplement, Oxford University Press.

*Hebridean Folksongs,* with Francis Collinson, Oxford University Press, Vol. I 1969, Vol. II 1977, Vol. III 1981.

*Highland Songs of the Forty-Five,* 2nd edition (revised), Scottish Gaelic Texts Society 1984, (John Grant 1933).

'Macrolepidoptera Cannae', *Entomologist's Record,* Vol. 81 pp. 211, 235, 292.

'Notes On Carmina Gadelica', *Scottish Gaelic Studies,* reprint of two articles and reviews.

'Our Barra Years', *The Scots Magazine,* Aug. and Sept. 1975, (private reprint).

*Songs Remembered in Exile,* Aberdeen University Press 1990, reprinted Birlinn 1999.

*Stories from South Uist,* told by Angus MacLellan, recorded by John Lorne Campbell and transcribed from the recording, 2nd edition, Birlinn 1997, reprinted 2001, (Routledge & Kegan Paul, 1961).

*Strange Things,* with Trevor H. Hall, Routledge & Kegan Paul 1965, reprinted Birlinn 2006.

*Tales from Barra, told by the Coddy,* foreword Compton Mackenzie, introduction John Lorne Campbell, Campbell 1960, 2nd edition (revised) 1961, reprints 1973, 1975, 1992.

*The Book of Barra,* with Compton Mackenzie and Carl H. Borgstrom, ed John Lorne Campbell, G. Routledge & Sons 1936, reprinted Acair 1998, 2006.

*The Furrow behind Me,* told by Angus MacLellan, South Uist. Recorded in Gaelic and translated from the recordings with notes by John Lorne Campbell, Routledge & Kegan Paul 1962, 2nd edition Birlinn 1997, reprinted 2002.

## By other authors

Barnett, T. Ratcliffe, *Highland Harvest,* James Clarke & Co 1937.

Botting, Douglas, *Gavin Maxwell, A Life,* HarperCollins 1993.

Cameron, James D., *For the People: A History of St Francis Xavier University,* McGill-Queen's University Press 1996.

Costello, Eileen, *Amhráin Mhuighe Seola,* Talbot Press, Dublin 1923.

Dictionary of National Biography, Oxford University Press 2004.

Dressler, Camille, *Eigg: The Story of an Island,* 2nd edition, Birlinn 2007.

Gainford, Veronica, *Tayvallich and Taynish,* V. Gainford 1984.

Goodrich-Frier, Ada, *Outer Isles,* A. Constable & Co. 1902.

Grimble, Ian, *Clans and Clan Chiefs,* Blond and Briggs 1980.

Haswell-Smith, Hamish, *The Scottish Islands,* Canongate 2004.

Kennedy-Fraser, Marjory, *A Life of Song,* Oxford University Press 1929.

Linklater, Andro, *Compton Mackenzie: A Life,* Chatto & Windus 1987.

Love, John A., *Rum: A Landscape without Figures,* Birlinn 2001.

Mackay, D.N., *Clan Warfare in the Scottish Highlands,* Alexander Gardner 1922.

Mackenzie, Compton, *My Life and Times – Octaves 7 & 8,* Chatto & Windus 1968.

Mackenzie, Sir Compton, *The Windsor Tapestry,* Rich & Cowan 1938.

MacNeice, Louis, *I Crossed the Minch,* Polygon 2007.

Murray, Amy, *Father Allan's Island,* Harcourt, Brace and Howe, New York 1920.

Paterson, Raymond Campbell, *The Lords of the Isles,* Birlinn 2001.

Schafer, Bruno, *They Heard his Voice,* McMullen Books 1952.

Shaw, Margaret Fay, *Folksongs and Folklore of South Uist,* 3rd edition, Birlinn 2005 (Routledge & Kegan Paul 1955).

Shaw, Margaret Fay, *From the Alleghenies to the Hebrides,* Canongate Press 1994.

Strang, Alice, *Winifred Nicholson in Scotland,* National Galleries of Scotland 2005.

Sutherland, Donald, *A Highland Childhood,* Birlinn 1996.

Withers, Charles W.J., *Gaelic in Scotland 1698–1981,* John Donald 1984.

# Notes and References

## Foreword

1. Kathleen Raine, *A Valentine for John and Margaret*, 1978.

## Chapter 1: The Honoured Ancestor

1. An outline of Archibald Campbell's life is carried on the website http://www.knapdalepeople.com/inveryouth.htm.
2. Ian Grimble, *Clans and Clan Chiefs*, Blond and Briggs, 1980.
3. Letter from Archibald Campbell to General Howe, 19 June 1776 quoted at http://www.knapdalepeople.com/inveramrev.htm.
4. Letter to General Howe from Concord Gaol, 14 February 1777, quoted at http://www.knapdalepeople.com/inveramrev.htm.
5. Donald Sutherland, *A Highland Childhood*, Birlinn, 1996, p. 3.
6. Ibid. p. 7. John Lorne Campbell (JLC) cites this book, under its original title *Butt and Ben,* in his notebook as a good record of Argyll society at the time. He also warmly recommends Compton Mackenzie, *The Monarch of the Glen.*
7. The claim was accepted by Lord Lyon King of Arms in 1875, but contested by later historians, including Colin Campbell, younger brother of John Lorne Campbell. See Alastair Campbell of Airds, *A History of Clan Campbell*, Volume 2, Polygon, 2000.
8. JLC notebooks in the Canna House archive.
9. Notebook: *The end of Inverneill,* Canna House archive.
10. Sutherland, *A Highland Childhood,* p. 3.
11. Canna House archive.
12. Sutherland, *A Highland Childhood,* p. 4

## Chapter 2: A Divided Family

1. JLC notebooks in the Canna House archive.
2. Veronica Gainford, *Tayvallich and Taynish*, North Knapdale, V. Gainford, 1984.
3. Ibid.
4. JLC notebooks in the Canna House archive.
5. Ibid.

6. Ibid.

7. Around £12,000 at 2010 prices.

8. JLC notebooks in the Canna House archive.

9. Charles W.J. Withers, *Gaelic in Scotland 1698–1981*, John Donald, 1984, p. 100.

10. Ibid., p. 115.

11. Ibid., p. 71.

12. Ibid., p. 97.

13. Reports and Tables: Population, Ages, Conjugal Condition, Orphanhood, Birthplaces, Gaelic-Speaking, Housing, *1921 Census of Scotland*, Tables 63–65, discussed by JLC in a letter to 'George' in Canna House archive.

14. Withers, *Gaelic in Scotland* p. 23.

15. BBC Scotland Television, Gaelic & Features, *Fear Chanaidh*, 1994.

16. JLC notebooks in the Canna House archive.

## Chapter 3: Homeless and Jobless

1. John Lorne Campbell, *Highland Songs of the Forty-Five*, John Grant, 1933.

2. D.N. Mackay, *Clan Warfare in the Scottish Highlands*, Alexander Gardner, 1922.

3. It was republished in 1984 by the Scottish Gaelic Texts Society.

4. JLC notebooks in the Canna House archive.

5. Ibid.

6. Now in Oxfordshire.

7. JLC notebooks in the Canna House archive.

8. Ibid.

9. Ibid.

10. Ibid.

11. John Lorne Campbell, *Songs Remembered in Exile*, Aberdeen University Press, 1990.

## Chapter 4: A Classless Society

1. For example see John Lorne Campbell, 'Our Barra Years', *The Scots Magazine*, August 1975, p. 494.

2. Ibid., p. 496.

3. Francis Thompson, *The Uists and Barra*, David & Charles, 1974.

4. John later published some of them in his introduction to John Mac-Pherson's *Tales from Barra told by the Coddy*, 2nd edition, Birlinn, 1992.

5. From the obituary, quoted in John's introduction to MacPherson, *Tales from Barra*. Words in square brackets are added by John Lorne Campbell.

6. MacPherson, *Tales from Barra*, p. 21.

7. Sources for the life of Compton Mackenzie include Andro Linklater,

*Compton Mackenzie: A Life*, Chatto & Windus, 1987, and Mackenzie's own autobiography, *My Life and Times – Octave 7: 1931–1938* and *Octave 8: 1939–1946*, Chatto & Windus, 1968.

8. Louis MacNeice, *I Crossed the Minch*, Polygon, 2007, p. 93.
9. Mackenzie, *My Life and Times – Octave 7*, p. 191.
10. Campbell, 'Our Barra Years', p. 499.
11. Canna House archive.
12. Mackenzie, *My Life and Times – Octave 7*, p. 212.
13. Campbell, 'Our Barra Years', p. 501.
14. Ibid., p. 502.
15. Mackenzie, *My Life and Times – Octave 7*, p. 193.
16. *Outlook*, September 1936, p. 64
17. Mackenzie, *My Life and Times – Octave 7*, p. 617.

## Chapter 5: A Bird Blown Off Course

1. Margaret Fay Shaw, *From the Alleghenies to the Hebrides*, Canongate Press, 1994.
2. BBC Scotland Television, Gaelic & Features, *Fear Chanaidh*, 1995
3. Shaw, *From the Alleghenies*, p. 16.
4. Letter dated 20 July 1926, Canna House archive.
5. Letter dated 28 July 1926, Canna House archive.
6. Letter dated 3 August 1926, Canna House archive.
7. Margaret Fay Shaw, *Folksongs and Folklore of South Uist*, Routledge & Kegan Paul, 1955, third edition Birlinn, 2005, p.1.
8. There is a discussion of the forms of Gaelic song in Shaw, *Folksongs and Folklore*, p. 77.
9. Eileen Costello, *Amhráin Mhuighe Seola*, Talbot Press, Dublin, 1923.
10. Shaw, *From the Alleghenies*, p. 58.
11. Shaw, *Folksongs and Folklore*, p. 5.
12. Shaw, *From the Alleghenies*, p. 61.
13. Ibid., p. 61.
14. Shaw, *Folksongs and Folklore*, p. 6.
15. Ibid., p. 7.
16. Ibid., p. 16.
17. Letter dated 11 March 1930, Canna House archive.
18. Ibid.

## Chapter 6: Recording a Vanishing Culture

1. Compton Mackenzie, *My Life and Times – Octave 7: 1931–1938*, Chatto & Windus, 1968, p. 165.

2. J.L. Campbell, *Songs Remembered in Exile*, Aberdeen University Press, 1990, p. 2. Ten of the songs were published in J.L. Cambell (editor and translator), Annie Johnston, John MacLean, *Gaelic Folksongs from the Isle of Barra recorded by J.L. Campbell*. Linguaphone Institute for the Folklore Institute of Scotland, 1950.

3. Campbell, *Songs Remembered in Exile*, p. 60.

4. Ibid., p. 74.

5. Ibid., pp. 37–39. See also James D. Cameron, *For the People: A History of St Francis Xavier University*, McGill-Queen's University Press, 1996.

6. Ibid., p. 39.

7. Ibid., p. 39.

8. Ibid., p. 43.

9. John edited and published the diaries of the first Catholic teacher to be appointed to a school in South Uist; see F.G. Rae, *A school in South Uist: Reminiscences of a Hebridean Schoolmaster, 1890–1913*, Birlinn, 1997, Introduction, p. xviii.

10. Dr Moses Coady, *Masters of their own Destiny*, Harper & Row, 1939.

11. Ibid., p. 17

12. Campbell, *Songs Remembered in Exile*, p. 50.

13. *The Sea Leaguer*, No. 6, December, 1937, given to the author by John Lorne Campbell.

14. Ibid., p. 10.

15. John Lorne Campbell & Sir Alexander MacEwen, *Act Now for the Highlands and Islands*, Oliver & Boyd, 1939.

## Chapter 7: Absent Neighbours

1. Raymond Campbell Paterson, *The Lords of the Isles*, Birlinn, 2001, pp. 194–5.

2. Ibid., p. 150. This was not the end of the story: Clanranald went on to sell everything except the clan castle and its tiny island.

3. John A. Love, *Rum:A Landscape without Figures*, Birlinn 2001, p. 197–8.

4. Ibid., p. 231.

5. Ibid., p. 242.

6. Camille Dressler, *Eigg: the Story of an Island*, Birlinn, 2nd edn, p. 80.

7. Ibid., p. 99.

8. Ibid., p. 118.

## Chapter 8: The Isle of Canna

1. See for example, 'Garden of Eden changes hands', the *Scotsman*, 12 June, 1981.

2. Hamish Haswell-Smith, *The Scottish Islands*, Canongate, 2004.

3. See J.L Campbell, *Canna, The Story of a Hebridean Island*, 4th edn, Birlinn, 2002, p. 239.

4. T. Ratcliffe Barnett, *Highland Harvest*, James Clarke & Co., 1937, p. 41–2.

5. By coincidence a member of the same family that sold Taynish to John's ancestor, Sir Archibald Campbell. See Campbell, *Canna*, p. 132.

6. Camille Dressler, *Eigg: the Story of an Island*, 2nd edn, Birlinn, 2007, p. 84.

7. Ibid., p. 162.

8. MacNeill papers from the collection of Mr Gilmour Thom.

9. Robert Thom's diary 1847–48, from the collection of Mr Gilmour Thom.

10. 'Obituaries', *Glasgow Herald*, 8 May 1911.

11. Campbell, *Canna*, p. 169.

12. MacNeill papers from the collection of Mr Gilmour Thom.

13. Campbell, *Canna*, p. 173.

14. Dressler, *Eigg*, p. 120.

## Chapter 9: Into Ownership

1. Sources for this chapter include John Lorne Campbell's notebooks, the 'Annals of Canna', his unpublished account of the purchase and early years of the ownership of the island, and the Log of the *Gille Brighde*. All are in the Canna House archive.

2. Sir Compton Mackenzie, *The Windsor Tapestry*, Rich & Cowan, 1938, p. 538.

3. *Time* magazine, 4 July 1938.

4. Sir Compton Mackenzie, *My Life and Times – Octave 7: 1931–1938*, Chatto & Windus, 1968, p. 254.

5. Ibid., p. 250.

6. Ibid., p. 246.

## Chapter 10: Into Debt

1. J.L. Campbell, 'The Annals of Canna', unpublished notebook, Canna House archive.

2. Margaret Fay Shaw, *From the Alleghenies to the Hebrides*, Canongate Press, 1994, p. 120.

3. J.L Campbell, *Canna, The Story of a Hebridean Island*, Oxford University Press, 1984, pp. 172–3.

4. Shaw, *From the Alleghenies*, p. 119.

5. Ibid.

6. Ibid., p. 121.

## Chapter 11: War and Hard Times

1. John Lorne Campbell's notebook, Canna House archive.

2. Compton Mackenzie, *My Life and Times – Octave 8: 1939–1946*, Chatto & Windus, p. 59.

3. Ibid., p. 60.

4. J.L. Campbell, 'The Annals of Canna', Canna House archive.

5. Margaret Fay Shaw, *From the Alleghenies to the Hebrides*, Canongate Press, 1994, p. 128.

6. Bruno Schafer, ed., *They Heard His Voice*, McMullen Books, 1952.

## Chapter 12: Turning the Tide

1. Douglas Botting, *Gavin Maxwell, A Life*, HarperCollins, 1993, p. 95.

2. Alice Strang, *Winifred Nicholson in Scotland*, National Galleries of Scotland, 2005, p. 25.

3. J.L. Campbell, 'The Annals of Canna', unpublished notebook, Canna House archive.

4. Letter to Francis Collinson, 5 July 1951, Canna House archive.

5. Letters in the Canna House archive.

## Chapter 13: A Voice for the Voiceless

1. Senator T.K. Whitaker, lecture given to the Glens of Antrim Historical Society, 3 April 1981.

2. J.L. Campbell, 'Report on the recording of Hebridean Folksongs since 1936', Canna House archive

3. J.L. Campbell, 'Angus MacLellan MBE 1896–1966', Scottish Studies, Vol. 10, Part 2, School of Scottish Studies, University of Edinburgh, 1966, pp. 193–7.

4. *Glasgow Herald*, 28 May 1947.

5. Letter to Seamus Delargy, 30 June 1951, Canna House archive.

6. Letter to Francis Collinson, 21 February 1951, Canna House archive.

7. Letter to John Lorne Campbell, 10 October 1950, Canna House archive.

8. Letter to Alan Lomax, 14 November 1950, Canna House archive.

9. Letter to John Lorne Campbell, 20 November 1950, Canna House archive.

10. Letter to Francis Collinson, 5 July 1951, Canna House archive.

11. Letter to Annie Johnston, 19 July 1951, Canna House archive.

12. Letter to Sidney Newman, 19 July 1951, Canna House archive.

13. Letter to John Lorne Campbell, 30 July 1951, Canna House archive.

14. Letter to John Lorne Campbell, 27 July 1951, Canna House archive.

15. Letter to Francis Collinson, 30 July 1951, Canna House archive.

16. Letter to John Lorne Campbell, 10 September 1951, Canna House archive.

17. Letter to John Lorne Campbell, 15 September 1951, Canna House archive.

18. Letter to Calum Maclean, 16 January 1952, Canna House archive.

19. Letter to John Lorne Campbell, 22 January 1952, Canna House archive.

## Chapter 14: The End of Inverneill

1. 'Notes on the financial history of Inverneill', private notebook, Canna House archive, 1955.
2. 'The end of Inverneill', private notebook, Canna House archive, 1955.
3. Ibid.
4. Sources for this chapter, unless otherwise stated, are John Lorne Campbell, 'The true story of the sale of Inverneill and Taynish', private notebook, and J.L. Campbell, 'The Campbells of Inverneill and the Johnston Die Press Company etc', unpublished article, both in the Canna House archive.
5. *Financial Times*, 5 May 1903.

## Chapter 15: Illuminating the Celtic Twilight

1. Kathleen Raine, 'Eileann Chanaidh', *The Hollow Hill*, Hamish Hamilton, 1964.
2. Letter from J.L. Campbell to D. Ellis Evans, April 1980, *Folklore*, Vol. 108, 1997, p. 103.
3. J.L. Campbell and Trevor Hall, *Strange Things*, Routledge & Kegan Paul, 1968, p. 7.
4. J.L. Campbell and Hugh Cheape, *A Very Civil People: Hebridean Folk History and Tradition*, Birlinn 2004, p. xiii.
5. J.L. Campbell, *Gaelic in Scottish Education and Life*, Saltire Society, 1945, pp. 82–92.
6. Ronald Black, ed., *Eilein na b-Oige, The poems of Fr Allan McDonald*, Mungo, 2002.
7. 'Songs of the Hebrides', *The Scots Magazine*, January 1958, p. 308.
8. F.G. Rea, *A School in South Uist,* Birlinn, 1997, p. 6.
9. Marjory Kennedy-Fraser, *A Life of Song*, Oxford University Press, 1929, p. 121.
10. Ibid., p. 110.
11. Campbell and Hall, *Strange Things*, p. 8.
12. Sir Robert Rait and Dr George Pryde, *Scotland (Modern World series)*, 1934, p. 302, quoted in J. Lorne Campbell with Francis Collinson, *Hebridean Folksong*, Oxford University Press, 1969, p. 27.
13. Campbell and Collinson, *Hebridean Folksong*.
14. Ian A. Olson, 'Collinson, Francis James Montgomery (1898–1984)', Oxford Dictionary of National Biography, Oxford University Press, 2004.
15. J.L. Campbell, *Fr Allan MacDonald of Eriskay, Priest, Poet, Folklorist*, Oliver & Boyd, 1954.
16. 'The late Fr Allan MacDonald, Miss Goodrich-Freer and Hebridean Folklore', *Scottish Studies*, 1958, pp. 175–88.

## Chapter 16: Recognition and Contentment

1. Olsen, Oxford Dictionary of National Biography.
2. Letter to John Lorne Campbell, 25 February 1951, Canna House archive.
3. Letters to Bruce Phillips and James Stormonth Darling, 21 April 1980, National Trust for Scotland archive.
4. Margaret Fay Shaw, *Folksongs and Folklore of South Uist*, Routledge & Kegan Paul, London 1955.
5. The story is detailed in Karl Sabbagh, *A Rum Affair*, Allen Lane, London, 1999
6. Ibid. p. 75
7. Ibid. pp. 82–3
8. Ibid. p. 163. See also *Entomologist's Record* Vol. 87 1975 p. 161. *On the Rumoured Presence of the Large Blue Butterfly. Maculinea Arion L. in the Hebrides.*
9. *Outlook* September 1936 pp. 64–66.
10. *The New Alliance*, May–June 1944 p. 10.
11. *The Scots Review* December 1948, p. 125.
12. Letter to Stewart Rule & Co., 1 June 1959, Canna House archive.

## Chapter 17: Fighting for a Lifeline

1. 'Statements on behalf of the Island of Canna', 20 July 1959, Canna House archive.
2. 'Memorandum on Canna Transport', 1960, Canna House archive.
3. 'Statement on the transport facilities that will be lost to the Island of Canna under the proposed reorganisation of MacBrayne's shipping services and British Railways' freight service withdrawal, 1963', Canna House archive.
4. Camille Dressler, *Eigg; the Story of an Island*, Birlinn, 2007, p. 165.
5. The *Guardian*, 2 May 1979, p 14.

## Chapter 18: A Succession Problem

1. Letter from Robin McEwen to Jamie Stormonth Darling, 10 April 1956, National Trust for Scotland archive.
2. Memo by Jamie Stormonth Darling, 23 April 1956, National Trust for Scotland archive.
3. Letter from Jamie Stormonth Darling to John Lorne Campbell, 1 April 1975, National Trust for Scotland archive.
4. Memo by Jamie Stormonth Darling, 3 August 1979, National Trust for Scotland archive.
5. Heads of Agreement between John Lorne Campbell and National Trust for Scotland, 14 May 1981, National Trust for Scotland archive.

6. Letter from John Lorne Campbell to Ray Perman, 20 December 1980, in possession of the author.

7. Ibid.

8. Report by Blair Kelly, 19 March 1973, National Trust for Scotland archive.

9. Letter from Peat, Marwick, Mitchell to National Heritage Memorial Fund, 10 April 1981, National Trust for Scotland archive.

10. Letter from Jamie Stormonth Darling to Brian Lang, 10 April 1981, National Trust for Scotland archive.

11. The *Scotsman*, June 1981

12. Letter from Jamie Stormonth Darling to John Lorne Campbell, 2 October 1981, National Trust for Scotland archive.

13. Memo from Charles Cameron to Lester Borley, 30 August 1983, National Trust for Scotland archive.

14. Letter from John Lorne Campbell to Jamie Stormonth Darling, 21 September 1981, National Trust for Scotland archive.

## Chapter 19: The Old Order Changes

1. Letter from John Lorne Campbell to Jamie Stormonth Darling, 5 October 1981, National Trust for Scotland archive.

2. Letter from Donald John MacKinnon to Jamie Stormonth Darling, 27 April 1982, National Trust for Scotland archive.

3. Letter from John Lorne Campbell to Kate Hardie, 24 January 1983, National Trust for Scotland archive.

4. Letter from John Lorne Campbell to Jamie Stormonth Darling, 22 November 1982, National Trust for Scotland archive.

5. Jamie Stormonth Darling memo, 15 November 1982, National Trust for Scotland archive.

6. Letter from Margaret Fay Shaw to Jamie Stormonth Darling, 10 March 1983, National Trust for Scotland archive.

7. Letter from John Lorne Campbell to Ray Perman, 2 October 1984, in possession of the author.

8. Letter from Lord Wemyss to Jamie Stormonth Darling, 21 May 1982, National Trust for Scotland archive.

9. Letter from John Lorne Campbell to Jamie Stormonth Darling, 12 April 1983, National Trust for Scotland archive.

10. 'The National Trust: a good idea gone wrong?' *Glasgow Herald*, 30 November 1989, p. 15.

11. *Canna Management Plan: 1994–99*, National Trust for Scotland archive.

12. Letter from John Lorne Campbell to Angus McIntosh, 4 August 1986, Canna House archive.

13. 'Campbell's Kingdom', *Country Living*, date unknown. National Trust for Scotland archive.

## Chapter 20: Despair and Recovery

1. Letter from John Lorne Campbell to Fitzroy MacLean, 4 August 1986, Canna House archive.
2. Memo from Charles Cameron to Lester Borley, 25 August 1983, National Trust for Scotland archive.
3. Undated note (after 1981), Canna House archive.
4. Letter from A. Bryant to M. Mackechnie, 21 January 1991, Canna House archive.
5. Memo from Anthony Bryant to Lester Borley, 20 April 1992, National Trust for Scotland archive.
6. Letter from Margaret Fay Shaw to Kate Hardie, 21 April 1992, National Trust for Scotland archive.
7. Letter from Margaret Fay Shaw to the author, 19 July 1994.
8. Published after John's death as *A Very Civil People*, Birlinn, 1999.
9. Letter from Margaret Fay Shaw to Ann Berthoff, 24 September 1994.
10. J.L. Campbell, *Canna, The Story of a Hebridean Island*, Oxford University Press, 1984, p. 95.
11. Ibid., p. 96.
12. Letter from Margaret Fay Shaw to Ann Berthoff, 19 February 1995.
13. Letter from Margaret Fay Shaw to Ann Berthoff, 28 December 1995.

## Chapter 21: Who Can Tell His Place of Dying?

1. Extract from 'Am Bàs' (Death), Fr Allan MacDonald, *Bardachd Mhgr. Ailein, The Gaelic Poems of Fr Allan MacDonald*, transcribed and edited by J.L. Campbell from his MS and published privately by J.L. Campbell, 1965, in Canna House archive.
2. The *Scotsman*, 29 April 1996, p. 9.
3. Lorn MacIntyre, 'Obituary for John Lorne Campbell', the *Herald*, 27 April 1996, p. 14.
4. *Folklore*, Vol. 108, 1997, p. 103.

## Chapter 22: Essay: Return to Canna

1. 'Lives in a Landscape', BBC Radio 4, 11 December 2009.
2. Ibid.

# Index